THE RESEARCH PAPER
A Common-Sense Approach

Thomas E. Gaston
Purdue University

Bret H. Smith
Auburn University

PRENTICE-HALL, INC.
A Division of Simon & Schuster, Englewood Cliffs, NJ 07632

Library of Congress Cataloging-in-Publication Data

GASTON, THOMAS E. (Thomas Elmer), 1931–
  The research paper.

  Includes index.
  1. Report writing. 2. Research. I. Smith,
Bret H., 1958–   . II. Title.
LB2369.G28 1987   808'.02   86-30612
ISBN 0-13-774100-6

Editorial/production supervision: Virginia Rubens
Interior design: Jayne Conte and Meryl Poweski
Cover design: Karen Stephens
Manufacturing buyer: Ray Keating
Cover photo: Bob Llewellyn/Four by Five, Inc.

Printed in the United States of America
10   9   8   7   6   5   4   3   2   1

Acknowledgments appear on page xiii, which constitutes
a continuation of the copyright page.

ISBN 0-13-774100-6 01

Prentice-Hall International (UK) Limited, *London*
Prentice-Hall of Australia Pty. Limited, *Sydney*
Prentice-Hall Canada Inc., *Toronto*
Prentice-Hall Hispanoamericana, S.A., *Mexico*
Prentice-Hall of India Private Limited, *New Delhi*
Prentice-Hall of Japan, Inc., *Tokyo*
Prentice-Hall of Southeast Asia Pte. Ltd., *Singapore*
Editora Prentice-Hall do Brasil, Ltda., *Rio de Janeiro*

Contents

Dedication and Acknowledgments

Professor Gaston dedicates his work on this book to Dorothy, who made all things grow; to Nancy, who gave him new roots when his own growth faltered; and to Pam, Tommy, Ted, Patricia, Judy, Andy, Bob, Amy, Lauren Elizabeth, Clarence, and Mabel—all of whom, in their own ways, are growing just about right.

Professor Smith's dedication is to the members of his family: Lew, Ardeth, Heidi, Melinda, Eric, Karen, Stephanie, Pete, and Pete, whose love, patience, prayer, and encouragement were always beyond praise and will therefore never be absent from memory.

Though this book has only two authors, it has literally hundreds of contributors, all of whom have our sincerest thanks for the help they have given. In particular, we would like to express appreciation to Professor Leonora Woodman, who, during her tenure as director of composition at Purdue University, permitted us to field-test some of the more novel materials in this text in Purdue's English 102 classes. Our thanks go also to the instructors of those classes, Srinivas Aravamudan, Mary Campbell, Joseph Faulkner, Suzanne Fox, and Nicholas Kaldis. Their detailed reports and thoughtful critiques contributed much to the final "debugging" of some of our best exercises.

This book grows directly out of a position paper written by the present authors in collaboration with Robert Kennedy and benefits in several respects from his contributions to that paper, which will soon be published in James Ford's *Teaching the Research Paper* (Metuchen, NJ: Scarecrow Press).

Our indebtedness extends also to Deborah Brassard, Robert Durante, Wendy Hamilton, Mark Letourneau, Brian Price and Jane Thielman, whose questions as beginning instructors under Professor Gaston's mentorship first led him to codify for others the underlying principles that are reflected in this textbook.

The opportunity to codify them for himself was first afforded by the wise leadership which always made him feel "easy in harness" during his baptismal years at the University of Kentucky and, later, by the numerous workshops and faculty meetings sponsored by the University of Kentucky Community College System where he spent many profitable hours swapping ideas with some of the best composition teachers to be found anywhere. That their contributions to this book are too diffuse and pervasive to be specifically acknowledged diminishes neither their importance nor his appreciation.

Valuable proofreading and critical assistance was provided by several family members and friends including Dorothy Gaston, Theodore Gaston, Nancy Gaston, Brooke Horvath, Alfield Ingberg, Stephanie Medich, Ardeth Smith, Heidi Smith, Melinda Smith, and Margaret Woodworth. Technical assistance from Dr. Lewis Smith made some of the examples from medicine and biology both more accurate and more apt than they otherwise would have been.

Steward Saunders and Ellen Neville of the Purdue University Library System helped us to understand more thoroughly the intricacies of the Dewey Decimal and the Library of Congress cataloguing systems. Our debt to them is great indeed.

So is our debt to the numerous colleagues who reviewed the manuscript at various stages and generously shared their reactions, suggestions, and criticisms. Their advice was uniformly sound, and we have incorporated most of their suggestions into this final version. Only in a few places did they disagree in their perceptions and force us to make difficult decisions. For those decisions and any remaining defects in the book we must take responsibility. For advice that distinguished itself for both quality and quantity, we are indebted to the following: Gary Acton, Eastern Montana College; Jay Balderson, Western Illinois University; Therese Brychta, Truckee Meadows Community College; Duncan Carter, Boston University; Peter Dusenbery, Bradley University; James E. Ford, University of Nebraska, Lincoln; Raymond MacKenzie, Mankato State University; Robert Martin, Portland State University; Walter S. Minot, Gannon University; George Otte, Baruch College, City University of New York; and Martha Simonsen, William Rainey Harper College.

For placing us in touch with those reviewers, for understanding when tragedy and illness forced repeated delays in our writing, and for teaching us much about the publishing business, we are indebted to Phil Miller, Prentice-Hall's excellent English editor, and to his able assistant, Jane Baumann, who went out of her way on numerous occasions promptly to supply needed assistance and materials without once pointing out that as often as not she was being asked to rescue us from the consequences of our own inefficiency.

And finally, we acknowledge our gratitude to the several authors and publishers listed below, who have permitted us to reproduce the fruits of their labors so that in the pages of this book we could better repay future students for what we have gained from their predecessors.

Adams, Sam. "Vietnam Cover-up: Playing War with Numbers." © *Harper's Magazine* May 1975: 41–44, 62–73. Reprinted by permission.

Table from *Advertising Age* (copyright). Source: McCann-Erickson, Inc., New York, N.Y. Compiled for Crain Communications, Inc.

Asher, J. William. *Educational Research and Evaluation Methods.* Boston: Little, Brown and Company, 1976.

Book Review Digest, entry starting "Diggett, Charles." Book Review Digest Copyright © 1983, 1984 by The H. W. Wilson Company. Material reproduced by permission of the publisher.

"The Cargo Cults," *Time,* 8 June 1959: 74–75. Copyright 1959 Time Inc. All rights reserved. Reprinted by permission from *Time.*

Dunkin, Paul S. *Cataloging USA.* Chicago: American Library Association, 1969. Reprinted by permission.

Erwin, Dabney. "Hypnosis in Burn Therapy." *Hypnosis 1979: Proceedings of the 8th International Congress of Hypnosis and Psychosomatic Medicine,* Melbourne, 1979. Ed. Graham D. Burrows, David R. Collison, and Lorraine Dennerstein. New York: Elsevier/North-Holland Biomedical Press, 1979. 269–276. Reprinted by permission.

"Moonshining as a Fine Art" from *The Foxfire Book. Hog Dressing, Log Cabin Building . . .* Edited with an introduction by Eliot Wigginton. Copyright © 1968, 1969, 1970, 1971, 1972 by The Foxfire Fund, Inc.

Article on "Hypnosis" in *Encyclopedia Americana* reprinted with permission of *Encyclopedia Americana,* Copyright 1984, Grolier, Inc.

Article on "Hypnosis" in *Encyclopaedia Brittanica: Micropaedia,* 15th ed. (1974) reprinted by permission.

Excerpt on "Hypnosis" from *The New York Times Index* copyright © 1980 by The New York Times Company. Reprinted by permission.

Article on "Hypnosis" from *The Oxford English Dictionary* reprinted by permission of Oxford University Press.

"Intelligence: This Fish is a Smarty." *Newsweek* 4 July 1960: 59. Copyright 1960, by Newsweek, Inc. All Rights Reserved. Reprinted by permission.

Excerpt from Koestler, Arthur, *Act of Creation* reprinted by permission of The Sterling Lord Agency, Inc. Copyright © 1964, 1976 by Arthur Koestler.

Extract from *Phoenix II: Uncollected Papers of D. H. Lawrence,* Edited by F. Warren Roberts and Harry T. Moore. Copyright © 1959, 1963, 1968 by the Estate of Frieda Lawrence Ravagli. Reprinted by permission of Viking Penguin, Inc.

Midge, Isadore Gilbert. "Reference Works and Reference Books" as reprinted in Eugene P. Sheehy, *Guide to Reference Books,* 9th ed. Chicago: American Library Association, 1976. xiv-xv.

Advertisement "You're Number One" reprinted by permission of Quality Stores, Inc., N. Muskegon, MI.

Excerpt "Trials (espionage)" from *Readers' Guide to Periodical Literature* reproduced by permission of The H. W. Wilson Company.

"Reported Crime in Metropolitan Areas, 1982" from *The World Almanac & Book of Facts,* 1984 edition, copyright © Newspaper Enterprise Association, Inc., 1983, New York, NY 10166.

Excerpt from Sagan, Carl, *Cosmos,* reprinted by permission of Random House, Inc.

Excerpt from Toffler, Alvin, *Future Shock,* reprinted by permission of Random House, Inc.

Preface:
To the Teacher

The bias of this book is a simple one. We believe that students have a right to be taken seriously. Accordingly, we do not believe that their views, their interests, and their ambitions should be dismissed too quickly. Certainly they should not be ignored altogether by those of us who describe ourselves as humanists and assume responsibility for such important aspects of their personal competence as the use of the library, the assessment of evidence, and the writing of research reports.

That is why the first two chapters of this book are devoted to explaining why and how the skills learned in writing a research paper will help all students reach their own educational, intellectual, and personal goals. That is why the examples used throughout the book are drawn not merely from literary research or from academic research, but from the full spectrum of human activity. And that is why we have declined to present an idealized view of the research process, preferring instead to tell the truth as best we could about a process that is not always neat, predictable, and orderly.

In this book, as in our own classes, we try to demonstrate in the most compelling terms that research is connected at the highest level to the continuum of human progress, and we invite students to see themselves as potential contributors to that process. At the same time, however, we make clear that at the lowest and most concrete level the essential skills to be covered can help immensely with such mundane projects as getting through college and succeeding on the job.

That is why this book begins and ends with material not normally covered in similar texts. It begins, in effect, with an effort to connect the research paper as the teacher conceives it to the real world as the student understands it; and it ends with an invitation to the student to consider the value and the possible future uses of what he or she has learned. This material, while pedagogically valuable in our experience, is not essential to the integrity of the rest of the book.

Though our own experience convinces us of the value of placing the research paper in its rhetorical context at the beginning, instructors who wish to move more quickly to discussing the selection of a topic, the shaping of a research question, the introduction to the library, and the essentials of documentation can easily do so by skipping the first two chapters until such time as they want to address the questions raised in those pages. Similarly, no loss to the *usual* coverage of the research paper follows if the last chapter is omitted.

We are quite aware that in recent years some excellent English instructors have shifted their focus away from library research towards various kinds of empirical investigation. Those instructors may find their patience stretched a bit when they note that our chapter on primary research, hefty through it is, does not appear until after the essentials of the traditional library-based research report have been thoroughly covered. This postponement was necessary to keep the emphasis where we still believe it belongs: on library research.

Still, the book is consciously and intentionally a middle-of-the road text. The very catholicity to which it aspires could not be achieved without a reasonably adequate treatment of several alternative modes of primary research. Most instructors will find, we think, that the treatment of this material in chapter 10 is sufficient for beginning students in a composition course. For reasons of their own, however, they may want to assign chapter 10 earlier in the course than its present placement would seem to suggest. We know of no reason that doing so would diminish in any way the value of what is covered, there or anywhere else in the book.

Another point at which instructors will surely want to use their own judgment is in the assignment of exercises from this book. The discussion questions, exercises, and writing assignments are numerous and varied. They range from drill with details of documentation to discussion questions concerning far-reaching ethical implications of modern research and the rhetorical practices of those who write about it.

In such a mix, obviously, not all assignments will be appropriate for all students. Yet we consider this one of the strengths of the book, for we believe that a text can be nothing more and should be nothing less than a professional tool for teachers, and we have tried in these pages to expand, not restrict their options.

And finally, because we find that—next to the excitement of research—the excitement of teaching is one of the things that make life most worth living, we invite all who are willing to do so to share with us their own reactions and those of the students whom they introduce to research with the help of this book.

1

Why Research Is Important to You

You cannot live in the United States today and remain unaffected by research. You are born in a hospital which is itself a constantly changing assembly of life-sustaining equipment created and kept up-to-date by research. You grow up, shopping daily in malls which, as a result of research, will sell thirty-two times as many different products on the day of your death as they did on the day of your birth.

No matter what your occupation or where you pursue it, your work will be continuously affected by research. If you work for a corporation, your employer's future will depend in large part on how wisely it spends its share of the $18,428,000,000 that American industry invests each year in research and development. If you work for a small business, you are sure to be affected by the the millions of smaller research projects that businesses use to learn the market value of real estate, to clarify tax laws, to find packaging techniques that sell products, and to develop whatever other information they need to earn their profits. In a very real sense, your job is likely to be created by research, sustained by research, and—if someday technological unemployment catches up with you as it has thousands of others—destroyed by research.

It has been estimated that between 1900 and 1960, the total amount of human knowledge just about doubled. Since then, as Alvin Toffler points out in his book *Future Shock,* the rate at which we are compiling knowledge has been increasing at a dizzying pace.

Today, for example, the number of scientific journals and articles is doubling, like industrial production in the advanced countries, about every fifteen years, and according to biochemist Philip Siekevitz, "what has been learned in the last three decades about the nature of living beings dwarfs in

1

extent of knowledge any comparable period of scientific discovery in the history of mankind." Today the United States government alone generates 100,000 reports each year, plus 450,000 articles, books and papers. On a world-wide basis, scientific and technical literature mounts at a rate of some 60,000,000 pages a year (31).

During the entire year in which Columbus discovered America, only about a thousand books were published. In the mid-sixties, the total reached a thousand books a *day*—and the rate, as Toffler points out, continues to accelerate. About a century after Columbus, Sir Francis Bacon, a brilliant English lawyer and scholar, could still seriously expect to read all that was known. Today, though, only a fool would claim, as Bacon did, "I have taken all knowledge for my province."

Futurists—scholars who study present trends and use them to predict the future—tell us that society in the information age is likely to evolve so that the major social rift is not so much between the "haves" and the "have-nots." The advantaged class, they say, will become those who have access to the new information, the "knows." Those without such access will become the new class of deprived citizens, the "don't knows."

Simply by going to college, you have assured yourself a chance to remain "in the know." You will not do this, of course, by reading everything printed. You will do it by learning to identify and locate what, for your purposes, you really need to read. Your essential reading, if not your day-to-day work as a college graduate, is almost certain to keep you in touch with ongoing research. The exact way you apply what you learn from this book may vary according to whether you choose a career in the humanities, in journalism, in business, or in one of the professions.

But even if your job never requires you actually to do research, you can be sure that you will eventually need to know what is covered in the following pages. For in almost every modern organization, the way to the top leads farther and farther from the shop and more and more towards paperwork. It is upon information and communication, above all else, that modern business depends. Those in positions of responsibility must receive information, combine it, reflect on it, and make the right decisions about it. Much of that information, naturally, is based on research. Even those executives and professionals who never conduct research themselves will still be called upon to read and evaluate reports. And research reports are what this book is about.

WHY WHAT WE KNOW IS NOT NECESSARILY SO

To be understood at all, the research report must be understood in context. One good way to understand how you and your future research fit into the big picture is to consider some research findings that may help you compare yourself with the "typical" student. The book *Forms of Intellectual and Ethical Development in the College Years* by William G. Perry, Jr. summarizes psychological studies that show a remarkably consistent pattern of intellectual growth among college students. Because nobody can pretend to tell you about your private experiences as a human being, you may find that you are an exception. Even so, it will help you understand the nature of research if you know a little about this pattern.

Most students begin college with the assumption that knowledge and information are the same thing. They assume, unconsciously, that their professors have more knowledge *because* they know more facts. This assumption leads them, naturally, to expect that college teaching will consist mainly of lectures in which professors deliver information for students to remember and perhaps later to use. Thus they consider information to be a measurable "product," the college to be some sort of delivery vehicle, and themselves almost to be inanimate computers, waiting passively to take delivery on, and store, that information.

The most obvious error in this view is that facts are not uniform and interchangeable parts in our structure of knowledge. A man who knows two facts ("Arkansas produces 85% of the bauxite mined in the United States" and "Nashville, Tennessee, was first established as Fort Nashborough") is not necessarily twice as knowledgeable as a man knowing only one. To constitute knowledge, facts must be understood, connected, evaluated, and assigned a place in a whole pattern of organized information. Therefore, students' education cannot really begin as long as they see their job as one of taking delivery on unquestionable "truth."

It is, in fact, in their changing attitudes towards questioning that students show genuine educational development. At first, most students see the professor's every question as a test, used to check their understanding and recall of the information given them. Then they begin to see that often the instructor asks questions because he or she is more interested in their reasoning than in the specific answers they come up with. At this mid-point in their growth, they frequently suspect their teachers of toying with them. They assume that the professors really "know" the answers, but purposely withhold them in order to teach students to think for themselves. Finally, though, most students come to realize that their best instructors have not been playing games. Their changing assumptions about knowledge have brought them to the most important truth there is to learn: no secret hoard of answers exists.

The professors' only real knowledge consists of their ability to shape questions that can and should be answered. In order to ask such questions, researchers must first evaluate and organize the information they have. Second, they must remain aware of what they do *not* know. And third, they must formulate their questions so that the answers gained from their research will add to their present understanding. Professors cannot hand students the truth because nobody can possibly know "the truth, the whole truth, and nothing but the truth." What good professors try very hard to share with their students are their methods for continually grasping more and more partial truths. All they have to share, finally, are the findings and methods of their research.

Their real advantage, therefore, grows directly out of their questioning attitude. For true scholars know that virtually all human knowledge is tentative. Before his death in 1947 at the age of eighty-seven, the famous philosopher Alfred North Whitehead often entertained groups of students and scholars in his home. Again and again, he would stress to the students his amazement that almost nothing he had learned as an undergraduate at Cambridge University in the early 1880s was still considered true in the 1940s.

You would be an exceptional student indeed if, after reading these paragraphs, you suddenly transformed yourself into a restrained and disciplined thinker about all subjects that came to your attention. For most people, that growth comes later, more slowly and less surely. But you can sharpen your understanding of research a great deal simply by considering the implications of that fact which Whitehead found so fascinating.

VIRTUALLY ALL HUMAN KNOWLEDGE IS TENTATIVE

If our best and surest knowledge becomes so quickly outmoded, it necessarily follows that we cannot simply rely on the wisdom of our forebears. Unfortunately, the wisdom of yesteryear comes to us tangled indistinguishably with yesterday's errors and dogmas. Intellectual and economic progress requires that old beliefs be challenged, for nobody can know in advance which of our present certainties will ultimately prove to be misplaced. Certainly no one today would attempt to cure depression by removing "bad blood" from the patient. Yet for more than a thousand years, physicians practiced bloodletting as confidently as today's doctors apply antiseptic.

Indeed, the case of antiseptic has about it a certain apt irony. It happens that less than twenty years ago researchers discovered that the antiseptic lotion then routinely given to hospital patients was toxic when absorbed through cuts and abrasions on the skin. One day the use of that lotion constituted our most enlightened medical practice. A year later, its use would have been considered near-quackery. Research is an ongoing quest for knowledge which by its nature must often undermine "information" from the past in order to establish new truths.

Those long years during which hospitals unwittingly used a toxic antiseptic illustrate the wisdom in a quip by an anonymous frontier humorist. "It ain't the things we don't know that works the mischief," he said. "It's the things we know that ain't so." That observation deserves thinking about. It reminds us that our beliefs and assumptions are *always* intermixed with our knowledge and that harm can result if we forget this fact. The following exercise gives you an opportunity to test the generalization that all human knowledge is tentative, so that you can clarify your understanding and decide for yourself the extent to which you agree.

EXERCISE 1.1:   Knowledge, Beliefs, and Assumptions

PART ONE: WHAT DOES IT MEAN TO "KNOW"?

Directions: Each of the following statements was considered known truth at one time or another. Some are still about as certain as human knowledge can be. Others are generally considered rank foolishness today. Most are now believed by some but not all people. Rate each statement according to your estimate of its acceptance today.

Use the number below	to indicate your estimate that this percentage of Americans still believe a statement.
1	Less than 15%
2	15%–40%
3	About 50%
4	60%–85%
5	More than 85%

1. All matter is made up of *four* elements: earth, air, fire, and water. (Considered "known" about 300 B.C.)
2. Occasionally it rains toads and earthworms. ("Known" about 100 B.C.)
3. There are spirits which inhabit matter and which can, under the right conditions, be "distilled" out of such substances as camphor, turpentine, etc. ("Known" about 1500.)
4. God made man for a purpose. (Considered established knowledge about 1400.)
5. To those who surrender their souls, the devil gives the powers of witchcraft. ("Known" about 1600.)
6. Hypnosis does not exist. ("Known" about 1800.)
7. Life must come from life. ("Known" about 1875.)
8. All matter is composed of atoms, which in turn are composed of electrons. ("Known" about 1900.)
9. The subconscious mind exerts a steady and important influence on our daily lives. ("Known" about 1920.)
10. The oriental practice of acupuncture for pain relief and medical treatment has no basis in scientific fact. ("Known" about 1960.)

PART TWO: QUESTIONS FOR DISCUSSION AND REFLECTION

1. One thing demonstrated by part one of this exercise is that, at any given time, some human knowledge is being superseded by newer discoveries and interpretations. Where, then, does this new knowledge come from? What obstacles must it overcome before it can be accepted?

2. Throughout history lives have been lost, injustices done, and suffering extended because people "knew" things that were not true. Can you see how any of the beliefs listed above could have contributed to such misfortunes?

3. Do you agree with the point of this exercise: That virtually all human knowledge is tentative? Why? Is this just another way of saying that *real knowledge* is impossible? If so, why should we continue our educational and research activities? Why not just give up and quit?

PART THREE: WRITING ASSIGNMENTS

1. Have you ever personally observed a situation in which a well-intentioned but misinformed person caused harm by holding inflexibly to an erroneous dogma, superstition, or assumption? Write a one-to-three-page account of the event, identifying the dogma and explaining the harm done.

2. In view of the tentativeness of human knowledge, what is the proper role of argumentation and persuasion in modern life? Does one person actually have a right to undertake to change the views of another? If so, in which circumstances do you think such persuasion is justified, and what persuasive methods do you think it proper to use? Consider these questions carefully. Then take *one* conclusion you reached and explain, in a two-to-four-page paper, how you reached it and what light it sheds on the role of research in modern life.

COMMONLY ACCEPTED SOURCES OF "TRUTH"

What most people accept as "truths," at any point in history, will be found upon examination to derive from one of four sources. First, some beliefs are just accepted by convention, i.e., "everybody knows it." In the United States everybody "knows" that it is "normal" to stand about three feet away when talking with a casual acquaintance. Citizens of many Latin American countries "know," however, that so much distance is a sure sign of aloofness. Their conventions are different; yet both beliefs are correct because they accurately reflect the conventions of the respective cultures. Second, some beliefs are based on authoritarian pronouncements by a source which is seldom or never questioned: A Bible, a Koran, a *Mein Kampf*, a Communist Manifesto, or even a constitution. Third, some "truths" are accepted simply because they seem intuitively right. These include many spiritual and religious perceptions, perhaps most personal values, and almost all esthetic insights. Surprisingly, however, they also include mathematical relationships and scientific hypotheses which, often enough, are conceived of *before* the experiments and proofs that will later be called upon to demonstrate them. Finally, some beliefs are based on the logical consideration of observable evidence. This, of course, is the domain of systematic research and the subject to which most of this book will be devoted.

EXERCISE 1.2:   Where "Truths" Originate

Directions: Use the glossary below to select the letter that correctly identifies the source of each of the "truths" listed.

Use this letter	to indicate that the source is
S	social convention
A	authoritarian pronouncement
I	intuitive perception
R	rational interpretation of observable evidence

1. "Numerology can hardly be called superstition. Aristotle wrote at length on the virtues of the number seven; many great philosophers believed that they could predict the future with their mathematics, and Kepler, the seventeenth-century scientist who discovered the elliptical orbit of the planets, was a devout believer in the magic of numbers." The heavy reliance on the opinions of Aristotle and Kepler show that the speaker relies on what source of "truth"?

2. Men of the nomadic tribes of Arabia demonstrate their virility to each other by seeing who can drink the filthiest water. The importance of an ability to drink filthy water goes unquestioned among these nomads because their "truth" originates in what source?

3. Before it was definitely decided to arrange the numbers on push-button telephones as they now are, designers tried placing them in a variety of ways: circular, two vertical rows, two horizontal rows, diagonal patterns, etc. Experimentation proved that most people made fewer mistakes with today's four rows of three buttons each. On which source of truth did telephone manufacturers depend when they decided to adopt the now-familiar design?

4. In some cultures, including some regions of the United States, people solve their most important personal problems by means of bibliomancy. Here is the definition of *bibliomancy* given in the 1968 edition of *The Random House Dictionary of the English Language:*

   "*bibliomancy* (bib'le o man' se) n. divination by means of a book, esp. the Bible opened at random to some verse or passage which is then interpreted. biblio + mancy."

   What source of "truth" is relied on by those who use bibliomancy to solve problems?

5. "I turned my chair to the fire and dozed. Again the atoms were gambolling before my eyes. This time the smaller groups kept modestly in the background. My mental eye, rendered more acute by repeated visions of this kind, could now distinguish larger structures, of manifold conformation; long rows, sometimes more closely fitted together; all twining and twisting in snakelike motion. But look! What was that? One of the snakes had seized hold of its own tail, and the form whirled mockingly before my eyes. As if by a flash of lightning I awoke. . . . Let us learn to dream, gentlemen."

The above quotation is from Friedrich August von Kekule, whose dream of the serpent with its tail in its mouth caused him to conceive today's accepted description of the molecular structure of the benzene ring. From which source of "truth" did this scientific discovery originate?

6. After hundreds of years, the accumulated inaccuracies in the old Julian calendar began to cause real problems. So in 1752 England responded by adjusting its calendar to the newer, more accurate Gregorian version, which had already been adopted in Catholic Europe. When this correction was made, however, people rioted in the streets and shouted, "Give us back our fourteen days."

The fact that most people, including those eighteenth-century rioters, think of officially endorsed units of time as immutable, perhaps even God-given, shows that they place great trust in what source of "truth"?

7. The history of science records many conspicuous cases of researchers ahead of their time who became martyrs and public tragedies. "Robert Mayer, co-discoverer of the Principle of the Conservation of Energy, went insane because of lack of recognition for his work. So did Ignaz Semmelweiss, who discovered, in 1847, that the cause of childbed fever was infection of the patient with the 'cadaveric material' which surgeons and students carried on their hands. As an assistant at the General Hospital in Vienna, Semmelweiss introduced the strict rule of washing hands in chlorinated lime water before entering the ward. Before this innovation, one out of every eight women in the ward had died of puerperal fever; immediately afterwards mortality fell to one in thirty, and the next year to one in a hundred. Semmelweiss' reward was to be hounded out of Vienna by the medical profession—which was moved, apart from stupidity, by resentment of the suggestion that they might be carrying death on their hands. He went to Budapest, but made little headway with his doctrine, denounced his opponents as murderers, became raving mad, was put into a restraining jacket, and died in a mental hospital."

This quotation from Arthur Koestler's *The Act of Creation* suggests that the old "truth" which blocked advancement in these cases probably derived from which source?

8. In the May, 1975 issue of *Harper's* magazine, CIA intelligence analyst Sam Adams wrote that he made an amazing discovery in the mid-1960s. Just as the American government was leading the country deeper and deeper into the Vietnam War, he used techniques worked out for analyzing captured enemy documents to learn that the number of enemy soldiers was about *ten times* greater than allowed for in official U.S. estimates. Because the country was so divided in its support of the war, Adams says, his figures were suppressed by collusion among leaders in the Army, the CIA, and probably the White House.

Adams says that his continued efforts to get his well-supported figures taken seriously were responsible for his being transferred to what was then an insignificant job, writing a history of the rebel movement in nearby Cambodia. (Meanwhile, the enemy had seized the offensive in Vietnam and, within a very few months, had pressed near to final victory.) Soon after his assignment to the Cambodian section, Adams discovered that the official

U.S. estimate of the number of communist rebels in that country was also unrealistically low.

". . . Using exactly the same methods that I'd used on the Vietcong estimate before Tet (only now the methods were more refined), I came to the conclusion that the size of the Cambodian Communist Army was not 5,000 to 10,000 but more like 100,000 to 150,000. In other words, the U.S. government's official estimate was between ten and thirty times too low."

Adams reported that his estimates came from a systematic analysis of captured enemy documents. This being true, his estimate of the actual numbers of enemy troops came from which source of "truth"?

9. Adams submitted the figures mentioned in question 8 to his superiors in a memorandum report. The following is his account of what happened then:

"My memo was ready in early June, and this time I gave a copy to John Court of the White House the day before I turned it in at the Agency. This proved to be a wise move, because when I turned it in I was told, 'Under no circumstances does this go out of the room.' It was the best order-of-battle paper I'd ever done. It had about 120 footnotes, referencing about twice that many intelligence reports, and it was solid as a rock.

"A week later, I was taken off the Khmer Communist Army and forbidden to work on numbers anymore. *A junior analyst began reworking my memo with instructions to hold the figure below 30,000.* The analyst puzzled over this for several months, and at last settled on the same method the military had used in lowering the Vietcong estimates before Tet. He marched two whole categories out of the order of battle and 'scaled down' what was left. . . . The CIA published the memo, and that number became the U.S. government's official estimate" [italics added].

If Adams is correct in saying that CIA leaders instructed his successor to hold their estimate below 30,000 regardless of the evidence, then what was the real source of the "truth" in the figures that were finally given to the American people?

10. In 1597, King James I published a scholarly book on witchcraft. After explaining why no special mercy could be shown to women, children, or unfortunates convicted of witchcraft, even when they were personally known to the magistrate, James repeated his insistence on the death penalty. Here is a modern English version of what he wrote:

"When the chief magistrate needs their testimony in further trials, he may continue torturing them for such time as suits his needs. He may not, however, delay longer than necessary in putting them to death. For to spare their lives and not to strike when God bids strike and thus to severely punish so odious a treason against God is more than unlawful. It is doubtless no less sin in the magistrate who pardons them than it was in Saul's sparing of Agag, which was comparable to the sin of witchcraft itself, as Samuel alleged at the time."

Considering that King James' book claims to be science, takes much of its evidence from the Bible, and presents reasoning that has the force of law, on which source of truth, in your opinion, does his argument chiefly rest?

THE ADVANTAGES OF BEING REASONABLE

The fact that this book is about research in no way implies that the other approaches to truth are necessarily wrong. Human experience is so varied that each approach must at one time or another be relied upon. Where there is no need to raise important questions, social convention is a perfectly sound basis for solving occasional problems to the satisfaction of everybody. Where solid evidence is lacking and the results of being mistaken are not serious, intuition may be one's best guide.

When questions of great moment demand immediate answers, there may not be time to assemble and consider all the evidence. In the midst of military combat or social upheaval, it may be more important to arrive at *some* answer quickly than to take longer and choose the best one. The police officer working a traffic accident, the mayor contending with a riot, and the general responding to a surprise attack must, in a sense, shape the truth by the orders they give. Such authorities are a little like baseball umpires. Whatever they call a strike is a strike; what they call a ball is a ball. That is the way it has to be.

Under normal conditions, however, rational inquiry is the acknowledged and preferred source of knowledge in our culture. An American salesperson trying to persuade a buyer to use a new product knows that he or she must present research demonstrating that the product is cheaper or better. Governmental procurement officers and purchasers for businesses expect such data, and so do informed consumers. That is why such huge amounts are spent by corporations, universities, and government laboratories to develop the needed data.

When existing laws are questioned or new ones proposed, Senate and House committees subpoena expert witnesses to give testimony under oath on the relevant issues. The process is one of research, and the reports that are issued, though much longer, are developed by the same procedures that you will learn from this book. An even more familiar example of research in action is the jury trial. Here, the opposing attorneys and the judge cooperate in assembling and presenting to the jury all the relevant facts: the physical evidence, the testimony of witnesses, the opinions of experts, the wording of the law, and the significance of past court decisions—in short, everything that the jury can properly consider to arrive at a rational decision.

A moment's reflection will convince almost any objective thinker that virtually every segment of our technological society depends heavily on, and values, research. Even people who have only the vaguest understanding of rational inquiry hold research in esteem and respect its findings. Why else would TV hucksters who peddle toothpaste and laxatives to the masses so often brandish research reports from book-lined studies or appear in white coats surrounded by a contrived aura of scientism?

WHAT, EXACTLY, IS RESEARCH?

Research is the method by which rational inquiry is used to generate new knowledge. The purpose of this chapter is to explain fully the meaning of this definition. First, however, it is important to be clear about what research is not. It is not, for one thing, a process leading to "pure" knowledge. A common mistake is to assume that the *only* way to arrive at valid truths is via objective, scholarly research. We have just seen, however, that a belief is not necessarily wrong just because it is highly conventional or is communicated with authority or seems intuitively obvious.

In fact all these avenues to truth figure prominently in well-conducted research. Even empirical science has its "received opinion," which is not unlike the common man's conventional beliefs; its authorities, whom lesser scientists hesitate to contradict; and its geniuses, whose intuitive flashes light up intellectual territory that must be systematically explored by whole generations of more pedestrian researchers.

The advantage of reasoned investigation is not that it increases the *possibility* of a true conclusion; beliefs derived from any of the four sources *may* be correct. Those not based on reason, however, come to us with no guarantee of their accuracy and offer us no basis for deciding whether or not to trust them.

An important advantage of research is that it *decreases* the *probability* of a false conclusion. By proceeding rationally and objectively, by bringing together what is already known, and by basing new claims on explicit reasoning, research produces the most probable conclusions to be drawn, in a form that can be *communicated* to any qualified reader. Indeed, when research is considered from the point of view of the total society, it may be this communicability that is its biggest advantage. Our beliefs, our faiths, and our intuitions, however valid, may be forever personal and inexpressible. But the reasoning we do from evidence can be shared and used as the basis for cooperative decisions.

HOW COMMON IS COMMON SENSE?

A lay person watching a science-fiction movie or visiting a "high-tech" laboratory is likely to be impressed chiefly by the equipment he sees. That is a mistake. Books and scientific equipment both serve only to extend the scholar's powers of observation or to help him or her think faster about observations already made. Research in any field lives not in the resources used but in the mind of the researcher. To put it differently, the most important equipment, in any field of research, is the human brain. And that, of course, is a bit of equipment that you already own.

In fact, research does not even use any special forms of thought. It only systematizes and extends the common sense of everyday life. At bottom, all research consists of four simple operations: (1) making relevant observations, (2) making intelligent guesses about the relations among observed facts, (3) testing those guesses, and (4) revising them in the light of test results. These four operations are not in the least strange or mysterious. They are as natural to humans as breathing.

Suppose that on a cold January morning you jump into your car praying that you can get it started before you freeze to the icy vinyl seat. You turn the key. A moan sounds under the hood. You try again (i.e., you replicate the expriment). Still nothing. So you make a guess based on your observations. Hypothesis: "The battery terminals are loose or corroded." But you lift the hood, trace the ground wire to the battery and find both connections in good shape. Scratch Hypothesis One. Hypothesis Two: "The battery is out of water." But you check the cells and find them full. Hypothesis Two also is rejected on the basis of experimental findings.

From here on, your research proceeds in earnest. Forming new hypotheses and checking them out one by one, you proceed until you find a loose starter wire. You tighten that, try the ignition again, and beam as the engine coughs to life and settles into a purr. If you are philosophically inclined, it may occur to you as you drive away that you still do not know for certain that the loose starter wire was the cause of your car trouble. Some other factor could have been operating, a short that comes and goes, say, or some similar mischief in the windings of the starter. But if you are like most people, you will assume that the starter wire was the culprit unless you have further trouble.

In effect, then, you do what a scientist does. You interpret your findings in light of the probabilities and trust conclusions based on your experimentation until contradictory evidence turns up. It will become clear in the next few chapters that *all* the specialized techniques of research, humanistic as well as scientific, are simply methods for increasing the range and accuracy of observations and for tracing more precisely the relationships among them. They are just better ways of finding the loose starter cable and surer ways of deciding whether it caused the engine failure.

WHAT RESEARCHERS THINK ABOUT

There are, essentially, three kinds of research, all of which are used to some extent in every branch of scholarship, science, and technology. You will see, as we proceed, that certain kinds of investigation are particularly suited to certain disciplines. But all researchers work with data of three kinds: (1) data from the past, (2) data from the present, and surprisingly enough, (3) data from the future.

Getting to the Truth about the Past

Reports of research using data from the past include histories, biographies, case studies, certain kinds of survey research, and literary and social criticism based on historical evidence. Historians and literary scholars spend innumerable hours in archives, reading through old newspapers, journals, and diaries, piecing together the events of bygone days. Often it is necessary to confirm dates and establish chronology by checking public records or by reading through private collections of letters and journals. Clues carefully teased from sources like these enable intellectual detectives to assemble the biographies and histories that make up much of our cultural heritage.

An adaptation of this historical method produces the *case study*, widely used in marketing, business management, clinical psychology, and medicine. A case study is a comprehensive history of a single subject of investigation, for example, a single patient or a small business. Case studies are usually used during the earliest stages of investigation, before the development of firm hypotheses and enough received opinion to guide more definitive work. The physician takes a detailed medical history, and the psychologist takes copious notes on a patient's early childhood, neither knowing in advance just which questions are likely to lead to the proper diagnosis.

A somewhat different method of collecting data from the past is used frequently in the social sciences. Special questionnaires or structured interviews are used in *survey* research, which is often designed to gather information from informants on such subjects as child-rearing practices or job histories. In such studies, the researcher reaches back through time, as it were, and brings together selected information from hundreds or perhaps thousands of persons, all total strangers to her and to each other.

Getting to the Truth about the Present

Some research concentrates on understanding the significance of data from the present. Examples include field studies, taxonomies, real estate appraisals, polls, surveys, and military status reports, all dealing with events that are currently taking place.

Field studies, for instance, are an important tool of anthropologists, who often attempt to understand the social structure of a tribe, subculture, or community by living among its members and making detailed notes of their daily routines. Ethologists also use field studies to help them interpret data from laboratory experiments and observations made of animals living in captivity.

A special type of present-oriented research concentrates on the classification of data. *Taxonomy,* as it is called, can be an important branch of study, for only when observations are properly grouped can they lead us to the generalizations that spark new discoveries. If you are a psychoanalyst, it makes a great difference whether you classify homosexuality as a neurosis, a psychosis, or a normal alternative in development. Taxonomic research is particularly important to botanists and zoologists, whose studies require them to classify every form of life.

A more familiar type of present-oriented research, possibly, is found in the surveys and polls used to gather facts about recent events. The Nielsen ratings of TV shows, for instance, are based on viewers' current preferences. And the question usually posed by pollsters like Gallup, Roper, and Harris is, "Who would you vote for if the election were held *today?*"

Getting to the Truth about the Future

In one sense, all research is oriented towards the future. Because scholars consider all knowledge tentative, the findings of any investigation remain unquestioned only as long as still newer findings agree with them. Four centuries after Shakespeare, literary critics are still refining their interpretations of his plays. They are able to do this partly because they continue to bring together more information about the man and his time. Just as important, however, is the fact that different critics emphasize different evidence in the plays, and even when considering the same lines often evaluate them differently. Still, the state of Shakespearean studies is not nearly as chaotic as this brief description would seem to suggest.

The main reason it is not is that, in its own way, literary scholarship is also oriented toward the future. Some years ago the great Shakespearean critic Walter Clyde Curry argued convincingly that the witches in Shakespeare's *Macbeth* were not real witches at all, but demons pretending to be witches. (Remember, in Shakespeare's time, just four centuries ago, witches and demons were both as real to most people as space travel is to us.) Curry reached his conclusion because he believed that, according to seventeenth-century science, only demons could disappear instantaneously, as Shakespeare's witches did. He understood the "research" of Shakespeare's day to hold that witches could not vanish in a flash. He correctly cited "experts" of the time who denied witches' ability to disappear at one place and appear at another without crossing the space in between. When witches seemed to vanish, according to these Elizabethan experts, they did so by somehow solidifying the air around themselves so that, though still there, they became invisible. On the basis of this evidence, Curry argued that a real witch might appear to fade away slowly but could not, in Shakespeare's understanding, vanish instantly.

Curry's conclusion was based on the assumption that it would necessarily take time to form such an airy curtain of invisibility. Because some points in the meaning of the play hinged on this point, however, Robert West and other later scholars continued looking for additional evidence. And in time they found good reason to question Curry's denial that real witches' disappearances could *appear* to take place in a flash. First of all, none of the "experts" of Shakespeare's day actually said that the air could not solidify instantly. Secondly, in the transcripts of actual court cases and in plays based on those cases, eyewitness testimony did sometimes describe instantaneous disappearances. On that point, then, Curry was wrong, and his resulting interpretation of *Macbeth* was to that degree suspect. Thus the way was cleared for a somewhat more accurate understanding of Shakespeare's masterpiece.

Notice, though, the pattern in this step forward. In presenting his original interpretation, Curry was in effect betting that whatever evidence turned up in the future would support his conclusions. Curry usually won his bets. He made a number of lasting contributions to Shakespearean scholarship. But on this one point he was mistaken. When additional evidence came in, it undermined what he thought he had established and thus demonstrated again the tentativeness of human knowledge. In this limited sense, then, all research is oriented towards the future.

In science, however, this practice of testing present knowledge against future observations is much more formal than in the humanities. Almost all scientific knowledge is expected, in some way, to meet the *criterion of predictability*. In fact, the function of scientific hypotheses and theories is to predict in advance what will be found when certain observations are made. These predictions are tested when the right observations are made in a special kind of future-oriented research called the experiment.

Experimental Research

Whether carried out in the laboratory or in the field, experiments are carefully planned and controlled observations. The observations must be decided on in advance, and the researcher must know which findings will confirm his or her hypothesis and which will disprove it. Laboratory experiments allow the researcher to control conditions much more exactly so that if the suspected causes are operating he or she is sure to find them. Field experiments, on the other hand, are conducted in more realistic settings. The variables cannot be as carefully controlled, but findings from a field experiment are more likely to have practical significance. That is why tire manufacturers road-test their products and why agricultural experiment stations try out new hybrids in adjacent fields. It is not uncommon for a superiority that has been demonstrated in the laboratory to be almost imperceptible in the field where unpredictable factors can work against it.

2

How and Why Research Is Reported

As you saw in chapter 1, research reports are written not only in school but also in a variety of important nonacademic settings. While you are in school, though, it is the academic reports that will be of most importance to you.

RESEARCH REPORTS IN ACADEMIC SETTINGS

In business, industry, government, and the professions, the purpose of research reports is to convey information to readers who want or need to know the findings they contain. However, this is not generally true of research reports assigned in school.

Student Assignments

In a very few courses—like this one—you will be asked to write research papers just to learn the method. Often, in beginning writing courses, the major purpose is to improve your general writing ability. You are asked to practice with research papers simply because they provide a good way to train you to make sense, in writing, of complex evidence. In more advanced courses, dealing with scientific, technical, and business writing, the purpose may also be to familiarize you with the variety of documents in which research is reported within and between organizations. Still, only a very few of your college courses will ask you to write research reports simply to learn how to write them.

More often, in courses like history, philosophy, literature, political science, and possibly psychology, you will be asked to write research reports as a kind of test. In your first few courses, your term papers will not be written primarily to inform your instructor of your conclusions. Most of the time, your instructor will know in advance more or less what your conclusions should be. The paper serves only as a record of the research you did and the thinking that you put into it. As such, it gives your instructor something tangible to react to in his or her effort to help you learn to think like a scholar in that particular discipline. That is the school report's main function.

Even so, there are two things worth noticing now about the research paper as a student assignment. The first is the normal progression you will follow if you choose to major in an academic subject in which term paper assignments are commonly used. Although you usually start out, in such a major, by reporting research that only tells the instructor what he or she already knows, this is not where you end up. By the time you are well into your upper-division work, it will be apparent that your instructors too are subject to human limitations. No more than you can they "take all knowledge for . . . [their] province." So when your research skills are polished enough, and you are far enough along in your work, you may well reach a point where your instructors are in fact learning from your reports. They will still be your teachers, informing you of overlooked sources, guiding your reasoning, pointing out new possibilities, etc. But more and more, they will be speaking to you on equal terms, as one researcher to another, in a joint effort to get at the truth.

The final point to make about the research paper as a student assignment is merely to underscore the moral in what we have been saying. Because report writing is likely to play an important part in your future college work, common sense would dictate that you learn all you can from this book. Obviously, the sooner you learn to write good research papers, the surer, the easier, and the more enjoyable your success in college will be.

Professional Reports

Later, if you happen to become a school administrator, teacher, or professor, you will soon realize that student assignments are only one kind of research report in academic life. The bigger the school system or university, the more it depends on its internal flow of research-based information. Whether new buildings are built or old ones closed depends in large part on the persuasiveness of those messages. To have a significant impact on either the administration or the curriculum, an individual teacher can usually make his or her voice heard only with memoranda and letters based on solid research.

At the college and university level, faculty advancement depends heavily on the research that a professor conducts and reports. One of the professor's most important duties outside the classroom is to attend professional meetings where colleagues read and listen to papers reporting their latest research. It is here that the new knowledge, which perhaps ten years later will make its way into introductory texts, is first made available. When scholars are considered for promotion, their lists of publications and papers read are among the most important yardsticks for measuring "productivity."

The conventions and techniques used in all such reports are the ones that you are studying in this book.

RESEARCH REPORTS IN BUSINESS, INDUSTRY, AND PROFESSIONAL PRACTICE

Despite their significant role in school work, however, by far the most important uses of research reports are in non-academic settings. In chapter 1 we repeatedly emphasized that, to an extent unprecedented in human history, the American economy runs on research. Reports are the means by which findings from that research are delivered to those who can put them to use.

THE RESEARCH PAPER AND ITS AUDIENCE

A good writer is always mindful of the interests, needs, and expectations of his or her reader. This is particularly true of the writer of research papers, for readers come to research papers with definite needs. They expect to meet these needs with information that will be presented to them in a conventional report style and format. So writers of research reports, to a greater degree than essayists, journalists, or most college theme writers, are bound by the conventional expectations of their readers.

In many other kinds of writing, the author can find ways to "coach" the reader into reading in a special way. If the informal essayist, for instance, obviously takes on the role of a president or a pet or even an inanimate object, he or she can expect good readers to "catch on," to go along with the pretense, and to try at least to read as if the fiction were true. If the writer is successful, readers will, by following the cues, become nostalgic, amused, or outraged, just as the writer wanted them to.

The writer of the research report, on the other hand, can seldom make such demands on readers. Normally, they expect to find their amusement, entertainment, and excitement elsewhere. They read research reports for information. Obviously this does not mean that they want to be bored. But it does mean that readers of research reports have some common values and expectations which writers should know about and respect.

COMMON EXPECTATIONS OF REPORT READERS

In general, readers of research reports want dependable and significant information on a subject of interest to them. A well-written report lets them know early whether or not it contains the information they need.

Features of Good Research Reports

Readers expect research papers to have the following characteristics:

1. *Clarity.* Above all else, the research paper should be clear. Its conclusions should be worded so that the reader knows exactly what claims are made and what evidence leads to those conclusions.

2. *Completeness.* Everything of relevance to the conclusions should be contained in the report. The writer is under a special obligation to mention the existence of contrary evidence that bears on the conclusions drawn.

3. *Relevance.* On the other hand, nothing should be included which is not necessary to help readers follow the reasoning that led to the conclusions. Other kinds of writing have room for occasional digressions, reminiscences, and asides. But readers of research expect writers to stick to the subject.

4. *Reasonableness.* Because research depends on reasoning soundly from demonstrable evidence, rationality is a most important feature of the research report. The researcher at times may work with evidence that is, by its very nature, charged with emotion. Case studies of rape or outrageous instances of political corruption, for example, may lead the writer to strong conclusions. In special circumstances, he or she may intentionally let strength of conviction show indirectly in the language. But in general, the research report will be more convincing to readers if it is clearly based on an objective consideration of evidence.

DIFFERING AUDIENCE EXPECTATIONS AND NEEDS

Although most readers of research reports share the expectations listed above, audiences vary in other ways. Your reports will be more successful if you adapt them to the values and expectations of your particular audiences. To help you do this, consider the following questions:

1. *How involved are your readers in the subject of your report?* Are they professionals who are eagerly waiting for you to provide information they need? Or will your report arrive unexpectedly in their mail where it may not even get read? The developer waiting for an appraisal report for which he has already paid wants to know the market value of the property he is considering. To him trick openings and clever techniques for keeping his interest will only be irritations.

On the other hand, a report to the public by a federal commission or a public service organization must compete for readers with all the popular books and magazines on the market. Similarly, an unsolicited proposal sent to an executive from a subordinate within the organization may not get much attention unless it is made readable and interesting.

In general, the more involved your readers are in your subject, the more objective, the more concise, and the more impersonal they will expect your report to be. The less interested the audience, the more important it is that you provide complete background information and take steps to gain their interest.

2. *How knowledgeable are your readers on this subject?* It is deadening for a layperson to plow through a report laden with the technical jargon of experts. Yet it is insulting to send to experts reports containing whole paragraphs of background information that would be taken for granted by any qualified professional in the field. The trick is to decide how much of your report will be news to your readers, to make those points clear, and to support them with evidence based on facts and research procedures with which they are familiar. In short, consider first the information your audience already has on your subject, and begin there.

3. *What do your readers **need** to know on this subject?* A famous author and U.S. senator once advised, "Write for people who know less about the subject than you do, but who don't want to know *everything*." Match the information in your report to the needs of your audience.

An environmental engineer writing a public report only needs to tell citizens whether their environment is polluted, how she knows, and what should be done. Everything she says must be true, of course, and it must follow logically from the evidence she cites. However, if she wastes words interpreting every nuance in her data and answering questions no layperson would think to ask, she will just tax her readers' patience. On the other hand, if she is recommending legislation to Congress or policies to the Environmental Protection Agency, then close reasoning from complete evidence is exactly what is needed. Such a report will be scrutinized by experts with the time and resources to help them reach the best possible decisions. They need all the facts.

4. *What is your status, in relation to your readers?* An army officer or an engineer writing to his own subordinates can reasonably expect that they will read his reports, even if the writing is a little dry. In fact, they may even accept his conclusions in the absence of complete evidence. (When this happens, of course, the effect is to tinge the research report—which should rely exclusively on an objective presentation of evidence—with an uncharacteristic element of directive or command.) But if he is writing to professional peers or superiors, it is important that the content and tone of the report reflect this. A conclusion is more likely to be evaluated on its own merits if there is no unfortunate impropriety in the handling or the wording of the report.

DEFINING THE AUDIENCE FOR SCHOOL REPORTS

Often when assignments are made for school reports, you are told what audience to address and what kind of document to write. Pay particular attention to any instructions you are given on this point. If you are given no special instructions, however, then here is a safe rule of thumb: *write for an intelligent layperson who knows good research report technique but has no special knowledge of your subject.* Write to interest this person in your subject as well as to inform her about it. Include the explanation and background that she would need. Present the evidence that would convince her of your conclusions. And document whatever she would be unlikely to accept at face value. Chances are, a report which does those things will make your instructor beam.

EXERCISE 2.1:   Zeroing In on Your Audience

Case One: It is midnight, one week before the senior prom and two weeks from your high school graduation. You, your steady, your two best friends and their dates are all crowded into your father's car on the way back from a late movie. Everybody is having a great time, laughing, telling jokes, and clowning as you approach a curve in the road ahead. Your left arm is resting in the window, and your right hand is guiding the steering wheel. Starting to turn, you meet unexpected resistance in the steering wheel. As the curve approaches, you try harder to turn the wheel. You have just realized that somehow your right arm has gotten hooked around that of the person next to you when WHAM!

Two days later you wake up in the hospital, your leg suspended in a cast, your head bandaged, and your mother beaming at you in delight. "When you are feeling better," she tells you after a while, "I will help you, and we must prepare two reports on the accident—one for the insurance adjustor and one for the police department."

The insurance adjustor must decide who is at fault and how badly your car was damaged. He wants to know, as precisely as possible, the exact nature of the impact sustained by the vehicle. The police are interested in determining whether any laws were broken or road hazards involved. Your mother has taught you not to lie or misrepresent the truth, but, being a good writer, she does not expect you to volunteer irrelevant information that your reader is not asking about or interested in.

Part One: Examine each of the statements below. Decide whether it should be included in your report to the *police* and be able to explain why, in terms of the audience expectations discussed in this chapter.

1. You were using the family car without your father's permission.
2. You did not mean to wreck the car.
3. The "Curve Ahead" warning sign was covered with vines, so that you did not see it and could not have read it if you had seen it.
4. The other five people in the car were shaken up, but nobody else was seriously hurt; all were dismissed after overnight observation in the hospital.
5. At first the doctors thought the concussion you got might lead to permanent impairment of your memory, but now they think this is less likely.
6. Depending on what the garage determines about the condition of the frame, your father's car may be totalled.
7. You were going 50 miles per hour in a 50-mile-per-hour zone when the car went out of control.
8. You were trying to turn towards the left when you found that your arm would not move.

Part Two: Which of the following statements should be included in your report to the *insurance adjustor* and which ones omitted? Again, be prepared to explain your decisions in terms of your reader's needs and expectations.

1. By the time you hit the telephone pole, you had probably slowed the car to 35–40 mph.
2. You will now have to miss the prom.
3. Police examinations of the skid marks indicate that the car was moving at a 45° angle when it slid into the pole.
4. The car always had a tendency to steer to the right.
5. Your steady is now planning to go to the prom with your chief rival.
6. The police do not plan to charge you with any offense in connection with the accident.
7. Your father is hoping that the garage will pronounce the car totalled so that the insurance company will pay for a new one.
8. Except for the collision with the pole, the car sustained no other impact.

Case Two: You are a housing inspector for your city housing authority. Recently you inspected several rental units belonging to Wilsen Frederick, a wealthy landlord, and found them unfit for human habitation. Though you gave Mr. Frederick sixty days to make the necessary repairs, he has complained to several local politicians, and you have the clear sense that he is out to get you fired. However, your boss understands the situation and is willing to back you all the way.

The boss asks you to prepare two reports: one for his eyes only in which you describe the landlord's practices in detail and offer your recommendations for dealing with his violations; and a second one which you are to prepare for your boss's signature. This second report is to be sent to inquiring politicians and is meant only to assure them that the complaining landlord has not been singled out for exceptionally harsh treatment or harassment as he claims.

The purpose of the report to your boss, then, is to explain what you, as a housing inspector, believe should be done to enforce the law in Mr. Frederick's case. The purpose of the second report is to defend the propriety of the actions already taken by the housing authority.

Part One: Decide which of the following information should and which should not be included in the report you write for *your boss's eyes only.* Be able to justify your decisions in terms of your reader's needs and expectations.

1. In the past two months, the housing authority has received eighteen complaints about properties owned by Mr. Frederick, fifteen from his tenants and three from neighbors upset over the deterioration in two of his houses on Alabama Street.

2. You promised the complaining tenants that their names would not be mentioned, since they expressed fear of Frederick's reprisals.

3. You have heard from several sources that Frederick plays cards regularly with the mayor and the chief of police.

4. Each of Frederick's six houses that you inspected had been the subject of two or more complaints, and you found serious hazards to health and safety in all of them.

5. Frederick also owns a large construction company in town.

6. He once studied for the ministry and is, in fact, still a deacon in one of the town's leading churches.

7. You only cited the three buildings with the most serious violations: one with no heat, one with no operating plumbing, and one with raw sewage standing in the basement.

8. You recommend that, for the time being, the housing authority make no change in its position but that, if Wilsen Frederick fails to repair the cited buildings in the allotted time or if he steps up the political pressure, you be instructed to cite also the other three buildings you know to be in violation, and that the housing commissioner invite the press to accompany you on your next inspection.

Part Two: Which of the following information should and should not be included in the report you prepare for your boss to distribute in response to *outside inquiries?* Be able to explain your judgments in terms of readers' interests, needs and expectations.

1. Wilsen Frederick is rumored to be connected with organized crime at the national level.

2. None of the inspections of Frederick's properties was initiated by the housing authority; all were in response to multiple complaints.

3. In the past three years, several buildings constructed out of state by Frederick's construction company have been found to be substandard.

4. In view of the seriousness of the violations, the housing authority could legally have shut down the cited buildings and moved out all the tenants immediately; it was not required to give Frederick sixty days in which to make the necessary repairs.

5. Frederick's other buildings that you inspected also showed serious code violations and could easily have been cited.

6. Frederick's son-in-law tried unsuccessfully several times to get a job as an inspector with the housing authority.

7. Some of Frederick's tenants work for him at the construction company and are afraid to have him know that they filed complaints against him.

8. The housing authority has no plans at present to depart from its policy of inspecting properties only when complaints have been received about them.

REPORTS THAT TAKE STOCK
AND REPORTS THAT TAKE A STAND

At bottom, almost all research papers can be classified into two groups: (1) those that reach firm conclusions and (2) those that do not.

The "Thesis" or Documented Argument

If you feel justified in taking a stand on your subject, then you should try to organize your paper around the most important conclusion that can safely be drawn from the available evidence. It is good practice to word this conclusion, at least for your own benefit, in one simple statement called the *thesis statement.* Everything in the main part of the paper, then, should contribute either to explaining or supporting that statement. In chapter 7, you will learn how to shape a thesis statement that fits your data. All that is necessary at this point, however, is that you understand that a thesis statement, as we use the term, makes a substantial claim based on *all the evidence presented in your paper.* The alternative to making a claim, of course, is to stand neutral, to reach no firm conclusions.

Organizing What We Know: The Report

It often happens in ongoing research that scholars find, either individually or collectively, that they have more information than they can make sense of. This usually means that the questions they are trying to answer do not yet suit the data they have. Sometimes it means that they have not subdivided their data properly. When the evidence is this confusing, good researchers know that they cannot create thesis statements just for the sake of having them.

If you have run down all the newspaper accounts of the unsolved 1873 Kelsey murder case and you really do not see anything that has gone unnoticed by the hundreds of crime enthusiasts who have reviewed the case over the past century, then you don't have a thesis. It is hardly research to single out one luckless soul whose name happened to be connected with the case and argue vehemently that he must have been the murderer. When the evidence will not support a thesis statement, you can usually organize your paper around a looser *purpose,* or *framework,* statement. Instead of stating an important conclusion, the purpose statement only tells your reader how your report will be organized.

EXAMPLES OF REPORTS BEGINNING WITH THESIS STATEMENTS

[*From a memo report instructing employees in the preparation of company reports*]

When possible, every report should be organized around a

thesis statement. A straightforward statement of the conclusion

makes the report clearer and easier to follow. It gives the

writer an "argumentative edge" that makes it easier to hold

readers' interest. And it guides him or her in decisions about what information does and does not belong in the report. Reports without clear conclusions are often hard to follow, even when they are well thought out. Nothing contributes more to giving the reader an impression of a logical mind functioning efficiently than the presence of a clear thesis properly supported.

[Note that the paragraph begins by requiring in unmistakable terms that reports have thesis statements whenever possible.]

[From a report addressed to professional educators]

Theoretically, the representative mountaineer should be a perfect example of what Wendell Johnson called "prescientific orientation." The evidence in the following pages demonstrates that he assumes reality to be static and unchanging, that he is rigidly conservative, authoritarian, inclined to worry over questions so vague as to be meaningless, and suspicious of the outside world. It will be seen that these characteristics are all defining features of the prescientific orientation.

[The first sentence commits the report to showing that Johnson's theory would necessarily require that the people described have a "prescientific orientation."]

EXAMPLES OF REPORTS BEGINNING WITH PURPOSE STATEMENTS
[From a report-writing guide]

After the data is gathered and the thinking is done, the researcher knows pretty well what must go into his report. The question then is how he is to organize what he has to say. In the following pages, we shall discuss three options that are available to him: (1) building his report around a thesis statement; (2) building it around a "framework" statement; and (3) using an empty sentence or pseudothesis, which seems to make an assertion but which actually serves only as a tool for keeping the discussion on track. First, though, we shall look at how thesis statements work in some actual reports.

[Notice that the underlined sentence in this example does not take a stand. It simply identifies the options available.]

[*From a report addressed to professional educators*]

As curriculum planners across the country consider whether once again to devote significant amounts of time to instruction in general semantics, many have expressed the need for fuller information. They want to know exactly what general semantics is, how it gained dominance in the curriculum in the 1940s and 1950s, what caused it to be dropped in the late 1950s, and what new claims it has for treatment in the public school curriculum today. <u>This report addresses each of these topics in the order named.</u>

[*Again, notice that the underlined sentence makes clear what topics will be discussed but takes no position. The reader cannot tell whether or not the writer favors reintroducing this material into the classroom.*]

When a writer is not prepared to take a stand, the limited commitment of a purpose statement, early in the report, is still useful. It gives the reader an "advance organizer" that alerts him to what is coming in the discussion ahead. And like the thesis statement, it keeps the writer aware of her commitments as she drafts the report. Each time she stops to reread what she has written, she is reminded of what remains for her to do.

You may have noticed that the third example above mentions an option not described in our discussion: the so-called pseudothesis. A pseudothesis is a sentence that has the grammatical form of a statement but asserts nothing significant about the topic. "The 1982 Healy murder case in Lafayette, Indiana was one of the most bizarre crimes in our nation's history." (What, exactly, do we mean by *bizarre*? How can we compare the "bizarreness" of crimes? What, in fact, does the statement *say*?) Another example of a pseudothesis: "There are seven different things that English teachers mean when they use the term *good writing*." Such a statement may or may not serve as a framework for organizing a sound report. It is impossible to decide just from reading the sentence. Despite its being a grammatical statement, it doesn't say anything significant.

When pseudotheses succeed, they function like framework or purpose statements, though in context they are usually less obvious and sometimes more diplomatic. Unfortunately, pseudotheses present pitfalls of their own, which we will discuss in detail later, when you are involved in shaping your own thesis statement. For now, be sure that you understand the basic difference between reports that take stands, with clear theses, and those that take stock, using noncommittal purpose statements.

EXERCISE 2.2: Choosing an Appropriate Format

Part One: Listed below are five statements, each of which could be used as the central statement of a research report. Decide which statements are worded as *theses* and which as *purpose* or *framework* statements.

1. The federal government should clean up the TPC pollution in southern Indiana.
2. Most current theories of psychology can be classified as being, at bottom, either cognitive or behaviorist.
3. There are two schools of thought on whether the community needs a gymnasium more than it needs a new courthouse.
4. The present study shows that white-collar workers who are trained to write adequate reports earn significantly more than their peers without such training.
5. The Civil Rights Commission has been packed with political appointees who are not in sympathy with the official purposes of the commission.

Part Two: Described below are several situations in which you might be called upon to write research reports. Decide for each case whether you think the purpose and the evidence available would make it more appropriate for you to take a stand (with a thesis) or simply to organize the available information (with a purpose statement).

1. You supervise an office of twenty-five clerical personnel. Three must be laid off, and your boss has asked you to investigate staff members' job performances and to prepare a confidential recommendation listing the people whom you think he should let go.
2. Your boss has asked you to suggest possible ways that the company could profitably use or dispose of one of its buildings.
3. You have just run a laboratory experiment that shows that injections of lactic acid slow nerve damage caused by rattlesnake venom. Your boss wants you to report your work in a scientific journal.
4. As a linguist, you know that after years of argument your colleagues have simply stopped discussing the question of how humans first acquired speech. They consider the question simply unanswerable. But the president of your college wants you to report on the evidence for the national PTA magazine.
5. A firm in Minneapolis is considering investing $5 million to perfect a miniature TV camera which can be housed in an artificial eyeball and connected surgically to the "vision nerves" leading to the brain. They have asked you, as an electrical engineer, to report to them on whether development of such a small TV receiver is technically feasible.

THE BURDEN OF PROOF IN RESEARCH

A key word, in discussions of research reports, is *claim.* Again and again, you will find us coming back to the question, "What claims are being made, and on what grounds do they rest?" The reason for this is that the burden of proof is always on the researcher. It is the researcher who asserts that he has generated new knowledge. It is he who asks readers,

in effect, to change their established ways of thinking. So it is the researcher who must produce the evidence that justifies his conclusions.

What Is Evidence?

The word *evidence* comes from two Latin forms; *ex-*, meaning "from,
away, outside," and *videre*, meaning "to see." The meanings of the parts,
therefore, almost define the word. Evidence is something outside ourselves, there to be seen by all qualified observers. Theoretically, all evidence is of two kinds: (1) facts and (2) logical conclusions drawn from
facts. In practice, however, report writers often rely on expert opinion
and treat it as if it were a third kind of evidence. You will probably use
all three kinds in the reports you write; so we will discuss each briefly.

Facts. A fact is a verifiable observation. That is, two qualified observers confronted with the same fact should report identical observations. If
you are reading carefully, you may have noticed the guarded wording.
Congratulate yourself if you felt an impulse to challenge, "But who decides which observers are qualified?" Philosophically minded students can
soon follow that fascinating question into deep water.

For our purposes, however, it is sufficient if we understand *qualified
observers* to mean simply people who are biologically and intellectually
competent to make the observation under consideration. Obviously, a
blind person could not verify your observation of a rainbow nor a deaf
one your perception of a concert. They lack the biological competence to
do so. Nor could we, if we happened to be in the cockpit of a spaceship,
verify the pilot's readings of speed and direction. Not having been trained
to read the instruments or even to know how astronauts keep track of direction, we are not intellectually competent to make such observations.
Only someone with the proper training would be qualified to verify the
pilot's readings—facts though they are.

Given the presence of qualified observers, there is usually less dis-
pute over facts than over other kinds of evidence. Still, disputes do occur—sometimes very emotional ones. When this happens, the issue is
nearly always whether or not a reported observation is factual, i.e.,
whether it is *verifiable*.

Suppose that Jones has been shot down in the midst of a Saturday
afternoon football crowd. Five people tell the police that the assailant was
Smith, a tall man in a blue sport coat. Four others report that they saw
the shooting done by a short man in a white knit shirt. When Smith, the
man in the blue coat, later claims in court, "I didn't kill anybody," the
judge has before him an issue of fact.

The district attorney's first job is to prove that Smith did the shooting. To make good on that claim, his or her "theory of the case" must, of

course, draw on the testimony of the five observers who saw Smith shoot Jones and must account in some way for the perceptions of those four who thought they saw someone else kill Jones.

In most report writing, though, facts themselves are not the issue. Usually, you will use facts as evidence. If you can show that they *are* verifiable, facts are normally your best evidence. As the saying goes, "You can't argue with the facts." However, you often have good reason to question their significance.

Logical Deductions Drawn From Facts. Suppose you are the district attorney in the shooting incident. Suppose, further, that when you talk to the four witnesses who blamed the killing on a white-shirted gunman, you easily disqualified them as observers. They were four high school buddies whose reports contradicted each other in other ways. Therefore, you decide, by the preponderance of the evidence, that one boy probably thought he saw something and has since half-bullied his buddies into corroborating his story so that they can all get their names in the paper. This leaves you, as district attorney, with five credible eyewitnesses to the killing, all of whom are willing to testify that Smith shot Jones. And suppose, finally, that when Smith comes to trial, he changes his story and openly admits the shooting. Does this close your case? Have you convicted your murderer?

Not by a long shot! Only your claim that Smith *killed* Jones has been supported. The fact of the killing alone does not support the conclusion that the killing was legally a murder. Before *that* claim could be supported, you would have to consider all the available facts. There are, after all, a number of perfectly legal reasons that Smith might have killed Jones. Was Smith acting in self-defense? Had Jones been intentionally provoking Smith over an extended period? Did Smith go insane? Could the shooting have been accidental? As your research leads you into questions like these, it is taking you away from incontestable facts and into the area of judgment.

To remain *evidence,* to be data capable of supporting rational inquiry, these judgments must advance logically, step by step. First one claim is established by factual evidence. Then the established claim becomes evidence which fits with other evidence into a pattern that supports a second claim. And thus you proceed until finally you have demonstrated that the only conclusion which accounts for all the evidence is the judgment that Smith's killing of Jones falls within the legal definition of murder. That is not only the method of research in the practice of law. It is the method of research everywhere. And a good research report is one which keeps its method clear.

Expert Opinion. One shortcut, as the researcher inchworms her way to the findings she is interested in, is to cite experts and to treat their opinions as if they were themselves evidence. When you stop to think, however, it becomes clear that an expert's opinion, being nothing more than his own research conclusions, is based on the same two kinds of evidence that are available to you. He, too, depends on facts and on logical conclusions based on facts. Expertise is only an acquaintance with a wider range of relevant facts and greater competence in reasoning soundly with them.

Still, it often shortens and tightens a report to cite experts instead of going directly to the facts to establish every little point in your case. This is especially true when the opinion cited is generally accepted, when the point only serves as a starting point for your research, or when the point thus established is not crucial to your conclusions. Different disciplines vary greatly in the degree and manner in which they accept the use of expert opinion in research reports.

In general, such citations are used much more sparingly in the so-called hard sciences than in the more speculative, less experimental sciences and humanities. Both a strength and a weakness of expert testimony is that readers tend to accept it as very credible evidence, even when the facts and reasoning behind it are not clear to them. To a lay audience, therefore, a striking quotation by an acknowledged expert appears to be very persuasive evidence. Notice, however, that insofar as readers accept what the expert says only *because* he or she is an expert, they are not actually following the process of research. They are, at that point, accepting truth from authority.

GOOD SOURCES AND BAD ONES

Did you notice that two of the three kinds of evidence mentioned in the preceding section are not the product of the researcher's own thinking? Facts are already "out there" to be observed. Thousands of them have already been observed and reported in standard reference works and technical journals. They are available to any researcher, in any nearby library. There, too, can be found numerous expert opinions about the significance of those facts. Before beginning to draw conclusions of his own, therefore, the wise researcher brings together what is already known. One important function of this book is to teach you to do that.

You will learn how to take a general topic, consider it, and shape it into a researchable question. You will learn how to sleuth around in a library until you have located the information that bears on your question. What is more, you will learn to do this with the greatest efficiency and the least effort, by "pyramiding" your findings so that each source leads you to the next in a sequence that homes in on the data you need for a precise answer to your question. You will also learn useful strategies for organizing, interpreting, and reporting the data you assemble.

But first, you need to learn to distinguish good data from bad. Not every person who passes himself off as an expert is one. Not everything reported as factual in print meets our definition of a "verifiable observation." As you assemble your evidence, therefore, you should also be evaluating it. In general, as you look over your sources, your preferences should run as follows:

1. *Prefer acknowledged authorities to self-proclaimed ones.* The best index to the expertise of a researcher is the reputation he or she has among colleagues in the field. Usually, a researcher whose work is sound is known and respected at least among other experts. Very occasionally, someone completely unknown and even untrained in a discipline will do a significant piece of research. But the chances are much greater that the unknown country doctor who claims to have a cure for cancer and the kitchen-trained biologist who celebrates the discovery of a new process in the study of blood chemistry are only fooling themselves. Often such books are well written, interesting, and very popular. Therefore, you will find them in your library, even if true experts in the field consider them valueless.

2. *Prefer an authority working within his or her field of expertise to one who is reporting conclusions about another subject.* It is commonplace for a person who achieves celebrity because of accomplishments in one area to write books and articles advancing views on quite different matters. The movie star who writes on foreign policy, the journalist who becomes an instant expert on cancer, and the fiction writer who turns to psychic research are familiar examples. Such people may have valuable things to say. But it is important to remember that on the subject at hand, they are not speaking as experts. Becoming famous for accomplishments in one field does not necessarily make one competent in another.

3. *Prefer first-hand accounts over those from sources who were separated by time or space from the events reported.* Eyewitnesses are generally better sources than second-hand accounts. Written accounts set down immediately after an observation or experience are generally more accurate than those written much later, after other influences have crept in and memories have faded.

4. *Prefer unbiased and disinterested sources over those who can reasonably be suspected of having a motive for influencing the way others see the subject under investigation.* Scholars find, for instance, that biographies by close friends and relatives of famous people, though often valuable, must be read with caution. The natural tendency to suppress unflattering facts often causes the omission of evidence of potential importance to the researcher.

5. *Prefer public records to private documents in questionable cases.* The date on which a scientist applied for a patent or copyright is probably better evidence for the date of a discovery than a personal letter in which he reported to a friend that he made the discovery, unless of course the letter contained a detailed account. Humans may have any number of reasons for shading the truth in personal correspondence, but white lies of all types are less common in public records.

6. *Prefer accounts that are specific and complete to those that are vague and evasive.* Often the researcher must be as attentive to what is not said in a source as to what is said. If a report from a tobacco company declared the evidence that smoking causes heart trouble to be inconclusive, and fails to cite experimental evidence, that omission would bear looking into. If the report failed even to mention the hundreds of medical studies that reached the opposite conclusion, then it should be considered suspect, not because of what was in it but because of what was not.

7. *Prefer evidence that is credible on its own terms to that which is internally inconsistent or demonstrably false to any known facts.* Whether intentional or unintentional, inaccuracies in any part of an account suggest the need for caution in accepting any part of the account at face value. A witness who would lie about one point would probably lie about another; a fanatic who deludes himself about one fact may well delude himself about another. Such reports need not necessarily be ignored. They may even contain some reliable evidence not available elsewhere, but such evidence should always be used with caution and confirmed from other sources where possible.

8. *In general, prefer a recently published report to an older one.* By their very nature some facts are constantly changing. By the time you read this sentence, the population of China will be very different from what it was when the sentence was written. If present hopes among cancer researchers hold up, by that time we may also know a good deal more about "targeting" chemotherapy so that medicines now unavailable will be able to single out and attack cells only if they are malignant. Only up-to-date sources can provide such crucial evidence. Try always to consult the most recent sources available.

9. *In general, prefer works by standard publishers to those from unknown or "vanity" presses.* Acknowledged experts in a field will usually have their reports accepted for publication by the standard publishers in that discipline. Because a few standard publishers specialize in books and periodicals in a very few scientific and academic fields, you may not always know whether or not a name that is new to you is really that of a standard publisher. Your librarian can often help you decide. Occasionally, significant research is printed by unknown publishing houses—even by "vanity presses," where the author actually pays a commercial concern to publish his or her work. In most fields of research, though, this is rare. Beware when reports from those sources contradict the conclusions you find in works from standard publishers.

10. *In general, prefer authors who themselves follow the report-writing conventions that you are learning in this book.* Careful scholarship shows in the documentation provided for the important facts cited; in the careful thought that goes to justify the clear, restrained claims made; and in the organized, objective way in which information is evaluated and interpreted. Look twice at reports that show carelessness or suggest an emotional overreaction to the evidence supplied.

11. *When possible, prefer an authority known to your audience to one that they have never heard of.* Obviously, you want to rely on the best authorities you can locate. But when you have a choice between two equally good sources, your report will be shorter and more direct if you quote the expert already known to your audience. This spares you the responsibility of demonstrating to your readers that the quoted person is in fact an expert.

EXERCISE 2.3:   Distinguishing the Real Experts

Directions: Consider each of the fictional situations described below. Apply what you have just read to help you to decide whether the work named is (1) a *fully qualified* source, which you would accept as expert opinion; (2) a *possibly qualified* source, which you would consider but not necessarily accept as expert opinion; or (3) an *unqualified source* which you would suspect or ignore. Be prepared to explain your decisions.

1. Sandra Soakhead is an acclaimed actress, who has won honors for her performances on stage, screen, and television. Currently she is appearing on TV talk shows to publicize her book *Folk Medicine and Beauty Secrets of the Ozark Women.*
2. A new desk dictionary has just appeared in the supermarkets. It is entitled *Mr. Webster's Authentic Dictionary of American English* and is published by Harvey Webster and Associates of Old Hickory, Tennessee.
3. Will Christopher is a retired electrical engineer who lives in your town and enjoys a worldwide reputation as an expert on residential wiring. In the library, you come across his 1947 book *Modern Residential Wiring.*
4. Through the mail, you ordered a book by a professional "survivalist" named Elvin Woodstock. His book, *Correct Visual Difficulties Yourself,* explains how simple eye exercises will correct all the common visual impairments.
5. The most eloquent book on the dangers of nuclear war that you have come across is *Tomorrow May Never Come* by Randy Howell, president of the New American Peace Coalition. You notice, however, that the book, though laden with facts, cites few sources for the huge body of evidence it marshals.

WHY DOCUMENTATION IS IMPORTANT

Even if you have been introduced to the basic facts about citations, bibliographies, and reference lists in high school, the chances are that you will find, as you work through the exercises in this book, that there is a good deal more to be learned. Only part of what remains deals with the details of citation form. More important by far is that you will learn *why* citations are important. When you have thought about their function as intellectual insurance against error, fraud, and incompetence, you will see why scholars take them so seriously. Responsible documentation is an ethical obligation in virtually every field of inquiry, for without it the intellectual cooperation basic to all research is undermined. For this reason, you should learn to use documentation correctly. It is an academic necessity based on decency and common sense.

A simple citation turns an assertion from a claim by the writer into objective evidence, already established by someone else, which the writer can invoke in support of her own claim. But still, that evidence is no better than the researcher whose findings are cited. This is the value of citations. They enable readers to decide for themselves how much trust to place in the evidence presented.

In later chapters you will learn exactly how citations are marked and sources are listed, arranged, and punctuated. You will be told about the function of style sheets and encouraged to master thoroughly all the intricacies of documentation. To many students, this may seem much ado about nothing, but we assure you that it is not. One of the ways that readers of research reports decide whether or not the writer is trustworthy is by noticing how well the documentation in the report matches the conventional expectations of scholars in that field. Every detail of punctuation is important, for the constant assumption is that "he who would be careless of little things would also be careless of great things." You should decide now that you will never undermine your own credibility by doing a sloppy job of documentation.

THE WORK AHEAD

By now, we hope that you see library research in a new way. We hope that you see it a little more as the professional scholar sees it. For library investigation is a variety of past-oriented research which is essential to the methodology of almost every academic discipline, every science, and every technology. When a city planner sits down to work on a feasibility study, when a chemist gets a hunch that she may know where to look for a new molecular structure, and when a CPA is asked a new question about the IRS code, they all head for the library. J. William Asher, an acknowledged expert on scientific research design, declares emphatically in his book *Educational Research and Evaluation Methods* that "a good library is as invaluable to a researcher in scientific problems as it is to the philosopher, historian, and scholar in the humanities" (219). Later, in describing the pattern of a scientific report, he makes clear that a "review of the literature" is almost always an essential first step in scientific investigation (228).

Only by considering what has already been done can the scholar be sure that she is even *engaged* in research. Research, we said in chapter 1, is the generation of *new knowledge*. Unless the researcher begins by familiarizing herself with what others have already investigated, she may simply repeat their work. This may not render her work useless, but it certainly diminishes its value. What is worse, if she is naively replicating work that was not well planned in the first instance, she may repeat errors that would have been easily recognized by a thoughtful reading of reports on the earlier research.

It is a waste of time to do again what has already been done, unless it will be done better, more definitively, or more elegantly. Even to judge whether that is the case, the researcher must be familiar with past work. That planner mentioned above does not want to waste time working out in Des Moines techniques which have already been perfected in Schenectady. The chemist will be disappointed to discover belatedly that she is the *second* discoverer of her molecule, and the CPA's professional reputation depends on his coming back from his firm's library with answers that his client can depend on.

For all these purposes and for a hundred others that you will encounter in the years ahead, if you are alert enough to recognize them, library techniques are an extremely important research tool. You can expect, therefore, to use the conventions for researching, documenting, organizing, and interpreting data that you learn in this course, or close approximations of them, no matter what field you enter.

How, then, shall we proceed? If you will take a moment now to leaf through the pages ahead, you will see that the remainder of the book is organized in a cyclic pattern. First you will visit the library and familiarize yourself with a few of its most basic research tools. Then you will use those few sources as the basis for a short research report of your own. The next time you are sent back to the library, you will be working with slightly more advanced references. Consequently, your resulting report can be a little more complex, for you will have been shown how to bring together evidence from several sources. Keep this cycle in mind, even if your instructor elects to let you omit some of the short reports. Then you will always see the purpose behind what you are learning.

You will soon find yourself quite at home in the library. When you are sure you can make its sources work for you, you will begin work on your own full-fledged research report. We will guide you step by step as you develop your reading list, take notes, analyze your data, draft your paper, prepare your citations, and turn your work into a finished research report.

The cycle, then, consists of three steps: (1) getting to know your library's facilities; (2) using those sources to do some research of your own; and (3) reporting your research in acceptable report form. By the end of the book, you will have been through the cycle several times. Chances are, you will find by then that you no longer need this text except for occasional reference. That will be a good sign. It will mean that you have thoroughly mastered a set of skills that will serve you well, in school and out, for the rest of your life.

3

Getting to Know the Library

It may be said, without too much oversimplification, that researchers use libraries for help with two tasks: (1) asking questions and (2) answering questions. Of these, as you will find in chapter 6, the more important and more difficult by far is asking good questions.

A constant respect for the difference between what is actually known and what is generally believed is the first requirement of a good researcher. The day-to-day reading of professionals who "keep up" in their fields helps them stay aware of the important unanswered questions that bear on their work. Experts often center their own work around questions they identify from hints picked up in such background reading. Exceptions exist, of course, but usually good questions grow out of a certain amount of browsing. This apparently aimless survey of a subject is commonly the researcher's beginning point.

In certain school assignments, however, including some in this chapter, the question-asking step is bypassed. Instructors may simply assign questions and send students to the library to find and report the answers. This procedure has several practical advantages. It allows beginning students to concentrate on the nuts and bolts of library research. It also protects them from tackling topics that are insignificant or poorly defined or impossible to deal with on the basis of information available at nearby libraries.

You should realize, however, that when you get assignments of this kind the research procedure they call for is incomplete. Real-life research makes it your responsibility to identify and define your own questions. Still, such question-answering assignments provide excellent guidance while you get acquainted with the library. That is why we use them in this book. Later, as you get your bearings, you will gradually take over responsibility for your own questioning. First, though, you must get to know your library.

KNOWING YOUR OBJECTIVE

The library is one of the great achievements of western culture. As Carl Sagan wrote in his prize-winning book *Cosmos,* a great library today contains ten thousand times as much information as is stored in human genes and about ten times that stored in human brains.

> If I finish a book a week, I will read only a few thousand books in my lifetime, about a tenth of a percent of the contents of the greatest libraries of our time. The trick is to know which books to read. The information in books is not preprogrammed at birth but constantly changed, amended by new events, adapted to the world. It is now twenty-three centuries since the founding of the Alexandrian Library. If there were no books, no written records, think how prodigious a time twenty-three centuries would be. With four generations per century, twenty-three centuries occupies almost a hundred generations of human beings. If information could be passed on merely by word of mouth, how little we should know of our past, how slow would be our progress! Everything would depend on what ancient findings we had accidentally been told about, and how accurate the account was. Past information might be revered, but in successive retellings it would become progressively more muddled and eventually lost. Books permit us to voyage through time, to tap the wisdom of our ancestors. The library connects us with the insights and knowledge, painfully extracted from Nature, of the greatest minds that ever were, with the best teachers, drawn from the entire planet and from all our history, to instruct us without tiring, and to inspire us to make our own contributions to the collective knowledge of the human species (281–282).

Almost any intelligent person can spend enjoyable hours searching out the curiosities and treasures of a library. Sooner or later most educated people discover for themselves these pleasures of the mind. As amusing as it is, however, such intellectual meandering is not research. Research is reading with a purpose. To undertake research is to begin, however casually, to work towards a goal. And the best way to reach a goal is to make sure at the outset that you know what your goal is.

UNDERSTANDING YOUR ASSIGNMENT

Library assignments come in a variety of forms. Some are very open-ended: "Do a short paper on some aspect of Social Security"; "Present an authoritative defense of your views on gun control"; "Prepare a critique of Tennessee's 1925 'Monkey Trial' concerning the teaching of evolution in the public schools."

Other assignments, though still dealing with broad topics, will require you to take a position. "How did union workers' attitudes towards Social Security change during the 1970s?" "Should handguns be registered?" "Were the goals of the American Civil Liberties Union achieved or frustrated by the outcome of Tennessee's 1925 'Monkey Trial'?"

Occasionally, in exercises to acquaint you with specific reference tools, you may even be given trivia questions. "How much money was paid to Social Security beneficiaries during President Carter's administration?" "What was unique about the radio coverage of the 1925 'Monkey Trial' in Dayton, Tennessee?" Be sure that you do not attend so closely to what the question asks that you overlook what it *tells*. If you are clever enough to recognize it, you will find, even in the most open-ended assignment, useful starting information. The instructor who requests a short paper about *some aspect* of Social Security is clearly implying that he or she expects you to tackle only a tiny portion of that unwieldy topic. Your success may well depend on whether you first whittle the topic down to something that you can research adequately.

An instructor who asks how union workers' attitudes towards Social Security changed during the seventies is telling you, indirectly, that a change took place and approximately when it occurred. Similarly, the question about the goals of the American Civil Liberties Union and the "Monkey Trial" should focus your attention immediately on the possibility that the ACLU was a behind-the-scenes participant in the trial. Seizing on the information given by the question itself will often save you countless hours of burrowing through data that are completely beside the point.

EXERCISE 3.1:   Defining Your Starting Point

Directions: Following each of the sample research paper assignments below is a list of statements. Some of these statements contain clues, suggested by the assignments themselves, as to how you might begin your research. Others, though possibly true, bear no logical connection to the assigned question. Decide which statements are useful clues logically derived from the topic and which are not logically related to the assigned question.

1. Your assignment in economic history is to provide a documented answer to the following question: "When and why did the internal combustion engine win out over the steam engine and the electric motor so decisively that it became obvious that gasoline engines would power the cars of the twentieth century?"

   a. At one time electric cars gave strong competition to gasoline-powered cars.

   b. The steam engine at one time threatened to prevent gasoline engines from getting a start in the car market.

   c. Hundreds of electric-powered taxicabs and delivery vehicles once operated in the streets of major American cities.

d. The gasoline engine had certain clear advantages that caused it to win out over steam engines and electric motors.

e. At a certain point it became clear to everyone that the gasoline engine was more practical than its rivals.

f. The electric starter, first used in 1912, was invented by Charles Kettering.

2. Your physical anthropology teacher has asked you to survey the sociological, psychological, and anthropological characteristics of human males and females. "Then, in a carefully documented paper addressed to a doubting young colleague of mine, you are to summarize at least four lines of research which suggest that sexuality is not a simple either/or matter but rather that most people fall somewhere on a continuum between complete masculinity and complete femininity."

a. Studies show that there is no evidence that females are more social or lower in self-esteem than males.

b. Geneticists have found that, in fruit flies, if an offspring has two X chromosomes, regardless of whether or not a Y chromosome is present, it will be female.

c. With human beings, however, if a Y chromosome is present, the offspring will be male, regardless of the number of X chromosomes that may be present.

d. There is no consistent evidence that females are more suggestible or less achievement-motivated than males.

e. Psychological studies do not support the claim that males are more analytic than females.

f. In some cultures, females are reported to be more aggressive than males.

MULLING OVER YOUR CHOICE OF TOPIC

Once you are clear about the assigned topic and have studied the research clues you find in it, take a moment to make certain that you understand exactly what your instructor expects. Always notice especially what *kind* of paper you are asked to write. Is your report to be an argumentative paper, like the gun control "defense"? Is it to be an objective assessment, like the critique of the "Monkey Trial"? Or are you asked for some other kind of response, a book review perhaps, or a feasibility study, or even a noncommittal assembly of the relevant information? Be very sure, before you begin work, that you know what is being asked of you.

Both assignments in the preceding exercise require students to interpret as well as to assemble data. Even a complete report on the triumph of the gasoline engine will not be likely to please the economic historian unless the writer makes the reported facts show when and why the gasoline engine eclipsed its competitors. There may also be aspects of the subject that your instructor particularly wants covered. Notice points like the anthropology instructor's request for a summary of "four lines" of research. On such small points as these hinges the difference between success and failure in academic writing.

Often during your first year or two of college, instructors will specify how many sources you are to use and perhaps even suggest a minimum number of citations. Be sure to note and follow all such requirements. Note especially anything your instructor says about when your work is due. If periodic checks or progress reports are planned, be sure to organize your work accordingly. Good research reports require systematic, sustained work. They cannot be rushed to completion in a last-minute flurry. Plan your work around the instructor's deadlines.

Perhaps the most important thing about your assignment is the amount and kind of choice it leaves you. The more freedom you are given, the more responsibility you have for self-discipline. Suppose a psychology instructor asks you to do a review of the literature concerning some abnormal state of mind. That is a very open-ended assignment. When you are sure you know what he means by a "review of the literature" and by an "abnormal state," you have about all the guidance you will get from the assignment. Your job is to make the freedom thus granted work for you and not against you.

Considering Your Present Knowledge and Interests

One way to put your freedom to use is to play to your strengths. If you already know something that bears on mental abnormality, maybe that can be your starting point. This might be a good time to follow up on that magazine article you read last year about Burmese firewalkers. Or maybe you would like to take this opportunity to find out whether your high school study of *idiot savants* (mentally handicapped people with isolated streaks of genius) really gave you the complete picture.

If you have no such prior knowledge to draw on, you should still try to follow your own interests as much as the assignment allows. You will live closely with your research project for days, often for weeks. Why bore yourself? Why randomly pull a term from a psychology glossary when you have an opportunity to work on something that really appeals to you?

Some topics may even appeal to you precisely because you do not know anything about them. You have heard wild and conflicting stories about hypnotism, say, but you never knew what to believe. Hypnotism is an abnormal mental state that engages your longstanding curiosity. Projects motivated by interests like that are much more likely to lead to good research reports.

Avoiding the Painful

On the other hand, it is possible for student researchers to be too interested in their subjects. Students who care too much about the outcome of their inquiry may be lured away from objectivity. Remember that research should lead to *new knowledge* based on *rational consideration* of observable evidence.

Before committing yourself to a research project, it is a good idea to imagine how you will feel if the evidence forces you to conclusions which contradict your personal preferences. Beginning researchers whose preconceptions are challenged by the evidence sometimes find it tempting to pick and choose only evidence that meets their personal needs. That, of course, is not research.

At first, until you have become comfortable with research and its techniques, it is better to stay away from religious, political, or social topics about which you feel strongly. The overwhelming majority of your research findings will be enlightening, gratifying, and rewarding. You will soon learn to value research as a safe and trustworthy way to get at truth in a wide range of human endeavors. But try not to complicate your first efforts by choosing topics on which you may have special difficulty in being objective.

Maintaining objectivity is sometimes a problem, even for experienced researchers. Consider, for instance, George McLean Harper, the literary biographer who devoted much of his life to studying and writing about the poet William Wordsworth. Harper admired and respected Wordsworth to an uncommon—some might say an excessive—degree. But when Harper came across some upsetting evidence concerning Wordsworth's youthful years in France, he did the scholarly thing. He went to France to ferret out the truth.

In time, he found what he had hoped he would not: undeniable evidence that while in France Wordsworth had fathered an illegitimate child. It is said that when he saw the indisputable evidence Harper actually wept. But the facts he discovered nevertheless appeared in the second edition of his scholarly biography of Wordsworth, for he recognized that other critics might well find in Wordsworth's illicit love affair valuable clues to the full meaning of some important poems.

Trimming Topics to the Proper Size

Another important point to consider when you select a topic is your need to choose one that is properly matched to the time and effort you are able to spend on your research. Usually this means that you must restrict your investigation to a relatively small part of the topic that first catches your interest. You will learn how to do this in chapter 6, when we discuss how to shape good research questions. At that point, also, you will be given hints for matching your research project to the available library resources, for it is a major disappointment to the enthusiastic beginner to find that the well-formed research question which has just caught his enthusiasm simply cannot be answered with materials available within a thousand miles of the local library.

EXERCISE 3.2: Matching the Report to the Assignment

Directions: Listed below are three research report assignments of the kind that you might be given in college or on the job. Practice applying the advice given above by answering the questions following each assignment.

1. (From your political science instructor) "Choose either the Democratic or Republican party. Find out how that party is organized from the national level down through the state level to your own precinct. Name the most important party officers at each level, tell how they are chosen, and briefly explain their duties."

   a. Does this instructor seem to want an interpretative, persuasive paper, or a straightforward, factual presentation?

   b. What special points does she want covered in this paper. Why is it unlikely that a paper omitting some of these points would meet the instructor's objectives for assigning it?

   c. Can you imagine that anyone given such an assignment would find the subject so threatening that he or she could not be objective about it? Why?

   d. Do you see any reason to think that it might be hard to get the information you would need for such an assignment from a nearby library? Why?

2. (From your boss) "Within the next year we are going to open a branch office in your home state. It happens that one of the places we are considering is your home town. The other is the state capital, though we could certainly consider a different possibility. Because you know the state better than the rest of us, I want you to study the most promising possibilities and present your recommendations in a properly documented report by the end of next month."

   a. Does your boss want an interpretative paper or an objective presentation of facts?

   b. What special points does he want covered?

   c. Is it possible that you would find it hard to be objective as you analyzed the data for this report? Why?

   d. Would you expect to have difficulty finding the material you need for this assignment in a local library? Why?

3. (From the instructor of your sociology course, on the day after a spontaneous and heated classroom debate on abortion) "Additional entry on your list of possible term paper topics: What, exactly, does it mean to be *human*? At what point between conception and death does the individual become truly human? Explain your answer in a reasoned position paper fully supported by sound evidence."

   a. What do you understand the instructor to mean by the term *position paper*? Does he expect opinions or facts or both?

   b. What special features does the instructor suggest that he will look for in the paper, and what special points does he want covered?

    c. Is it likely that some students will find it difficult to carry out this project with objectivity? Why?

    d. Do you suppose you would have difficulty getting the information you need from your local library? Why?

TAKING STOCK

In a full-fledged research project, then, you would have considered a great many things before you even approached a library. You would have in mind the report format you were to approximate and the expected treatment of your subject. You would be aware of the instructor's special requirements, including the schedule of deadlines. You would have studied the assignment for useful clues. And you would have pondered ways of approaching it that would enable you to make the most of your knowledge and interests without putting at risk personal beliefs that you may not be ready to reexamine.

Most of these are things you can do just by remembering the need to do them. A few others you cannot practice until you have been given more instruction and guidance. Before taking up those details, though, let us begin to get acquainted with the place on which most of these efforts will focus. Let us take a quick look at the library.

HOW LIBRARIES ARE ORGANIZED

A library is an organized collection of books. The key word in this definition is *organized*. The library is not valuable simply because it contains a lot of information. It is valuable because, once you know how, you can *locate* that information. Until you can find what you need in the library, you have not really made yourself heir to this most important part of your cultural heritage. But spend a few hours learning to be at home in the library, and you will acquire an ability of lifelong value.

Most libraries are organized by one (or sometimes both) of two systems: (1) the Dewey Decimal system or (2) the Library of Congress system. The chances are good that you will need, sooner or later, to work with both systems. So even though you do not need to know them in detail, you should familiarize yourself with the most important features of each.

The Dewey Decimal System

One Sunday morning in 1873 an Amherst College undergraduate allowed his mind to drift from the boring chapel sermon to a problem with his work as a library assistant. It should be possible, he imagined, to find a consistent and sensible way of organizing even a huge number of books so that any one of them could be easily and quickly found by a typical schoolboy. We continue the story in the boy's own words, as they appear in *Cataloguing USA* by Paul S. Dunkin.

> . . . the solution flasht over me so that I jumpt in my seat and came very near shouting "Eureka!" It was to get absolute simplicity by using the simplist known symbols . . . numerals . . . to number a classification of all human knowledge in print. (93)

At twenty-one, Melvil Dewey had just conceived the system of classifying knowledge that is now used in more libraries throughout the world than all others combined. Dewey's inspiration was to create a system which, though extremely simple, was capable of including all existing books and all possible new books.

Essentially, the Dewey system assigns to each book a "call number" based on its subject. All possible areas of knowledge were divided by Dewey into ten major areas. Each of these general classifications was then assigned a range of 100 numbers:

000–099	General Works
100–199	Philosophy
200–299	Religion
300–399	Social Sciences
400–499	Language
500–599	Pure Science
600–699	Applied Science and Technology
700–799	The Arts
800–899	Literature and Rhetoric
900–999	History

Each of these large classes was further divided into ranges of ten numbers each. For instance, the numbers set aside for applied science and technology in the above table are broken down like this:

600–609	Technology (Applied Science)
610–619	Medical Sciences
620–629	Engineering and Allied Fields
630–639	Agriculture and Agricultural Industries
640–649	Domestic Arts and Sciences
650–659	Business and Related Subjects
660–669	Chemical Technology, etc.
670–679	Manufactures Processible
680–689	Assembled Products, etc.
690–699	Buildings

The same principle is used in further subdivisions of each of these classes. Books on the medical sciences, numbered 610–619 in the above table, would be assigned third digits according to this breakdown:

611   Human Anatomy

612   Human Physiology

613   General and Personal Hygiene

614   Public Health

615   Therapeutics and Pharmacology

616   Medicine

617   Surgery

618   Other Specialized Medicine

619   Comparative and Experimental Medicine

By using decimals, librarians can extend these successive subdivisions as far as necessary to distinguish almost any conceivable subject matter. The Dewey decimal number for this text, for instance, would be 808.02. This places it in the 800s, the general classification for literature and rhetoric. The second digit, being a zero, indicates that the book treats its subject generally; it does not restrict its discussion to some narrow aspect. The third digit shows that the aspect being dealt with in this way is rhetoric, or writing. And the decimal numbers are those shown in the Dewey guide for books on research papers.

The Cutter Number.   Most libraries also assign a second number to each book. Called the "Cutter number," after the librarian who developed the system for identifying authors, this second number is preceded by the author's last initial. The number itself is taken from a table normally used only by professional librarians and is followed by one or more small letters designating the first letter(s) of the first important words in the title. For instance, the Cutter number for this textbook, if you found it in a library, would be this: **G219r**

In this case, the G stands for "Gaston," the last name of the first author; the number is taken from the Cutter table and is the correct one for that name; and the small r stands for "research," the first important word in the title *The Research Paper: A Common-Sense Approach.* Thus the complete call number for this book would be **808.02**
G219r

Though you do not need to be an expert, you will need to use call numbers to locate the books you need. That is quite simple, really, if you just remember the following guidelines:

1. Consider every symbol important, whether it be number or letter, capital or lower case.

2. Read all symbols, regardless of whether they are letters or numbers, in the order in which they appear.

3. Starting with the first line, read each line from left to right and take every line in turn, just as you would in reading anything else.

4. Expect books to be shelved in numerical order.

5. When letters appear in call numbers, expect the books whose numbers are the same up to that point to be shelved alphabetically.

The Library of Congress System

If you study the sample breakdowns of the Dewey classification system shown above, you will soon see that they are, in places, illogical and unbalanced. Why, for instance, should surgery have the entire 617 classification to itself, while all other medical specialties must share the 618 number? Such imbalances are of little importance to small libraries or to public institutions whose holdings are mostly general collections. But in a medical school library, where all patrons are interested in medicine but only relatively few in surgery, this imbalance would create a real logjam in the 618s. To avoid such difficulties, the libraries of many colleges, universities, and research institutions have converted to a more balanced classification system.

The Library of Congress (LC) system uses call numbers that begin with one or two letters followed by whole numbers from 1–9999. Like Dewey numbers, LC numbers may carry decimal extensions and may be followed by one (or even two) Cutter numbers. Often the year of publication is also added.

The major classifications in the Library of Congress system are these:

A   General Works
B   Philosophy, Religion, and Psychology
C   Sciences Auxiliary to History (Archaeology, Genealogy, etc.)
D   History: General and Old World
E   History: American and U.S., General
F   History: American and U.S., Local
G   Geography, Anthropology, Folklore, Dance, Recreation
H   Social Sciences: Sociology, Business, Economics
I   Political Science
K   Law
L   Education
M   Music
N   Fine Arts: Art and Architecture

P   Philology, Linguistics, and Literature

Q   Science

R   Medicine

S   Agriculture, Fish Culture, and Hunting Sports

T   Technology

U   Military Science

V   Naval Science

Z   Bibliography and Library Science

Within each classification, additional letters and numbers are assigned according to a very complex coding system. Here, for instance, is the LC call number for this book: **PE1068**

UG38

Except for the fact that it begins with letters instead of numbers, it looks much like the Dewey number you saw earlier. But these numbers are assigned according to a quite different system.

Fortunately, though, library researchers do not need to learn such details in order to use the LC system. You will find that the guidelines listed above for reading Dewey call numbers work just as well when you need to locate books shelved by the LC system.

Many libraries are slowly converting from the Dewey to the LC system. This means that part of their holdings are now shelved by one system and part by the other. To do respectable research in such a library, you must be conversant with both systems.

EXERCISE 3.3: Working with Call Numbers

1. Below are two call numbers for the same book.

   521   QC173.55
   C127e   C34

   a. Which sample is a Dewey number, and which is an LC number? How can you tell?
   b. What do you suppose this book is about? How can you tell?

2. In 1981, Robert Alter wrote a book entitled *The Art of Biblical Narrative*. With what digit would the Dewey call number for this book begin? What letter would begin its LC call number?

3. Refer to the chapter as you need to, in order to decide what "hundreds" classification of the Dewey system would match the LC letters below.

   D   Q   N   B

4. Listed below are ten call numbers. Separate the Dewey numbers from the LC numbers and arrange each group in the order in which the books would appear on the library shelves. Refer, if you need to, to the guidelines on pp. 46–47.

QB44.2   BV600.2   PS217
S235   B67   M93R5

        031   928.1
        K16   T911a4

QC173.55   154.7   154.72
C34   L497s   L616

        920.72   BC135
        W891h   D67

5. Make a get-acquainted visit to your library. Ask about their policy concerning student access to the stacks. Find out which parts of the collection students may browse in and which parts are closed. Learn the procedure for requesting and checking out books. Poke around in the open stacks, and study the call numbers on the books. Consult a floor plan or shelving guide, if the library has one. Make notes or draw a sketch of where the books bearing each series of call numbers are shelved. Then keep this directory for quick reference later. It will keep you from wasting time each time your research takes you from one part of the library to another.

THE MOST COMMON SOURCES

The library's reference works are the researcher's tools. To do good work, you must know and respect the advantages and limitations of each of your tools. Within a year or two, if you are like most students, you will be working easily with highly specialized reference books like those listed in Appendix D of this book. First, though, let us be sure that you know what you can accomplish with the common, everyday resources found in any library. Used with just a little creativity, they will win you quite a reputation as a literary detective.

The Card Catalog

We start with the card catalog for five reasons. (1) Discussing it now gives you a good chance to apply what you have just learned about call numbers. (2) Most but not all college students have used it before for the research projects they did in high school; so those who need a review should receive it now. (3) Some useful features of the card catalog are almost never learned in high school. (4) You can be sure, whatever your major, that sooner or later you will need to use the card catalog. (5) The card catalog is one of the most obvious physical features of the library; so it is convenient to get to know it first and to "place" everything else, mentally, in relation to it.

Essentially, a card catalog is nothing more than a file of cards on which are written descriptions of all the books in a library. Usually there are at least three cards for each book: one alphabeticized according to the first author's last name, one according to the subject dealt with, and one according to the first important word in the title. Books which fit logically under more than one subject heading may have several subject cards in the catalog.

Samples of all three cards are shown in Figure 3–1. Note that, except for the first line, the three cards are identical. Notice also that, in each case, the call number appears in the upper left corner. Study the sample cards and note the other information on them. Consider how and when such information might be useful to the researcher.

Often in small libraries the author, subject, and title cards are filed together in one alphabetical sequence. But in larger libraries they are usually separated. Keeping the card catalog up-to-date is an expensive and difficult job for the librarians. So if funds are low or personnel in short supply, the catalog may be unreliable. This is especially true of the subject

FIGURE 3–1

Using the card catalog.

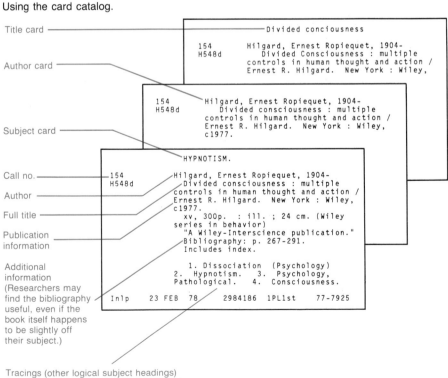

cards. So do not depend too heavily on them when listing the works available on your topic. Check the subject cards, of course, but complete your research plan by adding titles you find listed in other sources. Then check in the catalog for author or title cards on those titles. Often the library will own the right books but catalog them under unexpected subject headings.

Guide Cards. To save you time, most larger libraries have already subdivided the subject cards on their most popular topics. The cards are then separated by special "guide" cards labeling each subclassification, as shown in Figure 3–2 on the next page. Thus in the psychology library of one university the numerous books listed under the subject heading of psychology are subdivided like this:

Guide Card	Filed After Guide Card
Psychology	168 cards listing general works on psychology
Psychology. Addresses, essays, lectures	122 cards listing books containing addresses, essays, and lectures on aspects of general psychology
Psychology. Applied	25 cards
Psychology. Applied Addresses, essays, lectures	38 cards
Psychology. Comparative	55 cards
Psychology. Comparative Addresses, essays, lectures	39 cards
Psychology. Experimental	78 cards
Psychology. History	88 cards
Psychology. Industrial	80 cards
Psychology. Industrial Addresses, essays, lectures	52 cards
Psychology. Methodology	59 cards
Psychology of a . . .	198 cards listing books on the psychology of specific types of people and organisms
Psychology. Pathological	215 cards
Psychology. Pathological Addresses, essays, lectures	124 cards
Psychology. Physiological	146 cards
Psychology. Physiological Addresses, essays, lectures	60 cards
Psychology. Religious	61 cards

FIGURE 3–2

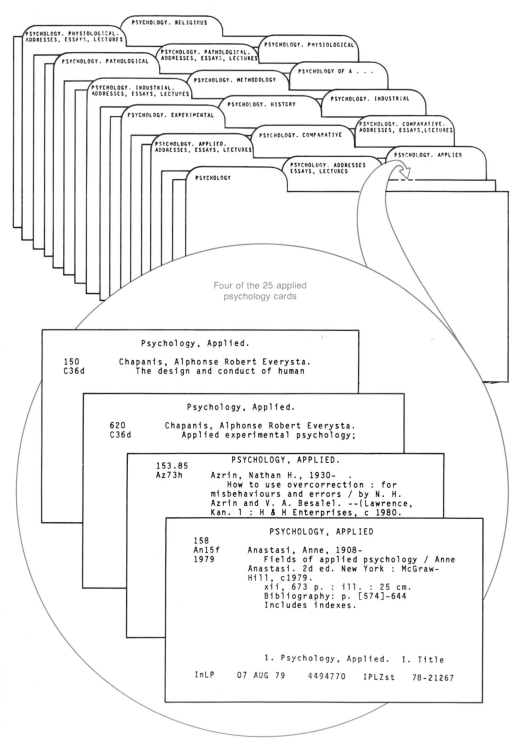

Four of the 25 applied
psychology cards

Psychology, Applied.

150   Chapanis, Alphonse Robert Everysta.
C36d   The design and conduct of human

Psychology, Applied.

620   Chapanis, Alphonse Robert Everysta.
C36d   Applied experimental psychology;

153.85   PSYCHOLOGY, APPLIED.
Az73h   Azrin, Nathan H., 1930- .
               How to use overcorrection : for
           misbehaviours and errors / by N. H.
           Azrin and V. A. Besalel. --(Lawrence,
           Kan. 1 : H & H Enterprises, c 1980.

                  PSYCHOLOGY, APPLIED
158
An15f   Anastasi, Anne, 1908-
1979   Fields of applied psychology / Anne
           Anastasi. 2d ed. New York : McGraw-
           Hill, c1979.
               xii, 673 p. : ill. : 25 cm.
               Bibliography: p. [574]-644
               Includes indexes.

               1. Psychology, Applied. I. Title

InLP   07 AUG 79   4494770   IPLZst   78-21267

Paying attention to guide cards makes it possible for you to skip quickly over numerous cards for books unrelated to your research topic. They are great time-savers for the busy researcher.

Cross-Reference Cards. Before or after the book cards under a subject heading, you will often find a card like the one shown in Figure 3–3. Use of such cross-referencing saves the library the expense of cluttering its catalog with numerous duplications. But you should remember that until you check under the other topics listed, your list of sources may remain incomplete.

Instead of putting such cross-reference cards in the catalog, most libraries using the LC system have a large two-volume work called *Library of Congress Subject Headings*. This book contains a standard set of cross-references that can be used in any library using the LC system. For instance, under "Hypnotism" it shows additional topics that should be looked up. Always remember to check the subject headings directory when working up your reading list in an "LC" library. (See Figure 3–4, p. 54.)

Despite the fact that, for the reasons stated, we discussed the card catalog first, it is not usually the best place to begin your research. Unless you have received different instructions or are already enough of an expert to pick your own beginning point, you will find that a general encyclopedia often provides an excellent introduction to your work.

FIGURE 3–3
Cross-reference card.

```
       Hypnotism

          see also

    Animal Magnetism        Rigidity(psychology)
    Crystal-gazing          Subconsciousness
    Hypnotism and crime     Therapeutics, Suggestive
    Mental suggestion
    Mesmerism
    Mind and body
    Personality, Disorders of
    Psychoanalysis
```

FIGURE 3–4
LC subject headings for hypnotism.

Hypnotism *(BF1111-1156; Hypnotism and crime, HV6110; Psychiatry, RC490-499)*	Psychology, Physiological
	Somnambulism
sa Animal magnetism	Subconsciousness
Autogenic training	Trance
Crystal-gazing	— Law and legislation *(Indirect)*
Forensic hypnotism	*sa* Forensic hypnotism
Hypnotic susceptibility	*xx* Forensic hypnotism
Hypnotism and crime	— Sounds
Magnetic healing	*xx* Sounds
Mental suggestion	— Therapeutic use
Mesmerism	*x* Hypnotherapy
Mind and body	*xx* Therapeutics, Suggestive
Psychoanalysis	**Hypnotism and crime**
Reincarnation therapy	*x* Crime and hypnotism
Rigidity (Psychology)	*xx* Crime and criminals
Stanford hypnotic susceptibility scale	Criminal psychology
Subconsciousness	Hypnotism
Therapeutics, Suggestive	**Hypnotism in dentistry**
x Autosuggestion	*xx* Anesthesia in dentistry
Braidism	Dentistry
Hypnosis	**Hypnotism in obstetrics**
xx Animal magnetism	*xx* Anesthesia in obstetrics
Clairvoyance	Obstetrics
Medicine	**Hypnotism in ophthalmology** *(Indirect)*
Mental suggestion	*xx* Anesthesia in ophthalmology
Mesmerism	Ophthalmology
Mind and body	**Hypnotism in surgery** *(RD85.H9)*
Mind-reading	*xx* Anesthesia
Psychical research	Surgery
Psychoanalysis	

General Encyclopedias and Dictionaries

American researchers have easy access to more first-rate encyclopedias and dictionaries than scholars in any other country. Unfortunately, however, the American public is besieged by cheap imitations of established reference works. Publishers of reliable encyclopedias and dictionaries invest huge amounts of money to get the best authorities to share their expertise and, in the case of dictionaries, to conduct extensive research of their own. Only the products of such responsible publishers can safely be used by researchers.

Most dime store and supermarket "bargains" are produced by profit-minded publishers who care little for accuracy. They pay hack writers to rewrite, popularize, and often distort material from today's standard works, or they deliberately market outmoded versions of standard works to which they buy rights for little or nothing. For these reasons, beginning researchers should be wary of any general encyclopedia or dictionary not listed in this book.

The standard encyclopedias are described briefly below. These works are revised extensively about every ten years, when new editions are issued. Between editions, several of their publishers also produce yearbooks to keep their information as current as possible. Of the five major encyclopedias available in this country, all but one is multivolumed, and of those all but one follow essentially the same organization. We will discuss first these common multivolume works.

> *Chambers Encyclopedia.* New rev. ed. 15 vols. Fairview Maxwell Scientific International, 1973. *Chambers* is the most authoritative of the British encyclopedias. It is particularly strong in the areas of biography, geography, and the humanities. One important point to keep in mind is that instead of keeping up-to-date by means of continuous revision like most multiple volume encyclopedias, *Chambers* keeps up to date by periodically issuing revised editions. Thus, depending on how long it has been since they issued a revised edition, some material may be dated.

> *Collier's Encyclopedia.* 24 vols. with annual supplements. New York: Macmillan Educational Corp., 1984. *Collier's* is no doubt the most readable of the major encyclopedias. Still, it is generally factual and up to date. Its last volume contains an easy-to-use index and annotated bibliography that often provides an excellent start for reading on a new topic.

> *Encyclopedia Americana.* International ed. 30 vols. with annual supplements. Danbury, Conn.: Grolier, 1984. Traditionally regarded as excellent on scientific and technical subjects, the *Americana* is longer and more comprehensive than *Collier's*. It is particularly good on subjects relating to the United States and Canada but, because of its revision practices, is sometimes out of touch with the latest scholarship. The last volume is given over to a comprehensive index. Excellent bibliographies appear at the end of most long and many short articles.

To use one of these general encyclopedias, check first in the correct alphabetical volume to see whether it contains a separate article on your subject. Use a little imagination, and try alternative titles if you do not find the one that first occurs to you. An encyclopedia with no article on "airplanes" might have a very good one on "aviation." Do not overlook such obvious possibilities.

At this point, you are reading just to get your bearings. So do not bother to take detailed notes unless you are sure you have found something useful. For the most part, you want a general orientation to the subject, a list of key concepts and names which might suggest ways to subdivide the topic, terms to look up later in your research, and some beginning entries for your working bibliography, or list of possible readings.

Often encyclopedia articles name important historical figures and current experts in a field. You can jot down their names and check later to see if there are separate articles on them. You can also check the author section of the card catalog to see whether the library has helpful books by the experts named. But first, be sure you note the bibliographical references that are especially recommended. Normally, these are listed at the end of the article; however, *Collier's* lists its bibliographies together in the last volume. Figure 3–5 shows you how a student might use the information in the *Americana* article on hypnotism in the first stages of a research project. Notice that books with titles clearly unconnected to your special interest are still worth noting at this point. You will be shown in chapter 4 how to use the bibliographies in *those* books to home in on your subject.

The above procedure must be modified somewhat for use with the *Encyclopedia Britannica*. The *Britannica* has a three-part organization unlike that of any other reference work. Despite the somewhat imposing titles of its sections, the *Britannica* is not difficult to use, and the value of its information is well worth the trouble of learning. Look for the following three parts:

Section	Size	Content
Propaedia	1 volume	"Outline of Knowledge." Contains guide to the *Britannica*.
Micropaedia	10 volumes	"Ready Reference and Index." Contains numerous short articles on specific subjects.
Macropaedia	19 volumes	"Knowledge in Depth." Contains long articles on broad topics.

Begin your research in the *Britannica* by going directly to the *Micropaedia* to see if your subject is listed there. (See Figure 3–6, p. 61.) If it is listed in the *Macropaedia,* it will also be listed here, and immediately after the boldface topic heading will appear the volume and page numbers of the *Macropaedia* article. After that, you will find a very brief discussion of the topic, a description of the contents of the *Macropaedia* article, and references to pertinent discussions in other articles in the other two sections of the *Britannica*.* When you have checked those references and noted the readings they suggest, you have pretty well gained what the *Britannica* can give you.

The one-volume *Columbia Encyclopedia,* 4th ed. (New York: Columbia University Press, 1975), though more limited in scope, is well worth consulting. Use it just as you would use any of the conventional multivolume encyclopedias.

---

*While this book was in production, in late 1985, a new edition of the *Britannica* appeared which introduced a modified *Micropaedia* and a conventional index. To use this latest edition properly, it is essential to start with the index, as with other encyclopedias.

FIGURE 3–5

Using an *Encyclopedia Americana* article to get started on a research project.

Note that, here and
throughout the article,
you are given an overview
of the subject.

Possible topic: medical
uses of hypnosis.

Possible topic: improper
uses of hypnosis.

Possible topic: hypnosis
and athletics.

Possible topic: what
is hypnosis?

Historical figure of
importance to subject.

Possible topic: hypnotic
susceptibility.

HYPNOSIS, hip-nō'səs, refers to a complex phenomenon that cannot even be described in a
few words and that is still harder to define.
Hypnosis is used by medical men to study their
patients' problems and to relieve symptoms such
as pain. It is also used improperly and with
great risk by quacks who allege, for example,
that they can enhance the performance of an
athlete or cure otherwise hopeless diseases. Still
another use or rather abuse of hypnosis is by
entertainers. A stage magician, for example,
may "put a subject to sleep" by having him watch
a light or an object and telling him he is growing sleepy. The hypnotist may then claim that
the subject is in his power as long as the trance
like state continues.

Calling hypnosis "sleep" is the earliest, simplest and least acceptable attempt at explanation.
This article will not give a definition but will
instead present facts about the phenomenon,
summarizing what scientific investigators know
about it.

Some students of the field believe that examples of hypnotism can be found in ancient
reports of religious ecstasy and religious trance.
However, very little hard information on the
subject is older than the work of Franz Anton
Mesmer in the late 18th century. Mesmer believed that a "rarefied fluid," which he called
animal magnetism, controlled health, he held
that he could cure disease by correcting imbalances in this fluid through the use of magnetism. Mesmer's theories about magnetism were
discounted by a French investigating commission,
although he did cure some patients. Later his
cures were ascribed to suggestion. Sometimes a
patient who believed he was being helped was
in fact improved. *Mesmerism* for many years was
the term for what is now called hypnosis.

Mesmer's results have been explained by the
claim that his patients were hypersuggestible.
This explanation, however, may amount to nothing more than substituting the term hypersuggestibility for hypnosis. Investigators in the
1950's and 1960's found that some subjects are
no more suggestible when hypnotized than when
not. Still, hypersuggestibility is probably the
most frequently observed phenomenon of the
hypnotic state.

TECHNIQUES OF HYPNOSIS

Who Can Be Hypnotized? Most workers in the
field believe that one of every three or four
persons can, under appropriate conditions, manifest hypnotic phenomena. Hypnotizability does
not depend on sex, age, intelligence, personality
type, emotional disease, or anything else so far
investigated.

As long as a subject's (or patient's) attention
can be gained, that person (if hypnotizable at
all) can be hypnotized. Good subjects can be

FIGURE 3–5 (*cont.*)

hypnotized with or without their knowledge and their conscious consent. All techniques utilize a gradual or rapid narrowing of the focus of conscious awareness. Theoretically, hypnotic induction is possible under the pretext of testing the ability to relax or while discussing interests or symptoms. During experimental closed-circuit telecasts, some members of television audiences have gone into hypnotic trance states while watching or listening to induction procedures. The U. S. television code since 1960 has banned portrayal of trance induction unless this is part of the plot of a play.

[There follow several paragraphs on techniques for inducing hypnosis, autohypnosis, and posthypnotic suggestion, which—though possible topics for research—are largely unrelated to the rest of the article.]

USES AND ABUSES OF HYPNOSIS

Possible topic: should stage hypnotism be outlawed?

For Entertainment. To the layman, hypnosis has an aura of mystery and magic. Overpopularization has led to oversimplification, and hypnosis more often than not is regarded as a parlor or theatrical trick, an instrument of the spiritist rather than as a powerful medical and psychological technique. The inherent dangers must be stressed. In one case, two girls in London were hypnotized by a New York stage hypnotist. They posthypnotically developed adverse reactions severe enough to require months of psychiatric treatment. The resulting public furor led Parliament to pass the British Hypnotism Act of 1952, limiting public displays of hypnosis.

The hypnotized subject may be openly susceptible to even veiled suggestion, he may have ready access to his more usually heavily veiled unconscious drives, and he may while hypnotized feel that all social and personal curbs on his behavior have been removed. For this reason the

Possible topic: the AMA's past and present positions on hypnosis.

American Medical Association in 1958 and the American Psychiatric Association in 1961 vigorously condemned all use of hypnosis for entertainment purposes. Unfortunately the dramatic manner in which hypnosis has been presented to the public obscures the fact that it is complex and potentially dangerous.

To Improve Performance. Some people look to hypnosis to increase physical strength or to improve physical, academic, professional, or artistic performance. For centuries hypnosis has been regarded an occult art bestowing on its practitioners secret Satanic power. Svengali, in George Du Maurier's novel *Trilby*, is the prototype of the all-powerful malignant hypnotist. By

Literary and historical figures possibly worth looking up.

his "arts" he makes a girl into a famous singer. It is worth noting that Du Maurier has Svengali rehearse Trilby while she is hypnotized, painstakingly teaching voice to her. He does not substitute hypnosis for voice training.

The hypnotized subject's motivation to perform may become pronounced enough for him to expend unusual effort in order to carry out his hypnotist's suggestions. But experimental evi-

FIGURE 3–5 (*cont.*)

dence shows that, if motivation is increased in other ways, the same person when not hypnotized may equal or exceed his performance under hypnosis.

This applies specifically in the field of athletics. In at least two cases, professional athletes did worse after hypnosis than before it. There is an additional danger. In its statement opposing the use of hypnosis in athletics, the AMA explained that hypnotized athletes may go beyond the limits of their physical ability and experience states of serious exhaustion; and because of posthypnotic suggestion they may be so intent on performance as to leave themselves open to injury.

Possible topic: one current use of hypnosis in medical or psychological research.

In Research. Hypnosis has proper uses in psychological and medical (including psychiatric) research. Only a trained psychologist or a trained investigator in medicine or allied health fields can competently conduct research of this type.

As an Aid in Treatment. Hypnotic techniques have legitimate uses in melical practice. Whenever hypnosis is used, however, it remains a psychiatric technique. There can be no nonpsychiatric clinical use of hypnosis, even though physicians in general practice and in the nonpsychiatric specialties may, and do, hypnotize patients for medical purposes.

Possible topic: hypnosis and mental illness.

Physicians hypnotize (1) to induce analgesia (decreased perception of pain) and anesthesia (absence of pain or other sensation); (2) to allay apprehension and anxiety; (3) to repress, or suggest away, symptoms; and (4) as an adjunctive technique in the treatment of psychiatric disease.

[The article next goes into an extended discussion of the use of hypnosis in medicine, research, and psychiatric practice. A few terms suggest research topics in those areas, but the omitted paragraphs contain little of interest for our purposes.]

Possible topic: hypnosis and the admissibility of evidence.

Hypnosis and the Law. Confessions obtained through the use of hypnosis have been declared by the courts to be inadmissible evidence. In the landmark case of *Leyra v. Denno*, which was fought all the way to the U. S. Supreme Court, a psychiatrist employed by a district attorney's office hypnotized a murder suspect, who then posthypnotically signed three separate confessions.

Historical event of possible relevance to topic.

The Supreme Court found that there had been mental coercion with violation of Section One of the 14th Amendment and Article Five of the Constitution. The prisoner was freed, for the only evidence against him was the confessions.

Possible topic: hypnosis and criminal investigation.

Hypnosis as an investigative tool has severe limitations. Hypnotized subjects, for example, may confess to crimes they have actually committed, to crimes they fantasy having committed, or to crimes their hypnotists think they have committed. They can falsify testimony against themselves and against others or be induced to persuade themselves that they remember committing crimes that in actuality they never committed.

FIGURE 3–5 (*cont.*)

DEFINITIONS OF HYPNOSIS

Outmoded definitions consider hypnosis a form of sleep; ground it in suggestion and call it hypersuggestibility; or explain it (Pierre Janet, Morton Prince, William McDougall) as due to dissociation. Another psychologist, Clark Hull, termed it "withdrawal of the subject's symbolic activities" through ideomotor and conditioned responses with hypersuggestibility nevertheless as its basis. The analysts (Sigmund Freud and others), define it as a transference phenomenon. Perhaps a hundred other definitions can be found in books and articles.

To the American Medical Association, hypnosis, according to its *Report on Medical Use of Hypnosis* (June 1958), is a "temporary condition of altered attention in the subject which may be induced by another person and in which a variety of phenomena may appear spontaneously or in response to verbal or other stimuli. These phenomena include alterations in consciousness and memory, increased suggestibility to suggestion, and the production in the subject of responses and ideas unfamiliar to him in his usual state of mind. Further, phenomena such as anesthesia, paralysis, muscle rigidity and vasomotor changes can be produced and removed in the hypnotic state." This is a phenomenonological definition. It states that certain sensory, motor, and memory abnormalities manifest themselves in hypnosis, but that they may not be present in a specific hypnotized subject. Thus the definition seems to reduce itself to this: hypnosis is what without definition most of us credit it to be.

One investigator (Theodore Barber) feels that hypnosis is an artifact of the investigatory process and is nonexistent. Martin Orne has shown that it can be simulated. Under certain conditions authorities cannot differentiate between hypnotized subjects and nonhypnotized subjects pretending to be hypnotized. Finally, every aspect of the subject is still controversial.

HAROLD ROSEN, M. D.
The Johns Hopkins University

Bibliography

Bernheim, Louis, *Hypnosis and Suggestion in Psychotherapy* (New Hyde Park, N. Y., 1964).

Chertok, L., *L'Hypnose: les problemes théoriques et pratiques* (Paris 1963).

Estabrooks, George H., ed., *Hypnosis: Current Problems* (New York 1962).

Gill, Merton M., and Brenman, Margaret, *Hypnosis and Related States: Psychoanalytic Studies in Regression* (New York 1959).

Group for the Advancement of Psychiatry, *Symposium No. 8: Medical Uses of Hypnosis* (New York 1962).

Hilgard, Ernest R., *Hypnotic Susceptibility* (New York 1965).

Meares, Ainslie, *Medical Hypnosis* (Philadelphia 1960).

Mesmer, Franz A. *Mémoire sur la découverte du magnetisme animal* (Paris 1779).

Rosen, Harold, *Hypotherapy in Clinical Psychiatry* (New York 1953).

Weitzenhoffer, Andre M., *Hypnotism: An Objective Study in Suggestibility.* (New York 1953).

Wolberg, Lewis R., *Hypnoanalysis* (New York 1945).

Experts named who have written on subject—possible leads for follow-up reading.

Source for possible follow-up reading.

Names of still more experts.

A reading list to begin with.

FIGURE 3–6
Getting started with the *Britannica.*

1. Look up your topic in the *Micropaedia.*

2. Check to see if there is a major article on that subject in the *Macropaedia.* The presence of a reference number indicates that there is, in volume 9 (number before the colon), and that it begins on page 133 (number after the colon).

3. Read description of major article.

4. Study "references in other text articles" and follow up on any of them that bear on your topic.

5. Look for "related entries" in the *Micropaedia,* which will be listed last if there are any (in this case there aren't). Follow up on any of those that seem promising.

hypnosis 9:133, a sleeplike state during which hallucinatory experiences, distortions in memory, and a wide range of behavioral responses may be induced through suggestion.

The text article covers the history of hypnosis and modern theoretical interpretations. The article also describes such hypnotic phenomena as muscular and physiological alterations, time distortion, delusions, attitude change, and age regression. An appraisal of the potentials, limitations, and dangers of hypnosis in medicine, dentistry, psychiatry, and criminal interrogation is also included.

REFERENCES in other text articles:
· animal immobility phenomena **2:**542d
· attention, stimulus, and CNV **2:**357g
· Christian Science defensive mental work **4:**563f
· deconditioning concept and usage **15:**148e
· déjà vu induction in normal individuals **11:**890b
· Freud's development of psychoanalysis **7:**739c
· hallucinations and withdrawal **9:**246b
· history of medicine before 1900 **11:**831c
· inflammatory response modification **9:**561g
· Janet's amnesia treatment **11:**886g
· New Thought applications of Quimby **13:**14d
· persuasion of the mentally disturbed **14:**125g
· psychiatry's history **15:**155e
· time perception variation **18:**423h
· treatment of conversion reactions **15:**171g

Dictionaries. Do not overlook the dictionary as a research tool. Every freshman should get one of the standard desk dictionaries and make it the mainstay of his or her personal library. Such dictionaries do far more than help with the spelling or meaning of unfamiliar words. To the informed user, they provide useful factual information on a variety of subjects, ranging from the population of Vietnam to the proofreading symbols used by American publishers.

Often, though, when the significance of your findings or the exact nature of your research question hinges on the meaning of a single term, you may need a different or a fuller definition than is contained in your desk dictionary. (See Figure 3–7, pp. 63–65.) For such purposes, the following sources are invaluable.

61

The Oxford English Dictionary. 12 vols. plus one vol. supplement and bibliography Oxford: Clarendon Press, 1933. Though dated, the OED (originally called *The New English Dictionary* or NED) is generally regarded as the best dictionary in any language. It is invaluable for tracing changes in the meaning of a word over time and for providing a complete record of its usage. Supplements published in 1972, 1976, and 1982 updated it and added American words to correct its characteristic emphasis on British usage.

Webster's Third New International Dictionary of the English Language Unabridged. Springfield, Mass.: G. and C. Merriam Co., 1976. This so-called unabridged volume, by the historical descendant of the famous lexicographer Noah Webster, gives less information than the *OED* but offers it in a more accessible form. On matters of spelling and usage, however, it is no work for the purist. It reports all recorded usages of a word and includes a minimum of guidance as to what is considered "correct."

The Random House Dictionary of the English Language. Ed. Jess Stern New York: Random House, 1962. Somewhat shorter and more readable than Webster's *Third,* this one provides somewhat more guidance on points of questionable usage.

Newspaper Indexes

Several major U.S. newspapers publish annual indexes listing every story or article they print. Usually these are kept up-to-date with frequent supplements. One, known as the *Newspaper Index,* lists stories from several papers: the *Chicago Tribune,* the *Los Angeles Times,* the *New Orleans Times-Picayune,* and the *Washington Post.* These indexes list and in some cases summarize the stories published in those papers.

The most commonly available source of this kind is the *New York Times Index.* Except for stories of purely local importance, the *Times* index is usually adequate. When it proves not to be, try one of the other newspaper indexes. (See Figure 3–8, p. 66.)

Such indexes are invaluable, even if your library happens not to have a file of the indexed newspapers. Often the summary included in the index will give you all the information you need. If not, you can usually follow up just as well with back issues or microfilm files of another newspaper that the library does own, once you get the exact place and date of the event from the index. For information about any topic important enough to have been written up in major newspapers, the indexes are your beginning point. However, like other reference tools they make extensive use of cross-indexing; so be prepared for a few detours.

Periodical Indexes

Because you want to base your research on the latest and best information, you will often find the material in books outdated and that in

FIGURE 3–7
Using the OED in research.

1. Look up all forms of the word under consideration.

2. Note variant spellings and synonyms for the word that are or have been current.

Hypnosis (hipnōu·sis). *Phys.* [f. Gr. type *ὕπνωσις*, n. of action f. ὑπνό-ειν to put to sleep. Cf. F. *hypnose* morbid sleep.]
1. 'The inducement or the gradual approach of sleep' (*Syd. Soc. Lex.* 1886).
1876 HARLEY *Mat. Med.* (ed. 6) 765 It invariably produced hypnosis and contraction of the pupil in him.
2. Artificially produced sleep: esp. that induced by hypnotism; the hypnotic state.
1882 *Quain's Dict. Med.* 973 The too ready adoption of hypnosis or Braidism may do harm rather than good. **1892** *Brit. Med. Jrnl.* 27 Aug. 459 The stages of hypnosis attained, varied from a slight degree of drowsiness to deep trance. **1893** *Pall Mall G.* 10 Jan. 2/1 The waking from hypnosis occurs through immediate action of the imagination, the command to wake up, or through sense [etc.]. **1898** *Times* 13 July 4/1 Any suggestion offered to a person during hypnosis has an exaggerated effect on his mind.

Hypnotic (hipnǫ·tik), *a.* and *sb.* [ad. F. *hypnotique* (16th c. in Paré), ad. late L. *hypnōticus,* a. Gr. ὑπνωτικός inclined to sleep, sleepy; also, putting to sleep, narcotic, f. ὑπνόειν to put to sleep. In 2, short for *neuro-hypnotic:* see HYPNOTISM.]
A. *adj.* **1.** Inducing sleep; soporific.
1625 HART *Anat. Ur.* I. ii. 31 Not neglecting hypnoticke, cordiall, and deoppilatiue medicines. **1758** J. S. *Le Dran's Observ. Surg.* (1771) 300 Hypnotic Draughts constantly repeated. **1878** T. BRYANT *Pract. Surg.* I. 249 The hydrate of chloral is a drug of great value as possessing hypnotic qualities without the evils attendant on other drugs of this class.
2. Of, pertaining to, or of the nature of hypnotism or ‘nervous sleep’; accompanied by hypnotism; producing hypnotism, hypnotizing.
1843 BRAID *Neurypnol.* 7 In respect to the Neuro-Hypnotic state induced by the method explained in this treatise. *Ibid.* 14 The method I now recommend for inducing the hypnotic condition. **1847–9** TODD *Cycl. Anat.* IV. 696/2 Some remarkable connection between the state of the eyes and condition of the brain and spinal cord, during the hypnotic state. **1874** MAUDSLEY *Respons. in Ment. Dis.* vii. 238 In the hypnotic or so-called mesmeric state. **1884** E. GURNEY in *Mind* Jan. 115 A gradual and continuous decline of hypnotic waking into hypnotic sleep. **1892** *19th Cent.* Jan. 24 To this day the..Fakirs of India throw themselves into a state of hypnotic ecstasy. **1898** *Times* 13 July 3/6 If they were going to suggest that the will had been obtained by hypnotic suggestion.
3. Susceptible to hypnotism; hypnotizable.
1881 *Standard* 29 Jan., The unfortunate young man was ..‘hypnotic'. **1892** E. HART in *Brit. Med. Jrnl.* 3 Dec. 1220 The confirmed and trained hypnotic subject is a maimed individual in mind and body.
B. *sb.* **1.** An agent that produces sleep; a sedative or soporific drug.
1681 tr. *Willis' Rem. Med. Wks.* Vocab., *Hypnotic,* a medicine that causes sleep. **1684** tr. *Bonet's Merc. Compit.* XIV. 48J Hypnoticks are oft necessary in this Disease. **1787** BEST *Angling* (ed. 2) 70 Evident to all who know the nature and operation of hypnotics. **1874** CARPENTER *Ment. Phys.* II. xv. (1879) 576 The droning voice of a heavy reader on a dull subject, is often a most effectual hypnotic. **1876** HARLEY *Mat. Med.* (ed. 6) 344 In moderate doses chloral hydrate is a pure hypnotic.
2. A person under the influence of hypnotism.
1888 C. L. NORTON in *N. Amer. Rev.* June 705 It is a recognized fact that the senses of hypnotics fall completely under the control of the hypnotizer. **1893** E. HART in *Brit. Med. Jrnl.* 11 Feb. 302 The hypnotic under the influence of suggestion is capable of becoming a dangerous lunatic of a new kind.

†Hypnotical (hipnǫ·tikăl), *a. Obs.* [f. as prec. + -AL.] = prec. A. 1.
1657 TOMLINSON *Renou's Disp.* 112 Their similitude to Hypnoticall medicaments.
Hence **Hypno·tically** *adv.,* in a hypnotic manner; by means of hypnotism.

FIGURE 3–7 (*cont.*)

3. Note historical figures associated with the term.

4. Look for and follow up on cross-references.

c 1700 D. G. *Harangues Quack Doctors* 15 It affecteth the Cure .. Hypnotically. **1883** 19*th Cent.* Oct. 708 It would be a conceivable hypothesis that the trance condition is produced hypnotically. **1891** *Daily News* 31 Mar. 5/1 The Hypnotiser.. hypnotically suggested her visions.

Hypnotism (hi·pnŏtiz'm). [f. HYPNOT-IC + -ISM. This word is due to Dr. James Braid of Manchester, who in 1842 introduced the term *neuro-hypnotism* for 'the state or condition or nervous sleep', and in 1843 used the shortened form *hypnotism*, when the context made the sense plain.]

1. The process of hypnotizing, or artificially producing a state in which the subject appears to be in a deep sleep, without any power of changing his mental or physical condition, except under the influence of some external suggestion or direction, to which he is involuntarily and unconsciously obedient. On recovering from this condition, the person has usually no remembrance of what he has said or done during the hypnotic state. The term is also applied to the branch of science which deals with the production of this state, and its causes and phenomena. See BRAIDISM, MESMERISM.

The usual way of inducing the state consists in causing a person to look fixedly, for several minutes, with complete concentration of the attention, at a bright or conspicuous object placed above and in front of the eyes at so short a distance that the convergence of the optic axes can only be accomplished with effort.

1842 BRAID in *Trans. Brit. Assoc.* (29 June), Practical Essay on the Curative Agency of Neuro-Hypnotism. **1843** — *Neurypnol.* 13 By the term 'Neuro-Hypnotism' then, is to be understood 'nervous sleep'; and, for the sake of brevity, suppressing the prefix 'neuro', by the terms— *Hypnotic*, will be understood 'The state or condition of *nervous* sleep'; *Hypnotize*, 'To induce *nervous* sleep'; *Hypnotized*, 'One who has been put into the state of *nervous* sleep'; *Hypnotism*, 'Nervous sleep'; *Hypnotist*, 'One who practises Neuro-Hypnotism'. **1847-9** TODD *Cycl. Anat.* IV. 695/2 Modes of inducing somnambulism .. practised .. under the designation of hypnotism. **1852** BRAID (*title*) Magic, Witchcraft, Animal Magnetism, Hypnotism and Electro Biology (ed. 3). **1883** 19*th Cent.* Oct. 696 Under the name of Hypnotism, the subject has after a long interval reappeared on the scientific horizon. **1892** *Brit. Med. Jrnl.* 27 Aug. 459 Hypnotism is an agent of great value in the treatment of chronic alcoholism. **1893** *Pall Mall G.* 10 Jan. 1/3 Hypnotism is the science which deals with the phenomena of a peculiar mental state produced by artificial means. **1898** *Times* 14 July 14/3 The habitual use of hypnotism on women is greatly injurious, both morally and intellectually.

2. The state thus induced: the hypnotized or hypnotic condition.

1843 [see sense 1]. **1847** *Nat. Encycl.* I. 760 This induced him [Braid] to give another name, Hypnotism, to the state in which persons are thus placed. **1860** *Illustr. Lond. News* 11 Feb. 139/2 Hypnotisme, or nervous sleep, now exciting so much attention in the French medical world. **1862** LYTTON *Str. Story* II. 215 The enchanters and magicians arrived.. at the faculty of.. inducing fits of hypnotism, trance, mania. **1876** C. M. DAVIES *Unorth. Lond.* (ed. 2) 98 Swedenborg had the power of inducing, in his own case, a state clearly the same as what we now call mesmerism or hypnotism.

3. Sleepiness or sleep artificially induced by any means; also *fig.*

1860 I. TAYLOR *Spir. Hebr. Poetry* (1873) 27 He has fallen into a sort of Biblical hypnotism, or artificial slumber, under the influence of which the actual meaning of words and phrases fails to rouse attention. **1875** H. C. WOOD *Therap.* (1879) 23, I have given a hypodermic injection of a grain of morphia to a man, inducing a degree of hypnotism. **1885** *Times* 15 Dec. 9 The country will be the gainer by the hypnotism of the one party and the forbearance of the other.

Hypnotist (hi·pnŏtist). [f. as prec. + -IST.] One who studies or practises hypnotism; a hypnotizer. Also *attrib.*

1843 [see HYPNOTISM 1]. **1884** *Proc. Soc. Psych. Res.* I. v. 12 Results which.. indicate a special sympathy or 'rap-

FIGURE 3–7 (*cont.*)

port' between a hypnotist or mesmerist and a sensitive 'subject'. **1890** *Athenæum* 10 May 603/1 The cleverest hypnotists have recently told us that they cannot induce a victim to commit an act altogether repugnant to his or her moral character. **1893** E. HART in *Brit. Med. Jrnl.* 18 Feb. 363 The hypnotist faith-curer of the hospital ward and the priestly faith-curer of the grotto are in truth utilising the same human elements.

Hence **Hypnoti·stic** *a.*, relating to hypnotists or hypnotism.

Hypnotize (hi·pnǒtəiz), *v.* [f. as HYPNOT-IC + -IZE: in F. *hypnotiser*.] *trans.* To put into a hypnotic state; to place under the influence of hypnotism; to mesmerize. Also *to hypnotize into* (a state or belief). Also *absol.*

   1843 [see HYPNOTISM 1]. **1847-9** TODD *Cycl. Anat.* IV. 703/1 Observations upon individuals hypnotised by Mr. Braid. **1880** *Brit. Med. Jrnl.* 4 Sept. 382 The natural normal state of those who may be readily hypnotised. **1892** *Daily News* 17 Dec. 5/5 They hypnotised themselves into believing in it. **1892** *Brit. Med. Jrnl.* 3 Dec. 1219 Anyone can hypnotise, and every one can hypnotise if he is patient enough, and either scientifically intelligent or ignorantly fanatic. **1896** *Voice* (N. Y.) 6 Feb. 2/4 Houses of Representatives have been hypnotized into subserviency.

Hence **Hy·pnotized** *ppl.a.*; **Hy·pnotizing** *vbl. sb.* and *ppl. a.* Also **Hy·pnotizable**, capable of being hypnotized. **Hypnotizability** (hi·pnǒtəizăbi·līti), capability of being hypnotized. **Hypnotiza·tion**, the action of hypnotizing, or condition of being hypnotized. **Hy·pnotizer,** one who hypnotizes.

   1888 *Amer. Jrnl. Psychol.* May 520 To furnish a criterion of the *hypnotizability of the subject. **1885** *Eng. Mechanic* 13 Feb. 512 The number of *hypnotisable subjects. **1883** *Proc. Soc. Psych. Res.* I. v. 67 After a very short course of *hypnotisation. **1892** *Spectator* 2 Jan. 26/2 Horses are very susceptible to hypnotization. **1843** *Hypnotized [see HYPNOTISM 1]. **1880** ROMANES in *19th Cent.* Sept. 475 When he clattered his teeth, the hypnotised patient repeated the movement. **1883** *Ibid.* Oct. 701 The 'subject' mimics or obeys his *hypnotiser in a quite mechanical way. **1889** *Athenæum* 25 May 661/1 He meets the monk Heliobas .. reputed hypnotizer and mesmerist. **1843** BRAID *Neurypnol.* 7 It was alleged that my mode of *hypnotizing was no novelty. **1883** *Proc. Soc. Psych. Res.* I. v. 63 The hypnotising process may carry a 'sensitive' subject in a minute.. into hypnotic sleep.

Hypnotoid (hi·pnǒtoid), *a.* [f. HYPNOT-IC + -OID.] Like or resembling the hypnotic state.

   1887 E. GURNEY in *Proc. Amer. Soc. Psych. Res.* Dec. 201 This young lady had a wonderful hypnotoid sensitiveness, by which she was sometimes able to make unconscious estimates.

---

newspapers too superficial for your purposes. For these reasons, most library research projects require some use of periodicals. The term *periodical* covers almost everything from mass readership magazines like the *Reader's Digest* to highly specialized journals written by and for experts, periodicals like the *Journal of Abnormal & Social Psychology* and *Shakespeare Quarterly*. Researchers cannot possibly comb through all of them to locate articles that bear on their subjects. They rely instead on composite indexes that list all articles in whole groups of related magazines.

   The most widely known of these, because it deals with the more popular magazines, is the *Readers' Guide to Periodical Literature*. The *Readers' Guide* indexes 150 common magazines and issues supplements every two

FIGURE 3–8
Using the *New York Times Index* for research.

1. Find topic in alphabetical listing.

2. Note cross references to other news stories involving topic.

HYPNOSIS **See also** Crime—NJ, Ap 13. Kidnapping, Mr 8, 12. Murders—NJ, Sell, Jane, Ap 13, My 18

Jane E Brody article on hypnosis; discusses what it is, who should perform it and its value in treating pain and other medical and psychological problems (L), Jl 2 III,9:1; Jane E Brody, in 1st of 2 articles on hypnosis, focues on its growing acceptance among health practitioners as form of therapy to treat diverse medical problems; 1 of most dramatic psychotherapeutice uses of hypnosis is emotional catharsis through 'age regression', although experts say it is far less useful than other modes of hypnotherapy (L), (O 7) III,1:5; Jane E Brody, in 2d article on hypnosis, discusses its use as tool by police in criminal cases; some experts charge that forensic use of hypnosis is rife with dangers and is often abused by well-meaning but poorly trained police officers (L), O 14 III,1:1

3. Read summaries of articles published on topic.

4. Note descriptions of summarized stories and dates and locations in newspaper.
   a. Letter in parenthesis indicates whether story is long (L), medium (M) or short (S).
   b. Month and day of publication shown.
   c. Section number is given in Roman numerals, followed by the page number, a colon and the column number.

5. Remember that once you get the approximate date from the *Times Index* and the place of an occurrence, you can acquire further details from any number of sources.

weeks. Thus it provides a convenient way to find what has been published recently on your topic in the popular press. You should learn how to use the *Readers' Guide,* for it is often helpful for any researcher—even an expert—to know what appears about his or her subject in the mass media. Moreover, many of the specialized periodical indexes that you will learn about in the next chapter are organized along the same lines as the *Readers' Guide.* Once you have become adept with it, you can easily adapt to those more advanced sources.

The following guidelines will help while you are learning:

1. *Expect the first item of each entry to be the title of the listed article.* When listings are alphabetized by author, however, the author's name appears as a heading.

2. *Expect the second item to be the author's name* unless the article is unsigned or is listed under the heading of the author's name, as explained above.

3. *Expect to find a page near the beginning of each volume on which its abbreviations are explained.* Make use of it when you need to, in order to make sense out of the numerous space-saving abbreviations used.

4. *Expect to spend extra time checking on the full name of the periodical in which each article appeared.* The abbreviations used in the index will not suffice for the citations and reference list of your report.

5. *Expect to pay particular attention to the numbers that appear just after the name of the magazine.* The number before the colon is the volume number. The page numbers appear after the colon. (You will need both for your list of works cited.)

FIGURE 3–9
Using the *Readers' Guide* to find pertinent articles.

TRIALS (espionage)
Another Dreyfus case? Rosenberg case. I. Edelman. Nation 175:615 D 27 '52
AP correspondent's trial called travesty of justice. U S Dept State Bul 25:92-3 Jl 16 '51
Atomic denials. Newsweek 37:21 Ap 2 '51
Bomb secrets? easy; Rosenbergs and Sobell. Newsweek 37:26-7 Mr 26 '51
Faceless men; Rosenbergs and Sobell. il Time 57:27 Mr 19 '51
Guilty as charged; Rosenbergs and Sobell. il Newsweek 37:23 Ap 9 '51
Guilty; Rosenbergs and Sobell. il Time 57: 23 Ap 9 '51
I was Stalin's prisoner; ed. by L. White. R. A. Vogeler. il Sat Eve Post 224:29+ N 17 '51
My friend, Yakovlev. Time 57:24-6 Mr 26 '51
Oatis trial. J. L. Fly. Nation 173:280-1 O 6 '51; Reply with rejoinder. C. Belfrage. 173:459-60 N 24 '51
On the record; espionage trial of Associated pressman William Oatis. Time 58:42 Jl 30 '51
Rosenberg case. A. G. Hays. Nation 175:422-3 N 8 '52; Reply. C. Belfrage. 175:503 N 29 '52
Spy's version of the a-bomb. il diag Life 30: 51-2+ Mr 26 '51
Story of the secret telephone line, a Communist technique at the Oatis trial. U S Dept State Bul 25:489-90 S 24 '51
Three and the atom; Rosenbergs and Sobell. il Newsweek 37:27 Mr 19 '51
Trial of William N. Oatis; with text of indictment and excerpts from proceedings. U S Dept State Bul 25:283-9 Ag 20 '51
What was Oatis' crime? W. M. Kotschnig. Vital Speeches 17:695-6 S 1 '51

Newspaper and Magazine Files

Most libraries keep back issues of some newspapers, journals, and magazines. So when the reading list you compile from periodical indexes and other sources is reasonably complete, you can begin looking up the actual articles. In recent years, most libraries have begun storing back issues of many of their periodicals on microfilm or microcards. One of the important things to investigate in your library is its periodical holdings in your field. You should find out early what magazines it has and where they are shelved.

Microform Sources

You should also find out what microform sources are available in your library. When asking, use the term *microform* because you have no way of knowing whether they have adopted microfilm, microfiche, or ultrafiche as their means of solving the storage problem for older and less-used publications. Microfilm reproductions are photographed on 35 mm film. Microfiche and ultrafiche reproductions appear on small laminated cards, with either 300 or 3000 pages per card. All these must be read with special instruments which the librarians will supply and show you how to operate.

You should become comfortable with microform sources. Libraries are making more and more use of microform to preserve deteriorating books, to save space in the filing of back issues of newspapers and periodicals, and to make certain other kinds of information more accessible. All doctoral dissertations, for instance, are now routinely copied in microform and sold to libraries in that form.

If you have not already thought about a topic for the major research project you will undertake for this course, you may want to do so now. The following exercises, designed to help you get acquainted with the basic library tools, will work just as well if you practice looking up entries of potential benefit to you.

EXERCISE 3.4:   Learning to Find the Evidence You Need

1. Suppose you are thinking of doing a paper on the question of whether the psychological differences between men and women are due to physiological inheritance or social learning. Study the two catalog cards shown in Figure 3–10 and list all the topics you find mentioned on them that you should look up.

2. What entries might you look under to find what *Collier's Encyclopedia* could tell you about the subject named in question one? Where would you expect to find the bibliographies in *Collier's*? How does their placement of bibliographies differ from that of the *Americana* and the *Britannica*?

3. Look up the word *undertaker* in the Oxford English Dictionary and study the definitions listed. You are familiar with the noun meaning "one who prepares corpses for burial, and arranges for, and conducts burial ceremonies." You have probably also heard the word *undertake* used as a verb, e.g., "He will undertake the challenge." What does the *OED* tell you about the historical connection between these two meanings of the same basic word?

4. Study the sample passage from the *Readers' Guide* for the period from April, 1951, to March, 1953, reproduced in Figure 3–9, p. 67. List the names and dates of publications which contain articles that you should look up if you are doing research on the selling of the plans for the atomic bomb. Give in each case the page numbers on which the article begins.

5. Be prepared to explain in your own words how you might use some of the sources described in this chapter to answer the following questions.

   a. During or just after World War II an airplane crashed into the Empire State Building. What was the exact date, whose plane was it, and what kind of aircraft was involved?

   b. Who were the country's leading sports heroes when the Great Depression came in 1929?

   c. What exactly was the difference between the "New Deal" and the "Fair Deal" in American political history?

   d. Was Richard Nixon impeached? What exactly is the meaning of the term *impeachment?*

   e. How did American scientists react after the first atomic bombs were used in warfare?

6. Visit the library, and locate the card catalog, the reference room, and the periodical room. Find out where back issues of periodicals are shelved and how they are catalogued. If you have any ideas about possible research topics, try looking up some logical headings in each appropriate source work that you have read about in this chapter. If not, browse through some sample volumes of each just to see how they are put together and how you would look things up in them. Remember where each of these works is shelved so that you can go directly to it when you need to.

7. Does your library have many microform sources? Find out what they are, where they are kept and how you go about using them.

FIGURE 3–10

Using the subject and cross-reference cards.

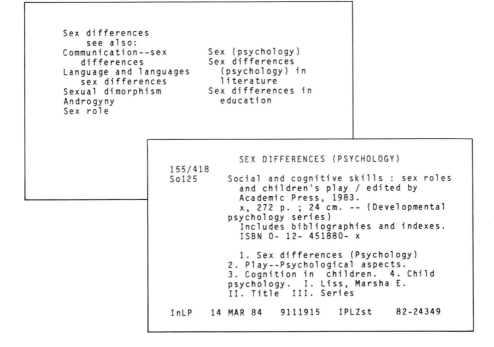

```
Sex differences
   see also:
Communication--sex        Sex (psychology)
   differences            Sex differences
Language and languages    (psychology) in
   sex differences        literature
Sexual dimorphism         Sex differences in
Androgyny                 education
Sex role
```

```
                    SEX DIFFERENCES (PSYCHOLOGY)
        155/418
        So125     Social and cognitive skills : sex roles
                    and children's play / edited by
                    Academic Press, 1983.
                    x, 272 p. ; 24 cm. -- (Developmental
                  psychology series)
                    Includes bibliographies and indexes.
                    ISBN 0- 12- 451880- x

                    1. Sex differences (Psychology)
                  2. Play--Psychological aspects.
                  3. Cognition in children.  4. Child
                  psychology.  I. Liss, Marsha E.
                  II. Title  III. Series

        InLP   14 MAR 84   9111915   IPLZst   82-24349
```

WRITING ASSIGNMENT: What Else Happened on That Special Day?

Practice using the sources described in this chapter by preparing a brief summary of the events that took place on one particular day within the past 100 years. Your report can take either of three forms.

1. **Create a Nostalgia Gift.** Think of someone, preferably an older person, to whom you would like to give a very personal gift. Pick a date of special importance in the life of that person. He or she will probably appreciate it more if you pick a date that is likely to be remembered, rather than a first birthday or other early childhood event. Use all the procedures and resources that you have learned in this chapter to find out what happened on that date. Then do a short three-to-four-page summary in which you report a representative cross-section of the day's events. Don't worry about footnotes or citations; simply report in your paper the names of your sources. Take enough notes on your reading to enable you to choose the most effective order in which to report your "nostalgia facts." Then simply plunge in.

On July 22, 1937, the newsstands showed copies of <u>Time</u> and

<u>Newsweek</u> with pictures of Adolph Hitler and Bing Crosby on their

covers. The <u>Nashville Tennessean</u> had a banner headline

announcing the closing of a CCC camp at Frankfort, and the

number one song in the country was . . .

Present the facts in such a way as to bring back graphic memories of what the world was like for your special person on that special day. Use as many paragraphs as you need for this. Then add two more that will turn your report into a nice, personalized gift. In the first, simply identify the reason this particular day is special. And in the second, tell why you wanted to compliment this person in this way. Try, if you can, to do these last two things in the same objective reportorial style in which you write the rest of your report. The imaginary paper begun above, for example, might conclude like this:

And in the home of a justice of the peace named William

Acres, in Madison, Tennessee, eight miles north of Nashville,

Thurston Gaston married Julia Nash.

So began a marriage that would last three decades, inspire

dozens of friends and acquaintances, and give joy to all who

knew them. It would, in fact cause their nephew "Squirt" to

remember them so fondly almost half a century later that he

would take this means of expressing his gratitude to his Aunt

Julia, who gave him so much and seemed never to suspect her own

inestimable value.

2. **Find Out about Your Own Birth Date.** Do a report similar to the one described above, but dedicate this one to yourself, and devote your paper to bringing your birthday to life. You missed out on a lot the first time around. Use the library to experience it again, this time as an adult.

3. **Play Historical Novelist.** One of the novelist's favorite devices for making imaginary events seem real is to surround them with historically accurate detail. Set the scene for such a treatment, but omit the imaginary characters and subjective interpretation that often accompany the facts in fictional presentations. Just take a comparatively recent date of notable historical importance and find out what else was on the minds of people on that date. What was the average American doing, for instance, on the day the Allied forces invaded Normandy in World War II or on the day the stock market crash brought on the Great Depression?

SINGLE-SOURCE RESEARCH REPORTS

Now that you know how to find books and articles on suitable research topics, it is time to begin thinking about how the information from those sources can properly be used in your research. In general, you will take information from sources for one of three reasons: (1) to use as data or evidence in support of conclusions that you reach on your own, either independently or by reasoning from the data you have assembled from such sources; (2) to present to your readers, in summary form, as an authoritative description of the best thinking on the subject; or (3) to make the conclusions of the source and/or the evidence presented for them the special subject of your own scrutiny. All of these are proper uses of the material you take from sources. What is important, though, is that you always make clear, to yourself and your readers which of those things you are doing at every point in your report.

Notice that it is not the material but the purpose of the researcher that determines the function that borrowed material serves in any given report. The newspaper article below, "Prior Cohabitation Linked to Unsuccessful Marriages," for instance, could easily be put to any of the three uses mentioned above.

Prior Cohabitation Linked to Unsuccessful Marriages

COLUMBUS, Ohio, Nov. 20. Couples who live together before marrying are less likely to have happy and successful marriages than couples who live apart until their wedding day, according to a university researcher.

"Practice doesn't make perfect," said Nancy Moore Clatworthy, associate professor of sociology at Ohio State University. She interviewed 100 couples in 1975 and concluded that "living together is not a good prelude to marriage."

The couples interviewed, aged 18 to 35, were selected at random. Eighty per cent were undergraduates or graduate college students and 20% were residents of the Columbus area.

Sixty-five per cent had lived together for an average of 2 1/2 years before marrying and had been married for two years. Ten per cent of this group had been married before.

The remaining 35% of the couples had not lived together before marriage and had been married an average of five years. It was the first marriage for all of them, but 50% had had sexual relations with their spouses before marriage.

"The findings do not support the hypothesis that a period of living together before marriage better helps to select a compatible mate or aids in adjustment to marriage," Dr. Clatworthy said in an interview.

She said the study indicated that couples who had not lived together before marriage were "just a little bit happier and more successful. There were fewer divorces."

The differences in the couples chosen were not significant, she said. All of them had basically the same problems, but those who had not lived together first "were higher on all scales, more involved and happier."

These couples, she said, "seemed to express a greater feeling of happiness and contentment and more pleasure with their partner than did the live-in couples."

Dr. Clatworthy said one explanation was that living together took the romance and mystery out of marriage.

"For instance, you find out living with somebody just how often they do have those sinus attacks and runny nose," she said. "Perhaps all we're seeing is the fact that the first years of marriage have already been experienced with all these problems in the live-in couple. The couples who are not living together prior to marriage are still in sort of a romantic haze."

In another 1975 study, Dr. Clatworthy interviewed 40 couples, most of them college students who had lived together but broke up before marrying. Two-thirds of the couples broke up for reasons similar to those that result in marital splits, she said.

This might indicate that living together and breaking up before marrying may prevent bad marriages and spare some couples from unhappiness later, "but you can't draw that conclusion," she said.

"Living together creates a whole new set of problems that they wouldn't have had if they had gotten married in the first place," she said.

Dr. Clatworthy said that before her most recent study she had begun to believe that living together before marrying might be a beneficial step in the courtship process.

Now, however, she said she believed it might be a harmful practice, especially for women.

"We notice that when live-ins break up the women are more likely to mention problems of the relationship than the men," she explained.

"On the other hand, our data showed that the women coped with the live-in situation better than the men. It was just that they complained about it more frequently.

"They said there was a lack of privacy, the partner didn't assume household responsibility. They claimed that they felt a loss of identity. And they also felt that there was boredom, that they had incompatible personalities."

She said women reported twice

as frequently as men that they felt dominated by their partner, that they were unable to be themselves, that their partner wanted them to be different and that their sexual needs and desires were incompatible.*

EXAMPLE OF ARTICLE'S USE AS EVIDENCE

A popular notion among young people today is that marriage ought to be "tried out" first, by a couple's agreeing to live together for a while to "see how things work out." A recent Associated Press story in the <u>Los Angeles Times</u> places Ohio State University sociologist Nancy Clatworthy on record as saying that instead of improving the chances for a successful marriage, premarital cohabitation actually creates additional problems. In taking this view, Professor Clatworthy merely echoes the conclusions that more and more experts are coming to, as they gather and analyze data about the so-called new lifestyle that appears to be sweeping the country.

Writer merely *reports* Professor Clatworthy's findings as one bit of evidence.

This writer obviously intends to go on and cite other experts who reached the same conclusion. Probably, therefore, she has no need to summarize Clatworthy's research or comment further on it. If this characterization of her findings is accurate, she has properly used her source.

EXAMPLE OF ARTICLE'S PRESENTATION IN NONCOMMITTAL SUMMARY

After interviewing 140 couples in two separate studies, Dr. Nancy Clatworthy of Ohio State University concluded in 1975 that living together before marriage does not, as is often supposed, improve the chances of a successful marriage.

In one study Clatworthy interviewed 100 married couples and compared the marital adjustments of those who had lived together

Note that the writer uses her own words and rearranges the facts in the original article so that their significance is made clear in as few words as possible. But what is said here is absolutely true to what Clatworthy is reported to have done and said in the original article. For many audiences, writers of research

*AP, "Prior Cohabitation Linked to Unsuccessful Marriages," *Los Angeles Times,* 21 Nov. 1976, Sec. 1, p. 19, cols. 1–5. Used by permission of The Associated Press.

reports would be
expected to pay some
attention to the design
of the research being
reported. But in this
paper for a lay
audience this writer
considers that
unnecessary. Note,
especially, the lack of
any interpretation or
personal comment
by the writer. She
contents herself
with reporting what
Clatworthy said and
did.

before marriage to those who had not. Although
the differences between the two groups were not
great, she concluded that those who had not lived
together were noticeably more happy and better
adjusted in their marriages and had fewer
divorces.

In a separate study, Clatworthy interviewed
40 couples who had lived together but separated
without marrying. She found that their reasons
for breaking up were quite similar to the reasons
often given by married couples who divorced
early. But she resists the conclusion that those
break-ups might in fact represent "bad marriages"
that never came to pass. That conclusion, while
not disproven, cannot properly be drawn from the
evidence, she says. And in explanation of her
scientific caution, she points out that the
couples living together must cope with a set of
problems that are unknown to married couples.

Example of Making the Source Itself the Subject of Analysis and Comment

[Suppose that the example above simply continues as follows.]

Notice that the writer
takes issue with the
published report that
she herself has just
accurately summarized.
But she makes clear
that she is not certain
just who her quarrel is
with.

Here she identifies
more precisely
the basis for her
disagreement with
the report.

Now she will go on to
detail points in the
report at which she

It is hard to tell, from the newspaper
account, just who is at fault, but something is
obviously wrong here. Possibly Professor
Clatworthy willingly sought publicity for her
research findings. But it seems more likely that
she was done in by an overeager public relations
man at the university or even by a poorly
prepared science writer who happened to hear her
report at a scientific meeting.

In any case, the newspaper account seems to
stress unduly those aspects of her work that are

thinks the bias she described is clearly shown. If she is successful in this, her point will be made, and she will have used this source in her *own* research in a way never anticipated by either the scientist or the reporter who wrote that particular account of her work.

likely to be comfortably accepted in middle

America and to strain unduly to deny those that

would cause consternation on Main Street in

Peoria. Let us look more closely at the

article. . . ."

PROPER AND IMPROPER USE OF SOURCES

In the chapters that follow, you will learn the many conventions that govern the proper use of sources in research. You will learn when to quote directly and when to summarize. You will learn when, why, and how to credit the sources you use. In short, you will learn the "good manners" of research reports.

The two most basic points, however, have to do with simple ethics and involve two report-writing skills that you should practice consciously in all future writing assignments.

Being True to Your Sources: The Summary

To save space and keep the reader's attention where it properly belongs, on *your* line of reasoning, you will often have to be very selective in choosing information for inclusion in your paper. But you must always follow the rule of fairness.

You must not pick and choose passages that you can put together in ways that the quoted writer would object to. Suppose critic Smith writes, "This play could well have been a modern masterpiece, but unfortunately it came nowhere near its potential." Quite obviously, it would be misrepresentation to report, " 'A modern masterpiece,' Smith said immediately after seeing this play." But more subtle forms of distortion are equally unfair.

Notice in the student's summary of the news article how careful she was to make everything she said square perfectly with the wording of the article. A careless writer might simply have assumed that Professor Clatworthy was personally responsible for the objectionable reporting of her work. But this student recognized that she would be misrepresenting the article if she concluded without knowing for certain that her objections were to anything the professor did.

The ability to summarize the research of others concisely, accurately, and understandably is one of the most important skills of the research writer. It requires that you select only the important points, that you omit most examples and evidence and concentrate on the main steps in the author's reasoning, and that you take special care not to read into the source assertions that it does not make.

The second important point in the responsible use of sources is that they must not be substituted for the report writer's own thinking. This means, for one thing, that your thinking, your opinions, and your wording must always be distinguished from the ideas and wording that you find in your sources. Failure to do this always plays havoc with the clarity of your report and may at times leave you open to a charge of plagiarism.

Plagiarism. To take credit for someone else's research or to copy or imitate closely his written presentation is to be guilty of a special kind of theft called *plagiarism*. By the time you have finished your own research project this semester, you are sure to be convinced that writing and research are both hard work. As with any other productive work, researchers and report writers are entitled to the fruits of their own labors. That is why it is illegal as well as dishonest to present someone else's work without proper acknowledgment.

If a significant amount of borrowed material is to be *published,* it is not enough just to credit the original sources. Permission must be obtained, and usually fees must be paid. In unpublished reports of the kind you will write in college, however, you need only to cite your sources according to the instructions in this book. Because it is so important, the failure to do this is considered a serious breach of academic honesty.

To avoid plagiarism, you need only remember to follow two rules: (1) give proper credit and (2) make fair use of borrowed materials. What do we mean by "fair use"? Just this: with only rare exceptions, a significant amount of your own thinking must be evident in every paper. "Fair use" means simply that you retain responsibility for deciding what you think about your topic—or at least how you will organize and make sense of what the experts think. It is your thinking that your research report is supposed to present. Fair use of your sources helps you do that better and more convincingly. But it does not permit you to shirk the responsibility.

The following practices constitute plagiarism; be sure to remember what they are and avoid them:

1. Using the exact words of a source without proper credit;
2. Paraphrasing or following closely the reasoning of a source without citing and giving proper credit to it.

The best way to avoid plagiarism, though, is to concentrate on what you should be doing with your sources. In future assignments, remember that second only to the importance of describing them accurately is the need to avoid depending on them too heavily.

WRITING ASSIGNMENT: A Single-Source Summary/Reaction Paper

You may write either one or two short papers to fulfill this assignment. If you do separate papers, one will be an objective summary of a source, and the other will be a "reaction" paper in which you refute, analyze, or otherwise comment on a source. Of course, even your reaction paper must contain enough of a summary of the source to enable readers who have not read it to understand and evaluate the comment you make on it. For that reason, you may find it easier to combine the two steps into one paper, opening with a summary and following with a personal commentary, something like that used in the last two examples based on the "Prior Cohabitation . . ." newspaper report on pp. 71–73. However, if you feel more comfortable picking separate topics and doing separate papers, feel free to do so.

Choose any one (or two), as appropriate.

1. Look up a magazine or newspaper article which bears on the research topic that you are thinking about for your major research in this course. Summarize and/or comment on it, as directed above, and submit a photocopy of the article to your instructor, along with your paper.

2. Suppose that, having once read the *Time* article reprinted on page 78, you mentioned the cargo cults today in psychology class. To your surprise, you found that neither your classmates nor your instructor had ever heard of them. For extra credit, you were assigned to do an objective summary of this article in sufficient detail to enable everyone to understand the essential facts about the cargo cult phenomena. Write that summary.

3. Consider what *you* think of the cargo cult article. Most people find, after reading this account, that they have some reaction to it worthy of development and explanation in two or three pages. Use the article as a source of data and evidence with which to support your own conclusions. Possibly the following questions will start you to thinking:

   a. Is the thinking of these natives essentially different from that of your fellow Americans? Why do you think so?

   b. What the GIs were doing purposefully, the natives attempted to imitate by turning the observed behavior of the Westerners into magic rituals. Which of the avenues to truth discussed in chapter 1 were the natives trying to follow?

   c. On those special days, when some local prophet has convinced the natives that the cargo *will* come and yet he fails to show up, the natives seem almost never to recant the faith. Instead, they try to modify it, to purify it, and otherwise to make it better so that it will finally work as they expect. Is this different from or similar to what American laypersons (and even American scientists) do when their expectations are not met? What makes you think so?

   d. One frequent reaction of the natives to their frustration when their cargo did not come as expected was to suspect that the Westerners were somehow cheating them out of the cargo that was justly theirs. Do you see

RELIGION

The Cargo Cults

Australian patrols venturing into the central highlands of New Guinea just after World War II found that their arrival set off a tremendous religious movement. The natives killed all their pigs—principal sources of food and symbol of social position—in the belief that after three days of darkness, "Great Pigs" would appear from the sky. Imitation radio antennas made of rope and bamboo were set up to receive news of the millennium, when black skins would turn white and all the harsh demands of life would miraculously disappear.

This was no isolated phenomenon. "Cargo cults" ("cargo" is pidgin English for trade goods) have been observed repeatedly in the islands of Melanesia (including New Guinea, the Solomons and the New Hebrides). All of them share the belief that black men will acquire the white man's magic to materialize goods from overseas without doing a lick of work. British Sociologist Peter M. Worsley writes of the cargo cults in the May issue of the *Scientific American,* and lists and locates 72 of them.

Central belief of the cargo cults is that the world is about to come to a cataclysmic end, after which God, ancestors, or some future hero will appear and establish a new order of things. In World War II, both sides benefited from this. G.I.s landing in the New Hebrides before taking Guadalcanal found the natives preparing airfields, roads and docks for the cargoes they thought were coming on magic ships and planes from the King of America, the potent Ruseful (Roosevelt). The Japanese were received by the Papuans of Dutch New Guinea with joy as harbingers of the new dispensation, but when it did not materialize, the Japanese had an uprising on their hands that had to be put down by force.

Secret Signs. The Melanesians took readily to European missions in the 19th century and expected Christianity to bring the "cargo." When this seemed indefinitely postponed, they began to believe that the white men were cheating them.

"White men did not work; they merely wrote secret signs on scraps of paper, for which they were given shiploads of goods . . . Plainly the goods must be made for Melanesians somewhere, perhaps in the Land of the Dead. The Whites, who possessed the secret of the cargo, were intercepting it and keeping it from the hands of the islanders . . . In the Madang district of New Guinea, after some 40 years' experience of the missions, the natives went in a body one day with a petition demanding that the cargo secret should now be revealed to them, for they had been very patient."

Modern Politics. To capture the secret, cargo cults usually contain some ritual imitation of European customs which may hold the clue to the white man's magic. Sometimes believers dress in European clothes and sit around tables with bottles of flowers on them, sometimes they pretend to write on pieces of paper. Many of the cults seek to bring on the new by destroying the old; they deliberately violate the ancient taboos of their people, kill their livestock, stop cultivating their fields. "Sometimes they spend days sitting gazing at the horizon for a glimpse of the long-awaited ship or airplane; sometimes they dance, pray and sing in mass congregations, becoming possessed and 'speaking with tongues.' "

But the cargo never comes. Then, instead of abandoning the cult, they tend to form splinter groups, organized around a "purer" faith. As long as the islanders' social situation remains unchanged, says Worsley, the cargo cults persist, but with the development of modern political forms, they begin to wither away. "In Melanesia, ordinary political bodies, trade unions, and native councils are becoming the normal media through which the islanders express their aspirations . . . It now seems unlikely that any major movement along cargo-cult lines will recur."

TIME, JUNE 8, 1959*

*Though the text is unchanged, it has been rearranged somewhat for this photoreproduction so that irrelevant intervening and surrounding material could be deleted.

signs in today's world that some of our suspicions may be similarly unreasonable? How so?

4. Select any controversial column, editorial, letter to the editor, or other expression of opinion that you find in a current newspaper or magazine. Summarize it, or comment on it, or both. Keep in mind your source and the need to be original in both wording and commentary.

4

Using More Advanced References

What you learned in chapter 3 was, in effect, how to start from scratch and quickly develop a kind of makeshift expertise on a completely strange topic. The sources you have just learned about will not make you an expert, but they will give you a start. For many of the questions you need to answer, that is enough. If you are being audited by the IRS and want to find out what you are in for, or if you want to get an idea of the living conditions at two or three locations where you have been offered jobs, you should be in fine shape if you just use what you learned in chapter 3.

By the time you are well into your college major, though, you will no longer start from scratch each time you do a report. To be sure, it never hurts and often helps to read a general encyclopedia article on your subject. Think twice when you are tempted to take a shortcut over territory you are not positive you remember thoroughly. If you find the necessary self-discipline in short supply, just remind yourself of the Nobel prize that got away.

In their book *The Double Helix,* the scientists James Watson and Francis Crick tell about their race with Linus Pauling to unlock the secrets of the DNA molecule. At one point, when they considered Pauling well ahead, they learned that he had apparently forgotten a key point of freshman physics that made all the difference. Consequently, it was they who made the breakthrough that might otherwise have won Pauling—already a Nobel prize winner—another award. If a failure to review the basics could rob a world-class scientist of a major discovery, there is good reason for the rest of us to be doubly sure we do our homework.

Sometimes, though, you can be certain that it would be wasting time to work your way through the start-up procedure described in chapter 3. When you are conversant with the background of your subject and quite clear on the question you want to research, you can safely begin with the works described in the pages that follow. Otherwise, you will consider them only after finishing your groundwork in the basic references discussed in chapter 3.

PUTTING SOURCES TO WORK

A former University of Kentucky librarian enjoys telling the story of what happened when he opened the library at the new community college that the university founded in Harlan County in 1961. Because his was, in some ways, the best library in that mountainous region, the librarian spread word in the community that all interested citizens were welcome to use it. So it happened that one of his very first noncollege patrons was a bright nine-year-old boy who appeared and asked, "Do you have any good books on alligators?"

"Why yes, as a matter of fact, I think we do," said the delighted librarian, and he began scurrying around among some unshelved books to find the titles he was looking for. A few minutes later, he presented his young scholar with four or five books, one of which was a hefty scientific text on alligators and crocodiles.

The boy dutifully took the books to a nearby table and began to leaf through them. But in a couple of minutes he was back at the librarian's desk, returning them. "What's wrong," asked the librarian, his disappointment clearly showing, "didn't you find what you had in mind?"

"Well, yes," said the boy, tapping the thick scientific tome, "but there is a lot more here than I want to know about alligators." That boy had the makings of a researcher.

Organizing Your Search

Just as the mountain boy came to the library with certain things that he wanted to know about alligators, the researcher works best with a clear, well-defined question that he wants to answer. For a while, early in his investigation, he may be unsure of that question. But he begins with a felt sense, a "notion" of what it is. And as he works, a number of possible formulations will come to his mind, until finally he sees the subject clearly enough to bring his question into sharp focus. At that point, he becomes sure of exactly what he wants to know about alligators. Even before that, though, he has a good sense of what he does *not* need to know about them.

It is particularly important, as the beginning researcher puts together his reading list, to work always towards that central question, around which his final report will swing. He must keep in mind that it is not only impossible to know everything about alligators. It is useless. So his job at this point is to locate readings that tell him what he wants to know for his purposes.

The difference between chasing intellectual butterflies and doing research is the difference between browsing and purposeful reading. Remember always that you are preparing your reading list for a *purpose*.

Using the Pyramid Principle

The name for such a purposeful reading list, by the way, is *bibliography*. So what you will learn in this chapter is how to complete a good bibliography. One secret to bibliographical research, as you have probably noticed, is working with the right sources. To avoid spinning your wheels uselessly, however, there is a second secret that you should know.

This secret, which has to do with the way you use your sources, is called the principle of the *pyramid*. Pyramiding works because of the fact that you check your sources one by one. So the number of bibliographical sources you use goes up by ones, just as the total goes up when you count. But from each bibliographical source you normally get several items for your list. Thus your bibliography grows in chunks, additions of anywhere from one to six or more entries at a time.

To see how quickly this works to your advantage, let us suppose that from your first check of all the appropriate sources listed in this chapter and the one preceding it, you only came up with one book and two journal articles related to your subject. (This is an extremely conservative estimate, but let us be extremely conservative.) Let us then suppose that, by leafing through these sources—even before reading them—and by studying the index of the book, the abstracts of the articles, and the bibliographies of all three, you found three usable references from each. Again, this is a very conservative estimate. You will, of course, get those references and examine them in the same way. Continue doing the same thing, and, as Figure 4–1 shows, your bibliography will have 81 entries by the time you run through the cycle four times and 243 entries if you complete a fifth cycle!

Because the principle of the pyramid works so decisively in your favor, there is no need to fear, as so many students do, that they will not find "enough information" for their papers. A much more real danger is that they will latch on to the first few sources they find that are remotely close to their topic and try by sheer willpower to fashion them into some semblance of a report. Such students seem to be hypnotized by the card catalog and the *Readers' Guide*. They will never learn research until they wean themselves from such elementary sources and put the principle of the pyramid to work.

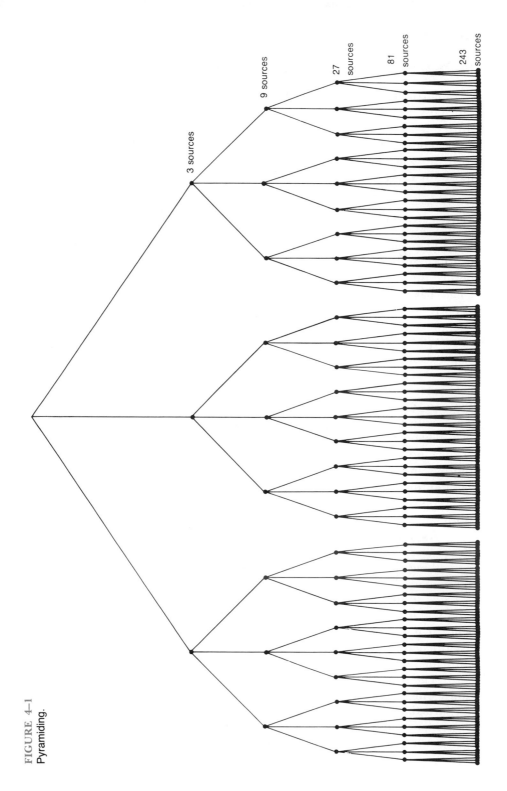

FIGURE 4–1
Pyramiding.

MORE ADVANCED REFERENCES

Fortunately for all of us, there are more good reference works than can possibly be described in an introductory book like this. But the sources described here and in chapter 3, coupled with the specialized bibliographies you will find in Appendix D, give you plenty to get started with. Do a little pyramiding from these sources, and you can research almost any topic that can be answered in the library.

Guide to Reference Books

The American Library Association's *Guide to Reference Books* is such a useful tool that one expert believes it should be covered in college classes before the card catalog is even mentioned. Now in its ninth edition, the *Guide* has been in print since 1902. Regular supplements are issued to keep it as current as possible. Though written for librarians, it is easy to use and well worth the time it takes to become comfortable with it.

What you get quickly from the *Guide* is a complete list of the most dependable reference books in almost any field. It does not claim to include everything, but virtually all works likely to be found in "a large general reference collection" are listed. This is usually more than enough to get you started.

Notice on the sample page reproduced in Figure 4–2 that the *Guide* lists bibliographies as well as directories, "fact books," collections of records, and historical accounts. This makes it one of the best places to begin pyramiding. Usually, you can tell right away whether a given work will be helpful on your subject. It is also an excellent way to chase down facts that you need in order to piece together an argument or to complete your understanding of some historical event.

As you work with the sources described in this chapter, and beyond them to specialized readings in your fields of interest, you will notice something interesting. A surprising number of the reference works recommended here are, in a sense, simply extensions of the basic works you learned to use in chapter 3. For instance, the dictionaries and encyclopedias you learned about there are intended for general readers. Here you will become familiar with a whole range of *specialized* dictionaries and encyclopedias, addressed to readers who want to become much more fully informed in restricted subject areas.

The *Readers' Guide to Periodical Literature,* the index to *popular* magazines which you learned about in chapter 3, has a half-dozen or so counterparts that publish similar indexes to specialized journals in almost every area of research. In a sense, too, the newspaper indexes and files, which you learned to use for pinning down dates and details, are extended and

FIGURE 4–2

Using the *Guide to Reference Books.*

representative, delegate, and resident commissioner to the 67th Congress, together with a recapitulation thereof, including the electoral vote.   JK1967.A3

U.S. Congress. Senate. Library. Electoral and popular votes for president and Congressional election statistics. Wash., Govt. Prt. Off., 1948. 24p.   **CJ99**

> Subtitle: Record of popular and electoral vote for president and vice-president by principal political parties and states, 1900 to 1943, and votes for senators and representatives by parties and states in elections of November 1942, 1944 and 1946, together with excerpts from the Constitution and statutes relating to elections.

◆Electoral votes for the president and vice-president, from 1789–, are included in the *Senate manual* (CJ79). A bibliography on the Electoral College is:

Szekely, Kalman S., comp. Electoral college; a selective annotated bibliography. Littleton, Colo., Libraries Unlimited, 1970. 125p.   **CJ100**

> Nearly 800 items relating to the history of the Electoral College, its organization, attempts at and proposals for reform, etc. Indexed.   Z7165.U5S95

Political parties

◆The standard histories of political parties, and the campaign textbooks issued by the principal parties, are the main sources of information in this field. Contents of the campaign textbooks vary, but usually contain party platforms, statements of the party's stand on principal issues, acceptance speeches of candidates, committee members, etc. Political and election statistics, accounts of national conventions, and texts of party platforms were given in the *Tribune almanac* (CG68) to 1914. Statistics and chief points of party platforms are given in the *World almanac* (CG75). Summary election statistics on federal offices are given in *Historical statistics of the United States* (CG71) and in the *Statistical abstract* (CG69). State manuals and legislative handbooks often give statistics of state and local elections.

Bain, Richard C. and **Parris, Judith H.** Convention decisions and voting records. 2d ed. Wash., Brookings Institution, [1973]. 350p., plus tables.   **CJ101**

> 1st ed. 1960, by Richard C. Bain.
> A handbook of presidential conventions, 1832–1972, with a section on each consisting of the political background, organization of the conventions, platforms adopted, nominations, balloting, etc. Appended are lists of nominees, convention officers, and voting records by state.   JK2255.B3

Barone, Michael, Ujifusa, Grant and **Matthews, Douglas.** The almanac of American politics. [Boston], Gambit, [1972]. 1030p.   **CJ102**

> Subtitle: The Senators, the Representatives—their records, states and districts, 1972.
> A political overview for each individual state is followed by a district-by-district summary of political background and information on the legislators. A very useful compilation.
> The *Almanac* has been continued on a biennial basis.   JK271.B343

Cox, Edward Franklin. State and national voting in federal elections, 1910–1970. [Hamden, Conn.], Archon Books, 1972. 280p.   **CJ103**

> Aims to provide voting statistics on a state-by-state basis in all three types of federal elections (presidential, senatorial, representative). In each category figures are given for the Democratic, Republican, and "other" party votes, together with percentages.   JK1965.C59

McKee, Thomas Hudson. National conventions and platforms of all political parties, 1789–1905; convention, popular and electoral vote. Also the political complexion of both

houses of Congress at each biennial period. 6th ed. rev. and enl. Baltimore, Friedenwald, 1906. 418p. 33p.   **CJ104**   JK2255.M2

Porter, Kirk H. and **Johnson, Donald Bruce.** National party platforms, 1840–1968. [4th ed.] Urbana, Univ. of Illinois Pr., [1970]. 768p.   **CJ105**

> 1st ed. 1956. An earlier work by Porter, with the same title, was published 1924.
> Offers a collection of copies of all the platforms of the major parties and of the principal minor parties.   JK2255.P6

Rosenbloom, David L., ed. The political market-place. [N.Y.], Quadrangle Books, [1972]. 948p.   **CJ106**

> A directory designed for those conducting political campaigns, giving names and addresses of elected officials, political party committees, media outlets, etc.   JK2283.R64

Wynar, Lubomyr Roman. American political parties; a selective guide to parties and movements of the 20th century. Littleton, Colo., Libraries Unlimited, 1969. 427p.   **CJ107**

> Lists books, monographs, and unpublished dissertations on American political parties and movements of the 20th century. Includes references to published platforms, proceedings of national conventions, etc., as well as secondary writings about the parties.   Z7165.U5W88

Biography

Who's who in American politics; a biographical directory of United States political leaders. Ed.1– , 1967/68–   N.Y., Bowker, 1967– . Biennial. (Ed.4, 1973/74)   **CJ108**

> Biographical sketches of political figures ranging from the president and nationally prominent personalities to local figures.   E176.W6424

Who's who in government. Ed.1– , 1972/73– . Chicago, Marquis, [1972–]. Biennial?   **CJ109**

> Offers biographical data on key men and women in all branches of the United States federal government, together with selected officials in local, state, and international government. Includes many names not found in *Who's who in America.* Index by field or subject specialty and by government department. More than 16,000 listings in the first edition.
> A publication with the same title was issued by the Biographical Research Bureau, 1930–32.   E747.W512

State and local government

Bibliography

Bollens, John Constantinus, Bayes, John R. and **Utter, Kathryn L.** American county government; with an annotated bibliography. Beverly Hills, Calif., Sage, [1969]. 433p.   **CJ110**

> A review of the literature, suggested approaches to new research, and bibliographical commentary on books, monographs, articles, and documents relating to American county government in general and to individual states.   JS411.B64

Council of State Governments. State bluebooks and reference publications (a selected bibliography). Lexington, Ky., The Council, [1972]. unpaged.   **CJ111**

> Gives information on the publication, frequency, and availability of directories, statistical compendiums, etc., of the individual states. For each state publications are grouped as: (1) Legislature and general state government; (2) Digests or summaries of legislative action; and (3) Guides, statistics, etc.

Government Affairs Foundation. Metropolitan communities: a bibliography, with special emphasis upon government and politics. Chicago, Public Admin. Service, [1957]. 392p.   **CJ112**

Margin annotations (left side):

Records of possible use to researchers

Directories like this one are frequently useful to researchers exploring contemporary subjects.

Historical accounts

Biographical information on well known personalities.

Such *annotated bibliographies* may be helpful in closing in on your own research question.

transcended by several more specialized "fact books" that you will learn about in this chapter.

All you should expect of yourself at this point is an awareness of the types of works in existence and an acquaintance with some specific ones of each type that might someday be useful in your own work. To accomplish this much, you should read this chapter, work its exercises, and study Appendix D to identify works listed there which are likely to be relevant to your studies.

Specialized Encyclopedias

Many research areas have their own specialized encyclopedias. In some cases, their articles may be beyond the reach of the young scholar, but they are usually fuller, more authoritative, and better documented than more general encyclopedias. Their documentation makes them good sources to check while you are pyramiding your own bibliography, even if you find yourself—for now—unable to cope with the articles on your subject in, say, *The International Encyclopedia of Chemical Sciences*. Besides, some of these specialized encyclopedias *are* comprehensible to the average college student. Probably anyone who can handle the *Britannica* can cope with the *Encyclopedia of Educational Research* and most of the *Encyclopedia of Religion and Ethics*.

Specialized Dictionaries

At this level of library research, the line between dictionaries and encyclopedias becomes obscure, if not invisible. For instance, the three-volume *Dictionary of Philosophy and Psychology* is much weightier, in every sense, than the one-volume *Columbia Desk Encyclopedia* that you learned about in chapter 3. But whatever their names, the specialized dictionaries are excellent tools for the creative researcher.

Good ones abound; and they cover almost every field of human knowledge. There are biographical dictionaries, like the one-volume *Webster's Biographical Dictionary* and the ten-volume *Dictionary of American Biography*, restricted to biographies of people no longer living. Others, like the *Dictionary of International Biography* and *Webster's American Biographies*, cover only those still living. Because of these restrictions, it is particularly important to check the date of publication when working with such a source.

A glance at the titles listed in Appendix D will show you that the range of dictionaries is almost unlimited. There are excellent etymological dictionaries (which specialize in tracing the derivations of words), dictionaries of slang and criminal argot, dictionaries of synonyms and antonyms, dictionaries of the occult, and scholarly dictionaries in almost every discipline from education to technology.

EXERCISE 4.1: Taking Stock of Your New Tools

PART ONE: CHOOSING BIBLIOGRAPHICAL SOURCES

1. Scan Appendix D or visit the reference room of your library, noting the titles of specialized dictionaries and encyclopedias among the listings. Pick a couple of each that might be of special interest to you for one of the following reasons:

   a. They bear on a subject to which you might devote your major research paper for this course.

   b. They deal with subjects in which you might consider majoring.

   c. They cover subjects in which you have always had a real, though amateurish, interest.

2. While skimming titles, jot down the names of the specialized dictionaries and/or encyclopedias which seem most likely to contain information about your own religious or philosophical commitment and/or background. If you prefer to keep this portion of the assignment less personal, feel free to substitute another religious denomination or philosophical position that you may have heard about but never fully understood. If you prefer a nondenominational topic of the same general kind, try looking up one of the following terms: *agnosticism, atheism, cynicism, idealism, mitigated skepticism, naturalism, pantheism, positivism,* or *skepticism.* Alternatively, you might want to look up some faith that is, to you, quite foreign: *Buddhism, Mohammedanism,* or *Shintoism,* for example.

PART TWO: USING BIBLIOGRAPHICAL SOURCES

1. Visit the library, taking your notes with you. Find the reference works you selected for Part One, remember where they are shelved, and take the volumes containing the entries you plan to look up to a work area at one of the tables.

2. Find the latest Supplement to the American Library Association's most recent *Guide to Reference Books* and take it with you to your work area.

3. Examine the *Guide* and learn to use it. Look up at least three works in it that relate to your planned research topic, your personal religion or philosophy, or one or more of your longstanding interests. Then use the card catalog and/or any other appropriate library resources to find out whether the library has your selections. Find those books and examine them to see how well they match the expectations you formed from your reading of the *Guide.* Keep a log of the steps in your search, and be prepared to report to the class on any shortcuts you might take next time. Sample a book or read at least one of the articles that you come across, and take brief notes to remind you essentially what it said and exactly where the material you read is located.

WRITING ASSIGNMENT: Reporting What You Learned

Write a three-to-four-page report on the religion, philosophy, or subject of special interest you investigated for Exercise 4–1. Address your report to an intelligent senior who knows no more about your subject than you did when you began. Do not try to use footnotes or include formal citations. Just mention in your paper the exact source from which you take specific facts or direct quotations. For instance:

> In the "Divination" article of the *Encyclopedia of Religion and Ethics,* James Hastings writes, "Dice, as we understand them, are but little used among savages; but the underlying principle—something which, if thrown may fall in any one of several different ways—is common enough."

Remember to make clear when you are borrowing from sources and when you are expressing your own ideas. Be sure that the bulk of the report is in your own words.

Yearbooks, Almanacs, and Specialized "Fact Books"

Brief mention was made in chapter 3 of the yearbooks that encyclopedia publishers produce to keep their information current. If you have not already examined a couple of these, you should do so now. When you need a quick summary of the latest developments in a field, they are invaluable. One researcher we know made a special trip to Chicago to look up a crucial point for a paper he was writing. Two days after submitting his report, he found the same information covered very well in the latest yearbook to his *Collier's Encyclopedia,* which he never bothered to check.

Usually, however, you will have to consult more specialized references to get all the information needed to complete your collection of data or to put your findings into perspective. The *Guide to Reference Works,* listed above, will direct you to literally hundreds of useful "fact books" of this sort. A few special ones, though, are so convenient and accessible that you should know them firsthand.

> *Facts on File: A Weekly World News Digest.* New York: Facts on File, October, 1930–. Besides giving a good summary of the news events of the preceding year, *Facts on File* includes cumulative indexes every five years which are invaluable for pinpointing the exact dates and locations of events on which you need to do further reading.
>
> *Information Please Almanac, Atlas, and Yearbook.* New York: A&W Publishers, Inc., 1946–. Like the *World Almanac, Information Please* is a treasury of useful factual information, from a short history of atomic energy to a list of figures prominent in the development of most modern knowledge and technology.
>
> *The Statesman's Yearbook.* New York: St. Martin's Press, 1864–. Though devoted primarily to reporting on the governments of the world, this work also provides a wealth of data on such topics as agriculture, commerce, and education.
>
> *Statistical Abstract of the United States.* Washington: U.S. Department of Commerce, 1878–. The standard summary of social, political, and economic statistics about the United States, *Statistical Abstract* also lists other useful statistical guides and sources. Sometimes these will have the information you need when the *Statistical Abstract* does not.

The World Almanac and Book of Facts. New York: Newspaper Enterprise Association, 1868–. Because it has been in existence for so long, this yearbook is a good place to check for historical as well as current facts.

EXERCISE 4.2:   Pinning Down the Facts

Directions: Use the problems below to sharpen your ability for the close reading, careful thinking, and objectivity that are essential to good research.

1. Reproduced in Figure 4–3 is the passage from *The World Almanac* that summarizes crime statistics in metropolitan areas. If your research centered on *violent* crime, what cities should come to your attention besides those for which statistics are reported in the table? In using these statistics, what possible sources of distortion should you keep in mind?

FIGURE 4–3
World Almanac summary of crime statistics.

918   Vital Statistics — Crime; Crime Rates

Reported Crime in Metropolitan Areas, 1982

Source: Compiled by the World Almanac based on 1982 Uniform Crime Reports, F.B.I.

The 25 Standard Metropolitan Areas listed below are those with the highest Crime Index totals. These totals refer to per capita reported crime rates for each of 7 kinds of major crime: the 5 listed below, plus aggravated assault and auto theft.

The rates are not an accurate index of crimes actually committed, however. They reflect reported crimes only. In many metropolitan areas an unknown number of crimes go unreported by victims; this is especially true of the crimes of rape, burglary, and larceny. Additionally, figures are often distorted for political reasons.

Metropolitan areas	Total	Violent[1]	Property[2]	Murder[3]	Rape	Robbery	Burglary	Larceny
Atlantic City, N.J.	12,889.7	987.5	11,902.2	14.1	58.9	433.8	2,629.3	8,467.3
Odessa, Tex.	10,710.0	696.3	10,013.7	29.8	61.2	232.6	3,285.8	5,893.1
Miami, Fla.	10,289.4	1,588.8	8,700.6	29.7	55.7	732.7	2,471.2	5,331.6
Las Vegas, Nev.	9,614.4	1,057.0	8,557.4	19.8	70.2	603.2	3,076.9	4,722.9
Gainesville, Fla.	8,842.5	990.4	7,852.1	11.3	87.1	173.0	2,170.0	5,420.1
Lubbock, Tex.	8,510.8	840.6	7,670.2	11.4	70.3	143.2	2,479.6	4,790.1
Bakersfield, Cal.	8,510.2	788.9	7,721.4	14.7	50.7	269.8	2,407.9	4,750.8
Savannah, Ga.	8,501.8	821.5	7,680.3	17.1	83.6	295.2	2,007.6	5,329.9
New York, N.Y.-N.J.	8,496.6	1,633.1	6,863.6	19.1	41.5	1,077.6	2,128.3	3,464.0
Sacramento, Cal.	8,356.4	640.9	7,715.5	7.9	47.3	289.0	2,239.6	4,921.2
Stockton, Cal.	8,236.9	623.5	7,613.4	19.5	44.4	250.2	2,366.4	4,829.1
Saginaw, Mich.	8,203.1	841.1	7,362.0	12.9	61.5	218.4	2,045.0	5,076.3
Detroit, Mich.	8,175.4	890.5	7,284.9	14.3	49.8	475.6	2,249.9	3,792.3
Ft. Lauderdale-Hollywood, Fla.	8,122.4	804.4	7,317.9	13.7	46.0	368.2	2,190.1	4,514.0
Orlando, Fla.	8,110.7	956.0	7,154.7	10.4	64.5	269.5	2,448.3	4,316.6
Los Angeles-Long Beach, Cal.	8,172.2	1,270.0	6,902.2	18.1	67.7	651.8	2,301.2	3,496.8
Little Rock-No. Little Rock, Ark.	8,149.5	810.2	7,339.3	11.9	67.6	256.0	2,143.9	4,762.0
Dallas-Ft. Worth, Tex.	8,047.6	718.0	7,329.6	15.9	63.4	290.7	2,228.4	4,571.7
Fresno, Cal.	8,013.6	757.7	7,255.9	13.3	56.9	302.2	2,366.6	4,390.9
Denver-Boulder, Col.	7,961.0	596.0	7,365.0	7.1	51.0	212.3	2,002.0	4,959.9
Portland, Ore.-Wash.	7,935.1	698.2	7,236.9	5.9	57.0	291.9	2,382.5	4,449.0
Riverside-San Bernardino-Ontario, Cal.	7,918.2	758.8	7,159.4	9.9	46.4	245.0	2,588.0	4,013.5
Flint, Mich.	7,857.7	846.8	7,020.9	8.2	53.4	209.2	2,311.0	4,388.2
Phoenix, Ariz.	7,819.4	539.5	7,279.8	8.5	40.1	193.7	2,084.6	4,767.9
San Francisco-Oakland, Cal.	7,775.3	875.4	6,899.9	10.0	51.1	443.5	1,881.2	4,490.8

(1) Violent crime includes murder and non-negligent manslaughter, forcible rape, robbery, and aggravated assault. Other metro areas in the top 25 in violent crime are: Baltimore, Md. (1,173.3); Columbia, S.C. (934.1); Charleston-N. Charleston, S.C. (919.4); Baton Rouge, La. (883.2); Jacksonville, Fla. (841.0); El Paso, Tex. (802.9); Florence, S.C. (802.5); Lakeland-Winter Haven, Fla. (802.0).

(2) Property crime includes burglary, larceny, and auto theft. Other metro areas in the top 25 in property crime are: West Palm Beach-Boca Raton, Fla. (7,882.4); Tucson, Ariz. (7,581.7); Des Moines, Ia. (7,432.9).

(3) Other metro areas in the top 25 cities in murder are: Houston, Tex. (28.2); New Orleans, La. (25.3); Longview-Marshall, Tex. (21.6); Jackson, Miss. (20.3); San Antonio, Tex. (18.5); Gary-Hammond-E. Chicago, Ind. (18.3); Midland, Tex. (18.0); Mobile, Ala. (16.3); Shreveport, La. (16.1); Birmingham, Ala. (15.9); Biloxi-Gulfport, Miss. (15.5); Charlottesville, Va. (15.4); Memphis, Tenn.-Ark.-Miss. (15.4); Lafayette, La. (14.2). Of these 25, all but 5 are in the South, in Texas, or in California.

2. Reproduced in Figure 4–4 is the section of the 104th (1984) edition of *Statistical Abstract* breaking down advertising expenditures by medium for the years 1965–1982. How much in dollars did total advertising expenditures increase during that period? What cautions must you keep in mind in interpreting these figures? Where should you go if you want further information about how they were compiled?

3. Visit your library and find the 1979, 1980, and 1984 editions of the almanacs listed in this chapter as well as the yearbooks for these same years for some of the standard encyclopedias listed in chapter 3. Leaf through both sets of books to get a general idea of what each covers. Then, find information in the almanacs so that you can answer the following questions:

   a. Most people have probably heard, by now, that Chicago's Sears Tower is taller than New York's Empire State Building. But is the Empire State Building still the tallest building in New York City? More specifically, what are New York's two tallest buildings, and how tall are they?

   b. Can twelve-year-old girls legally marry? Cite evidence that they can or cannot, and tell where and under what conditions your answer is true.

   c. Look up the table listing average salaries of full-time federal employees in a 1984 (or later) almanac. How many job categories are listed altogether? In how many of these does the average salary reported for

FIGURE 4–4
Statistical Abstract, breakdown of advertising expenditures by medium.

No. **968.** Advertising—Estimated Expenditures, by Medium: 1965 to 1982

[In millions of dollars, except percent. See text, page 553 for a discussion of types of advertising. See also *Historical Statistics, Colonial Times to 1970,* series R 106–109, R 123–126, and T 444–471]

MEDIUM	EXPENDITURES								PERCENT				
	1965	1970	1975	1978	1979	1980	1981	1982, prel.	1965	1970	1975	1980	1982, prel.
Total	15,250	19,550	27,900	43,330	48,780	53,550	60,430	66,580	100.0	100.0	100.0	100.0	100.0
National	9,340	11,350	15,200	23,720	26,695	29,815	33,890	37,785	61.2	58.1	54.5	55.7	56.8
Local	5,910	8,200	12,700	19,610	22,085	23,735	26,540	28,795	38.8	41.9	45.5	44.3	43.2
Newspapers	4,426	5,704	8,234	12,214	13,863	14,794	16,528	17,694	29.0	29.2	29.5	27.7	26.6
National	784	891	1,109	1,541	1,770	1,963	2,259	2,452	5.1	4.6	4.0	3.7	3.7
Local	3,642	4,813	7,125	10,673	12,093	12,831	14,269	15,242	23.9	24.6	25.5	24.0	22.9
Magazines	1,161	1,292	1,465	2,597	2,932	3,149	3,533	3,710	7.6	6.6	5.2	5.9	5.6
Weeklies	610	617	612	1,158	1,327	1,418	1,598	1,659	4.0	3.2	2.2	2.6	2.5
Women's	269	301	368	672	730	782	853	904	1.8	1.5	1.3	1.5	1.4
Monthlies	282	374	485	767	875	949	1,082	1,147	1.8	1.9	1.7	1.8	1.7
Farm publications	71	62	74	104	120	130	146	148	.5	.3	.3	.2	.2
Television	2,515	3,596	5,263	8,955	10,154	11,366	12,650	14,329	16.5	18.4	18.9	21.2	21.5
Network	1,237	1,658	2,306	3,975	4,599	5,130	5,575	6,210	8.1	8.5	8.3	9.6	9.3
Spot	892	1,234	1,623	2,607	2,873	3,269	3,730	4,360	5.9	6.3	5.8	6.1	6.6
Local	386	704	1,334	2,373	2,682	2,967	3,345	3,759	2.5	3.6	4.8	5.5	5.6
Radio	917	1,308	1,980	3,052	3,310	3,702	4,230	4,670	6.0	6.7	7.1	6.9	7.0
Network	60	56	83	147	161	183	230	255	.4	.3	.3	.3	.4
Spot	275	371	436	620	665	779	879	923	1.8	1.9	1.6	1.5	1.4
Local	582	881	1,461	2,285	2,484	2,740	3,129	3,492	3.8	4.5	5.2	5.1	5.2
Direct mail	2,324	2,766	4,124	5,987	6,653	7,596	8,944	10,319	15.2	14.1	14.8	14.2	15.5
Business papers	671	740	919	1,400	1,575	1,674	1,841	1,876	4.4	3.8	3.3	3.1	2.8
Outdoor	180	234	335	466	540	578	650	721	1.2	1.2	1.2	1.1	1.1
National	120	154	220	307	355	364	419	465	.8	.8	.8	.7	.7
Local	60	80	115	159	185	214	231	256	.4	.4	.4	.4	.4
Miscellaneous	2,985	3,848	5,506	8,555	9,633	10,561	11,908	13,113	19.6	19.7	19.7	19.7	19.7
National	1,745	2,126	2,841	4,435	4,992	5,578	6,334	7,067	11.5	10.9	10.2	10.4	10.6
Local	1,240	1,722	2,665	4,120	4,641	4,983	5,574	6,046	8.1	8.8	9.5	9.3	9.1

Source: McCann-Erickson, Inc., New York, N.Y. Compiled for Crain Communications, Inc. In *Advertising Age* (copyright). Percentages derived by U.S. Bureau of the Census.

women exceed that reported for men? How do you account for these figures? If you wanted to check your guess, how might you go about gathering data to find out whether you are correct?

WRITING ASSIGNMENT: A Short Narrative Based on Two Sources

In 1978, in Jonestown, Guyana, there occurred a major tragedy which some have called the "Jonestown massacre." Find accounts of this event in one contemporary almanac and one encyclopedia yearbook. Read the two accounts, and compare them on the basis of completeness, readability, and amount of background information included. Write a one- or two-page account of the event, in your own words, taking care to make clear which source you relied upon for each fact you include.

Government Sources

The *Statistical Abstract* is only one of thousands of government sources of use to researchers. Though cumbersome to draw on, the U.S. government is the largest single source of information in the world. Ahead of those who learn to make their way through its bureaucratic mazes lie rewarding careers as sociologists, historians, investigative reporters, consultants, and research specialists in literally hundreds of governmental and industrial jobs.

Over 17,000 documents are presently listed for sale by the U.S. Government Printing Office, and this total by no means includes all the official publications that can be acquired by diligent researchers. The superintendent of documents issues a monthly catalog of U.S. government publications currently for sale. In its prefatory section, you will find information on how to get copies of out-of-print documents. Since 1974, this catalog has been computerized as well as printed. The computerized version is made available to a cataloguing network of college libraries. Both versions now follow the Library of Congress subject headings you learned about in chapter 3. So it is relatively easy to find what publications are currently in print.

Sooner or later, you will probably find an occasion to consult the *Federal Register,* the *Index to the Code of Federal Regulations,* the *United States Code,* or the *United States Statutes at Large.* So you should remember their existence. Collectively, these works contain all our national law and all unclassified regulations concerning its administration. They are well worth checking if your research ever takes you far into the labyrinth of governmental records.

The one work to remember, in addition to *Statistical Abstract* and the monthly catalog of government publications, is Matthew Lesko's *Information U.S.A.* This book is especially valuable because it does more than list what governmental information is available where. It gives specific and practical advice about how best to go about getting the data you need.

Advanced Indexes

When you have practiced a bit with a fair sample of the reference works described here and become proficient with the *Readers' Guide,* your skimming and selective reading skills should be sharp enough to enable you to tackle almost any of the more advanced periodical indexes. You will find them listed under the appropriate subject headings in Appendix D.

One thing, though, is worth keeping in mind. Over the years, such works come and go, change their names, divide their areas of coverage, etc. So be sure to skim the prefatory information to ensure that the index you are using covered the kind of material you are looking for *at the time that material appeared.*

To give you an idea how important such an elementary precaution can be, consider the history of the very excellent work that appeared from 1907–1919 as the *Readers' Guide Supplement and International Index.* In 1920 it changed its name and, until 1965, was known as the *International Index to Periodicals.* From 1965–1974, it was given the much more descriptive title of *Social Sciences and Humanities Index.* Since 1974, however, it has been split in two. One part is the *Humanities Index,* and the other the *Social Sciences Index.* Both are excellent reference works. Together they index articles from over 500 scholarly and professional journals. But unless you remember the possibility of such a checkered past, you can easily waste time looking for what does not exist. Don't, for instance, expect to find articles published before 1973 listed in the *Humanities Index.*

Only an expert can keep up with such bibliographical metamorphoses within a field. But beginning researchers can remember to check prefaces and, if necessary, to ask librarians for help.

Book Sources

As your bibliography begins to pyramid, you will find more and more possible book entries turning up. Often you will wonder whether a given title is a sound scholarly work or a product of the lunatic fringe. You may be even more puzzled by some avant-garde works of fiction. Do they represent genius or mere eccentricity? While not a complete answer to this riddle, the *Book Review Digest* will at least let you know what professional reviewers said about a work within eighteen months of its publication. Sometimes that is enough to prevent a beginning scholar from confusing the latest fantasy about the authorship of Shakespeare's plays with literary scholarship or from dismissing out of hand responsible predictions about the coming information-based technology that sound, on the surface, preposterous.

One type of book source is so important in research that it requires special mention. This is the essay, or chapter, in a bound collection. Often just one or two of the articles in such an anthology will be of interest to you, but they may be crucial to your research. Yet from its title or subject listing in the card catalog you may not recognize the connection of the book to your subject. Not being a periodical, it will not be covered in any of the indexes we have discussed. How, then, does the careful researcher find such sources? Fortunately, there is a reference tool to cover just this need, the *Essay and General Literature Index*. Often the most authoritative, up-to-date information you find will be from such book chapters. So, if this is a possibility with your subject, don't consider your bibliography complete until you have checked the *Essay and General Literature Index*.

Biographical Sources

In your library reference room, you will find most of the authoritative sources of biographical or "life story" information about famous people. (We named several of the best ones in the "Specialized Dictionaries" section above.) In using these sources, always be aware of whether the subject of your investigation was living or deceased when the book was published and whether he or she was British or American. Many of the best works define their coverage along those lines.

EXERCISE 4.3: Following Your Leads to the Sources You Need

1. In the course of some research on counterfeiting, you learn that, during the 1930s, the U.S. government published a booklet entitled *Know Your Money*, filled with useful hints for spotting bogus bills. What information in this chapter would help you find out whether that pamphlet is still in print?
2. The Environmental Protection Agency has somehow confused your company with another one with a similar name. Since you have frequent correspondence with the EPA, this has caused the company several expensive bureaucratic entanglements over the past year. But every effort to straighten things out by phone has only confused them more. Yesterday, the boss pulled you off your regular research work and told you to drop everything until you could guarantee him that EPA's records on your company were completely accurate. You have decided that the best way to proceed is to request copies of their records on your company so that you can go over them yourself, identify the inaccuracies, and formally request the EPA to

correct its files. Use Lesko's *Information U.S.A.* to investigate your options, and answer the following questions:

a. Should you request copies of their records on you under the Freedom of Information Act or the Privacy Act? Why?

b. What should you do if they refuse to supply the requested records? On what pages do you find the answers to these questions?

3. A friend of yours is doing a research paper on hypnosis for her psychology class. Her boy friend recommended a book he had read titled *Hypnocop*, but your friend wonders whether this book is reliable enough to be given serious attention in a college research report. Upon looking it up in *Book Review Digest*, you find the listing reproduced in Figure 4–5. What advice would you give your friend about using the book?

4. Explain what kinds of materials you will find listed in the *Essay and General Literature Index* that might not be listed in other bibliographical sources.

5. Go to the library and examine some of the advanced periodical indexes mentioned in this chapter or that you find listed in Appendix D. Look up five possible readings on the topic you have in mind for your major research project. If you are still without a lead, you can for the time being work with any other subject you find interesting. For each article, copy down all the publication information exactly as you find it in the index.

FIGURE 4–5
Hypnocop review.

DIGGETT, CHARLES, 1927-. Hypnocop; true-life cases of the N.Y.P.D.'s first investigative hypnotist; [by] Charles Diggett and William C. Mulligan. 226p $14.95 1982 Doubleday

363.2 1. Hypnotism 2. Criminal investigation 3. New York (N.Y.)—Police
ISBN 0-385-17067-X   LC 81-43142

The author recounts his efforts to win approval of the use of hypnosis in investigating criminal cases in New York City. He tells the story of some of the 150 cases in which this forensic tool was used "including the David Berkowitz and Metropolitan Opera murder cases. . . . [Detective Sergeant] Diggetts success led to his appointment as the first head of the Hypnosis Unit of the NYPD in 1980." (Libr J)

———

"[While the author] is an enthusiastic proponent of hypnosis, Diggett is aware of its limits, pointing out, for instance, that since subjects can lie under hypnosis, independent corroboration of evidence obtained in this way is essential. Recommended for law enforcement personnel and laypersons interested in forensic hypnosis."
Libr J 107:1764 S 15 '82. Gregor A. Preston (120w)

"Sergeant Diggett retells dozens of cases, each of which exposes a different side of hypnosis. . . . William C. Mulligan has helped make the technical parts of 'Hypnocop' clear and the narrative parts juicy. But as Sergeant Diggett himself says, it's like magic: 'No one has ever been able to explain to me how or why it works.'"
N Y Times Book Rev p16 N 21 '82. Margaret Peters (340w)

WRITING ASSIGNMENT: A Short, Short Biography

Select some prominent person, living or dead, in whom you have either a personal or an academic interest. Look up that figure in at least three standard biographical sources. Prepare a two- or three-page report for your classmates giving the highlights of the person's life and explaining why you find him or her of special interest. Be sure to make clear which information you are taking from which source.

Appraising Unfamiliar Reference Works

When you have familiarized yourself with the sources discussed so far in this book, you have, as it were, passed the researcher's basic training course. You know your base camp in the library and the various directions in which you can branch out from it. However, the very object of that branching out is to lead you to still other references, works which have not been discussed or perhaps even mentioned in this book.

Not all those works will be worth your time. It is part of your responsibility as a researcher to evaluate them. What you learned so far will help some in making those decisions. At times, it may also help to consult the checklist shown in Figure 4–6 on pp. 96–97. This set of standards was actually developed for use by librarians. But many freshman have told us that using it saved time and trouble when they came across works that were new to them.

PREPARING CARDS ON YOUR SOURCES

From the outset, we have encouraged you to form a general idea of the topic for the full research report that you will write later in this course. To be sure, that topic may have to be modified drastically or even abandoned altogether. But as much as possible, we wanted you to practice using the basic reference tools by looking up information that you might actually put to use. If you were able to follow our advice and look up references of possible use, now is the time to record your progress.

In library research, we mark the trail of our investigation with a bibliography or list of references. As soon as you have become reasonably sure that you are going to draw on a work for your report, directly or indirectly, you should prepare a bibliography card on it. Go ahead and make cards in genuinely doubtful cases. It is faster in the long run to throw away four or five cards on works you did not use than to interrupt your later work at a much more vulnerable stage to take care of such a pesky detail. Be sure, too, that the entries on your cards conform in every detail to your assigned style sheet.

FIGURE 4–6

HOW TO STUDY
REFERENCE BOOKS*

Only constant and practical use of a reference book will make a student thoroughly familiar with its character and use, but the following suggestions will help him in his preliminary examination of the book.

1. Examine title page carefully for information as to
   a) scope of work as indicated in title
   b) author's name
   c) author's previous record (often indicated by list of degrees, positions, titles of earlier works, etc.)
   d) publisher
   e) date of publication. Check date of publication by reference to copyright date and date of Preface; while these dates offer no absolute guarantee of the date of information in the book, they sometimes help in determining this, especially in cases where they are considerably earlier than the imprint date.
2. Read Preface or Introduction for
   a) further information as to scope of work
   b) special features claimed
   c) limitations, if any
   d) comparison with other books on same subject.
3. Examine book itself for
   a) arrangement
   b) kind of entry
   c) cross references, i.e., extent to which included, whether given in main work or in separate list, etc.
   d) supplementary lists, noting number and kind and how connected with main work
   e) indexes, noting fullness and exactness of reference
   f) quality and kind of articles, noting whether they are popular or scientific, signed or unsigned, impartial or biased, and especially whether they are equipped with satisfactory bibliographical references in the form of either appended bibliographies, references throughout the text, or bibliographical footnotes. Several articles should be read carefully, compared with similar articles in other books. The student should, if possible, look up some subjects upon which he has either some special knowledge or means of securing accurate information. However important the form and convenience of arrangement of a reference book may be, the trustworthi-

*Midge, Isadore Gilbert. "Reference Works and Reference Books" as reprinted in Eugene P. Sheehy, *Guide to Reference Books*, 9th ed. Chicago: American Library Association, 1976. xiv–xv. Reprinted by permission.

FIGURE 4–6 (*cont.*)

    ness of its information is of still greater importance, and a knowledge of its comparative accuracy or inaccuracy is fundamental to any real knowledge of the book.

4. In examining both Preface and articles, note any evidence of lack of impartiality; e.g., if the book deals with a controversial subject, religious, political, etc., does it represent only one side; or, in the case of a biographical work, are the selection of names, kind and length of article, etc., determined in any way by the desire to secure subscribers.

5. In studying the arrangement of a book, note the possibility of variation in books which follow the same general arrangement; e.g., in a work arranged alphabetically, note what rules for alphabetizing have been followed. Among encyclopedias, for example, the *Britannica*[1] and the *Americana* follow different rules, and the student who does not observe that fact may miss the article for which he is looking. The alphabetizing of words containing an umlauted vowel is a possible source of confusion in many books, and in foreign reference books, in general, one should always remember points in which the foreign alphabetizing differs from the English. A fuller discussion of some of these points will be found on page [102] of this *Guide.*

6. If the work in question purports to be a new edition, note carefully the extent of revision claimed for it and check this by comparison with earlier editions. New or revised editions often present very special difficulties, and the examination should be extended enough to determine whether the revision is
   a) so complete and thorough that it supersedes the earlier work
   b) thorough, but with the omission of some material included in the earlier work which is still useful, in which case the two editions may have to be used together, or
   c) so insufficient and superficial that the earlier edition is still to be preferred.
   A reference worker needs such information about a book for two purposes:
   a) to decide whether or not the book should be purchased
   b) to be able to explain to readers who ask for a so-called new edition why its purchase was considered advisable.

THE STYLE MANUAL: THE SOURCE YOU ALWAYS USE

    In a sense, almost all research reports are originally intended for publication. Those that will not be printed in professional journals are nonetheless addressed to a circle of readers who stand in a very important relationship to the researcher. They are his professional peers and superiors, people who must accept his work if he is to prosper. To a large extent, they will judge him by the quality of those reports. So the convention among research scholars is that even working papers are prepared as if for publication.

This means that beginning researchers must understand the importance of the *style manual* or *style sheet* in publishing. As you do more of it, you will soon see that writing confronts you, almost from moment to moment, with a myriad of small decisions about what is "correct." Most of these decisions involve minute points of punctuation, formatting, and capitalization, for example, which are without intellectual importance in themselves. Which titles, for example, are italicized and which are put in quotation marks? Does the comma go before the final *and* in a series (e.g., *the red, white and blue*) or not?

Those who work daily with research reports know, of course, that such trivialities are unimportant *in themselves*. But they join with editors of all kinds in valuing *consistency* in such matters. So every publication of any significance has its own style sheet, to ensure that all its writers answer such questions in the same way. Large publications, like the big city newspapers and the monthly magazines, often write their own style sheets. Smaller ones frequently adopt an existing style sheet and follow it. In the case of the professional and technical journals that publish most research reports, the governing style sheets are not usually written by the publications themselves but rather by scholarly organizations.

The MLA Handbook and the APA Publication Manual

Thus a large number of journals in literature, art, philosophy, modern language studies, and other areas of the humanities will all follow the rules set forth in the *MLA Handbook,* which is the name of the style sheet developed by the Modern Language Association. Similarly, a host of periodicals in the sciences and social sciences follow the conventions described in the *Publication Manual of the American Psychological Association.*

There are a good many other style sheets governing publications in other academic fields, but the *MLA Handbook* and the *APA Publication Manual* are by far the most widely used. If your instructor has not already made clear which style sheet he or she expects you to use for your first documented paper, you should ask about that now. Most instructors ask beginning students to follow the MLA conventions. A good many others will also accept papers following the APA style, especially from students majoring in fields where that is the accepted standard. A few will even allow students majoring in fields like biology or chemistry, which have style sheets of their own, to acquire and use those style sheets while they are learning documentation.

It is not a major point, but we suggest that if your instructor is one of the latter, you accept the offer. Most students will go through college using one of the "big two" style sheets. That is why they are the ones this book covers in detail. The whole point in using a style sheet, though, is to learn to follow it *exactly*. So if you know in advance that your future work will require you to learn a different style and if your instructor gives you the opportunity to practice that style while learning research technique, consider doing so.

The working researcher wants his command of the style sheet to become second nature. He does not want to be annoyed by those decisions while trying to communicate the sense he has made of his data. If you start now using the sheet you will finally use in your work, you will begin that work with more useful practice behind you and without the nuisance of having to relearn a new version of the same basics.

On the other hand, your instructor may have excellent reasons for not giving you this option. Not all subjects can be treated equally well in all styles. If he feels that your subject is ill-suited to the style manual you have in mind or that the use of a different manual might needlessly complicate your learning, respect his professional judgment and follow his directions to the letter. The more important point is not which style sheet you learn but how you learn to regard it.

Why Details Are Important in Bibliography

One of the hardest things for many students to understand is *why* scholars make so much of the insignificant details legislated in style manuals with such hair-splitting precision. Why *is* consistency so important? What real difference does it make whether a comma in a citation goes inside or outside the parenthesis? The difference, obviously, is not a matter of truth. It is, however, a matter of courtesy and credibility among researchers—and for good reason.

Because research is the systematic pursuit of verifiable truth, the two things that it cannot tolerate are fraud and negligence. You are now learning the conventions that researchers have developed to protect themselves against dishonesty. Citations, footnotes, and bibliographies provide records that can be *checked,* assurances that reports presenting them are not based on distorted or manufactured evidence.

An unpleasant truth is that the incentives for successful fraud in research are real. Occurrences are frequent enough to keep all good researchers wary. For in a few instances financial rewards, promotions, and academic honors have been given to people who were later discovered to be out-and-out shysters. It is, therefore, a form of bad manners for researchers to expect colleagues to trust their unsupported claims. Research progresses on evidence; it follows that the burden of proof should be willingly accepted by the researcher.

Appropriate use of citations and references, therefore, shows that the writer accepts that responsibility and warrants the factual integrity of the report. To a certain extent, the strict adherence to a style sheet serves the same function. Not every carnival grifter or unschooled quack could or would bother to learn the intricacies of a standard academic style sheet.

Exactness in documentation also provides a further assurance. It suggests, at least, that a report was not hastily or carelessly prepared. In evaluating each other's work, researchers feel justified in assuming that one who would be careless in small things might also be careless of great matters. What is at issue, therefore, is *credibility*. That is why it is important to place every colon and every comma in every citation *exactly* as called for in your style sheet.

LISTS OF WORKS CITED AND REFERENCES

At the end of your research report, you should always list at least the works you actually drew upon. If you are using the APA style, this is titled the "Reference List" and is limited to works that you used in specific, identifiable ways. MLA style, on the other hand, normally heads it "Works Cited," assuming that all its entries are actually cited in the report. It is permissible under MLA style to present instead an inclusive list of all the books you drew upon, including those used for relevant background reading. Such a complete list of sources is titled "Bibliography." However, your list cannot properly be called a bibliography if it contains nonprint references, such as tape recordings, films, or personal interviews. In that case, use the broader title "Works Consulted." Unless these distinctions are important to the point under discussion, we shall use these terms interchangeably.

One advantage to preparing reference cards as you decide on your readings is that your bibliography is almost finished when your last reading is selected. All that remains is to alphabetize your cards and type them up in the proper list format at the end of your report. You will also find your bibliography cards to be your most convenient source of publication information for any footnotes you have to write.

In this chapter, you will learn the format for three of the most basic bibliographical entries: the book, the periodical article and the encyclopedia entry. Though we will explain both the MLA and APA formats, you should learn the one your instructor suggests for you and simply ignore what is said about the other.

Basic MLA Format

Sample Card for a Book Reference in the MLA Style

```
Maier, Henry W.  Three Theories of Child
     Development.  New York: Harper, 1965.
```

Notice that the bibligraphical entry contains essentially three kinds of information: (1) author identification; (2) exact title of the work; and (3) the facts of publication that an interested person would need in order to acquire the work.

Author Identification. First comes the last name of the author, followed by a comma. Then his first name, as it appears on the title page of the book, and his middle initial, followed by a period. That completes the author identification section of the entry for a simple, single-author book entry. If the work bears only the author's first two initials, you enter them in your bibliography, even if you happen to know his or her first name.

Exact Title. Two spaces after the period, you enter the exact title of the book, underlining it and capitalizing the first letter of each important word. If the book has a subtitle, put a colon after the title, and, one space later, begin the subtitle, which is also underlined. Follow the complete title with a period.

Facts of Publication. Two spaces after the title, write the city of publication. If the state or country in which the city is located is unlikely to be immediately recognizable, put its identifying abbreviation after the city, separated by a comma, and put the colon after the abbreviation.

One space after the colon, enter the name of the publisher, followed by a comma, the year of publication, and a final period. If only part of the work was used, enter the inclusive page numbers (e.g., 11–78) after the year and before the period.

Notice that the name of the publisher, Harper & Row, is here shortened to Harper. The *MLA Handbook* prescribes a set of shortened names for standard publishers. Find out from your instructor whether you are expected to use them; if so, be sure to allow yourself time to look them up. Notice that in the bibliography entry, the first line starts at the left margin and each later line is indented five places to the right. You will learn in later chapters that this format is *not* followed for footnotes or endnotes.

Sample Card for a Periodical Reference in the MLA Style

```
Reed, William F.  "The Prescription the
     Doctors Needed."  Sports Illustrated
     12 Feb. 1979: 12–13.
```

Notice, first, that the periodical entry is placed exactly like a book entry. That is, its second and subsequent lines follow the same "hanging indentation" form that you observed on the first card. They are indented five places to the right.

Notice, also, that the order of information is essentially the same in the two entries. First comes the author, last name, first name, and middle initial, punctuated just as it was on the book card.

Title of Article and Name of Periodical. Notice that the name of the *article* follows the author's name, in *quotation marks,* and that it is followed by a period that falls *inside* the second quotation mark. Two spaces after the article title, begins the name of the periodical which, like a book title, is *underlined,* but the name of the periodical, unlike a book title, is *not* followed immediately by any mark of punctuation.

Instead, the date, month and year of publication are entered in that order, with *no* intervening punctuation unless the month is abbreviated. In that case the usual period is used after the abbreviation. Immediately after the year comes a colon followed by the inclusive page numbers of the article and a final period.

Sample Card for an Encyclopedia Reference in the MLA Style

```
Schawlow, Arthur L. "Laser and Maser."

    Encyclopaedia Britannica: Macropaedia.

    1974 ed.
```

Author Identification. If the author is identified, begin with the last name, followed by the first name and middle initial, then a period. Remember that if you find initials instead of a name at the end of the article it is your responsibility to look elsewhere for the author's name. In most encyclopedias, you can check the index to learn the name that corresponds to those initials; in the case of the *Britannica,* look instead in the *Propaedia.* If no author information is available, begin with the title of the entry, as shown on page 104.

Title of Entry and Name of Encyclopedia. Two spaces later the title of the article is listed, followed by a period and enclosed in quotation marks. Two spaces after that list the title of the encyclopedia. In this case since the article comes from *The Encyclopaedia Britannica* you should also list the division (i.e., the *Macropaedia*) in which it appeared. The title of the encyclopedia and the division, if any, should be underlined, but *not* the title of the article. Follow this with a period.

Publication Information. Leave two more spaces and list the edition year, followed by the abreviation "ed" for edition and a period. No publisher's name or location is necessary.

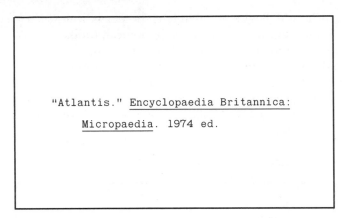

"Atlantis." <u>Encyclopaedia Britannica</u>:

<u>Micropaedia</u>. 1974 ed.

Basic APA Format

Sample Card for Book Reference in APA Style

Maier, H. W. (1965). <u>Three theories of child</u>

<u>development</u>. New York: Harper &

Row.

Notice that the reference contains essentially three kinds of information: (1) author identification; (2) exact title of the work; and (3) the facts of publication that an interested person would need in order to acquire the work.

Author Identification. First comes the last name of the author, followed by a comma. Then come the initials, each followed by a period. That completes the author identification section of the entry for a simple, one-author book. Note that you only enter the author's initials, even if the first name is given on the title page of the book.

Date. Two spaces after the writer's second initial, in parentheses, enter the year of publication. Put a period after the closing parenthesis mark.

Exact Title. Two spaces after the period, you enter the exact title of the book, underlining it and capitalizing only its first word. If the book has a subtitle, put a colon after the main title and, one space later, begin the subtitle, which is also underlined. As with the main title, only the first word of the subtitle is capitalized. Follow the complete title with a period.

Facts of Publication. Two spaces after the title, write the name of the city in which the book was published. If the state or country of publication is not obvious, put its identifying abbreviation after the city, separated by a comma, and put the colon that normally follows the name of the city after that abbreviation.

One space after the colon, enter the name of the publisher, followed by a final period. If only part of the book was used, enter the inclusive page numbers in parentheses immediately after the title and before the period. Abbreviate the word *pages* as *pp.*, as in Three theories of child development (pp. 11–78).

Note that the first line of the reference starts at the left margin. Each later line is indented three places to the right.

Sample Card for Periodical Reference in APA Style

```
Reed, W. F.  (1979, February 12).  The

prescription the doctors needed.

Sports Illustrated, pp. 12–13.
```

Notice, first, that the placement of the periodical reference entry is exactly like that for a book reference. That is, the first line extends all the way to the left, and later lines use "hanging indentation," to move three spaces to the right.

Notice, also, that the order of information is essentially the same as for book entries. The name of the author is handled first, in exactly the same way as for the book reference.

Two spaces after the author's second initial comes an opening parenthesis. Immediately after that is entered the year of publication, followed by a comma, the month, and the date if applicable. After that, the parenthesis is closed and a period is entered.

Title of Article and Name of Periodical. Begin the article title two spaces after the period that closes the date. Capitalize only the first letter of its first word, and place a period after it. Two spaces after the period, begin the name of the periodical, capitalizing every important word and underlining the whole title of the journal. Note that the title of the article is *not* underlined.

Sample Card for Encyclopedia Reference in APA Style

```
Schawlow, A. L. (1974). Laser and

    maser. In Encyclopaedia Britannica:

    Macropaedia (pp. 686-689). Chicago:

    Helen Hemingway Benton.
```

Author Identification. If the author is identified, begin with the last name, followed by the first and middle initials, both followed by periods. Remember that if you find initials instead of a name at the end of the article it is your responsibility to look elsewhere for the author's name. In most encyclopedias, you can check the index to learn the name that corresponds to those initials; in the case of the *Britannica,* look instead in the *Propaedia.*

Date. Skip two spaces and then enter the year of the edition you are citing, in parentheses followed by a period.

Title of Entry and Name of Encyclopedia. Two spaces later, list the title of the article. Remember that only the first word in the title and proper names should be capitalized when using the APA system. The title of the article should be followed by a period.

Two spaces later write "In" followed by the editor's name (first initial, middle initial and last name) if known. After this, list the title of the encyclopedia in which the article appeared, being careful to follow the APA rules for title capitalization. The latter title should be underlined. Then skip two spaces and write the page numbers of the article in parentheses. Place a period outside the closing parenthesis.

Publication Information. Leave two spaces and name the city of publication, followed by a colon. Skip a space, list the publisher's name, and close the entry with a period.

Unsigned Encyclopedia Articles. In a case where the author cannot be determined, such as in the *Micropaedia* or in articles found in *The Columbia Encyclopedia,* you simply begin your entry with the title of the encyclopedia article. All other punctuation and information remains the same, as in this example:

```
      Atlantis. (1974). In Encyclopaedia

         Britannica: Micropaedia (p. 304).

      Chicago: Helen Hemingway Benton.
```

EXERCISE 4.4:   Proofreading Bibliography Entries in the MLA Format

Below are five reference entries, supposedly in MLA style. Each of the entries contains several errors. Make the necessary corrections so that they conform to the format you learned in this chapter.

1. Snow, C. P. The physicists. Boston, Little: 1981.

2. "Nitrous oxide." Encyclopaedia Britannica: Micropaedia. 1974 ed.

3. Rosenblat, Roger. "Journalism and the larger truth," Time July 2, 1984: 88.

4. Alastair Campbell. <u>The Graphic Designer's Handbook</u>. Running
   Press: Philadelphia, 1983.

5. Davis, Dwight B. "Sports Mechanics: Olympians' Competitive
   Edge." <u>High Technology</u>. July 1984: pp. 34–41.

EXERCISE 4.5:   Proofreading Bibliography Entries in the APA Format

Below are five reference entries, supposedly in APA style. Each of the entries contains several errors. Make the necessary corrections so that they conform to the format you learned in this chapter.

1. Snow, C. P. <u>The Physicists</u>. (1981). Boston: Litle,
   Brown.

2. Davis, Dwight B. (July 1984). Sports mechanics: Olympians'
   competitive edge. <u>High Technology</u>, pp. 34–41.

3. "Hypnosis," (1974). <u>Encyclopaedia Britannica:</u>
   <u>Micropaedia</u>.

4. Campbell, Alastair. (1983) <u>The graphic designer's handbook.</u>
   Philadelphia: Running Press.

5. E. Rosenblat, R. (2 July, 1984). Journalism and the
   larger truth. <u>Time. 88.</u>

5

Bringing Sources Together— The Purpose of Citations

Most written communications are intended to make a point. If only two words appear on a billboard, they are very likely to be "Drink Coca-Cola." Take away the evidence and electioneering from a newspaper endorsement of a political candidate, and the editorial often reduces itself to "Vote for Ron Hubris!" The complaint letter you write, whether you choose to be courteous or argumentative, says—in essence—"I want my money back."

Usually, in support or explanation of that main point, writers bring together information from a number of sources: from memory ("This garbage can was guaranteed for five years"); from records ("Here is a copy of the sales receipt dated last July and a copy of the five-year warranty that came with it"); from first-hand observation ("The can cracked badly during the February cold"); and from their own reasoning with the information thus assembled ("Therefore, you owe me a refund").

GIVE YOUR PAPER A POINT

An important thing to remember is that research reports are not essentially different from other writing. Like other written messages, the research paper *must* have a point. Ideally, that point will make a definite claim: "Bruno Hauptmann was wrongfully convicted of murder"; "the maze-running behavior of the rats in Professor Festinger's experiment cannot be accounted for by reinforcement theory"; "William Carlos Williams' short story 'The Use of Force' contains imagery suggestive of rape."

109

Sometimes, however, when the state of the researcher's knowledge will not support such firm conclusions, the writer cannot make so definite a claim. But she must still give her paper a point. This can be done by organizing the data in order to clarify the issues, define the state of knowledge, or classify the points of view on a subject. Good research reports of this "suspended-judgment" type could take as their central points statements like these: "most theories about the causes of glaciers fall into one of three groups"; "the question over Sam Shepherd's guilt remains unanswered"; "psychologists are divided over the issue of whether reinforcement theory can account for the maze-running behavior of Professor Festinger's rats."

Readers of such stock-taking reports may not come away with the feeling that they understand fully the subject covered. But they should always understand it *better*. A report that does nothing more than gather relevant data and organize it for better understanding contributes its own kind of new knowledge to a field of inquiry. That increased understanding is the point of the report.

MARSHAL YOUR EVIDENCE

Like writers of other documents, report writers also draw on a wide range of sources. They, too, depend on memory, observation, written documents, and personal reasoning. What distinguishes research reports from other writing is that researchers try as best they can to put guarantees behind what they say. To a greater extent than other writers, researchers buttress their personal memories and observations with objective, impersonal, verifiable evidence.

The anecdotes and reminiscences that make for fascinating personal essays and after-dinner speeches have no place in research reports. Even an eyewitness should not cite his observation as the only evidence for an important point in a research paper if the facts can be verified independently. His readers may never have heard of the airplane that crashed into the Empire State Building in the mid-1940s. If he expects them to accept his conclusions about air safety because of something about that accident, he must establish with impartial evidence that it happened as he says. For access to that impartial evidence, he turns to the library.

Put Your Sources to Work

In the report, the researcher must put the information gathered from her reading to work. She must select it, summarize or (sometimes) quote it, and cite its sources, all in order to support *her point*. In this chapter you will learn how footnotes, endnotes, and parenthetical citations can help you demonstrate that you have adequate evidence for your assertions and conclusions. But do not make the mistake of confusing good report writing with footnote dropping or citation sprinkling. Only citations that put your information to *work* in some useful way belong in your report.

Report writing is, first of all, writing. It must make a point. It must be clear. Above all, it must be organized.

The Importance of Organization

No research report is better than the reasoning that goes into it. Research, being the *rational* pursuit of knowledge, depends for its success on reasoning based on verifiable evidence. The report is the record of that thinking. Only if the record is an organized one can the reader verify the worth of the thinking behind it.

In later chapters, when you begin sustained work on your first long research paper, you will be given point-by-point guidance to help you work with a large amount of information without losing your own sense of direction. For the time being, however, you will continue to write very short papers while practicing the fundamentals of documentation.

All such practice is pointless, though, unless you understand the logic behind what you are practicing. Perhaps the best way to demonstrate the fact that the report must have a purpose is to give you an opportunity to read one by a student who clearly did not understand what research was all about.

It is so easy for students who are just beginning with documentation to lose sight of the *purpose* of it all that good students, who would not otherwise do unsatisfactory work, often turn in papers like the one reproduced in Exercise 5.1. Do not worry about the handling of citations; just try to read it for logic and meaning. (The "United States" citations, by the way, are to the 1984 *Statistical Abstract*.)

EXERCISE 5.1: Why Citations Do Not Equal Research

```
                    The Difference Is Natural


    Women think differently than men. This is especially

true in the United States where there are 6,540,000 more

women than men (United States 33). Women also visit doctors

more (United States 111). But on the whole, they are

healthier and live longer than men (United States 35).
```

D. H. Lawrence said this many years ago: "Women have the logic of emotion; men have the logic of reason" (1). I think Lawrence's conclusion is logical. In fact, many famous women leaders do too. Phyllis Schlafly said so on nationwide TV recently (1). Virginia Woolf admitted that, when she first started, she could not write with power and imagination because she was too emotional. She said she felt like there was an Angel in the house coaxing her to write only ladylike things and making her afraid to write what men might disapprove of (236). This shows that women naturally look to men for leadership.

Look at what happened when a physician happened to tell Cynthia Ozick that women were naturally unstable for biochemical reasons. Instead of accepting his scientific evidence logically, she got angry and excited (40–44). The doctor was calm, as men usually are. But Miss Ozick could not discuss the subject rationally. On this subject, Gloria Steinem has said:

> A man has alimony and wifely debts to worry about, but a woman may lose so many of her civil rights that in the United States now, in important legal ways, she becomes a child again. In some states, she cannot sign credit agreements, use her maiden name, incorporate a business, or establish a legal residence of her own. Being a wife, according to most social and legal definitions, is still a nineteenth-century thing (24).

1. What is the *point* of this paper? Does it seem to have one? Show specific lines and passages that support your answer.
2. Does the evidence given in paragraph one support the claim made in the first sentence? Why? Are there other places in the paper where evidence does not support the contentions it is intended to? Where?

3. Note particularly the writer's handling of the opinion attributed to Phyllis Schlafly. Do you know who Ms. Schlafly is? How do you react to the writer's effort to have her speak for "many famous women leaders"? Do you find his report of her comments fully believable? Why?

4. Do you understand what the writer is talking about in his report of Cynthia Ozick's "irrationality" in paragraph 3? How does this affect your general trust in the writer? Assuming that the source would support his argument, how might he have made it work better for him?

5. Do you see any connection between the final Gloria Steinem quote and the rest of the paper? How does that make you, as a reader, react at this point?

6. Below is one student's suggested revision of the first paragraph. Do you think it represents an improvement? Explain your answer in terms of what you have learned from reading this book.

> In the United States today, there are 6,540,000 more women
>
> than men (United States 33). They differ from men in many ways.
>
> They visit doctors more (United States 111). Yet they are
>
> healthier than men, and they live longer (United States 35). The
>
> evidence suggests, also, that——in some ways at least——they
>
> think differently.

7. Some instructors call papers like the one above "intellectual crazy quilts." Now that you have experienced one from the reader's point of view, can you understand the reason for the name? Do you see how important it is that research writing be, first of all, clear, purposeful writing?

WHAT IS DOCUMENTATION?

In research papers, the word *documentation* is used for the entire set of conventions by which writers connect the evidence they take from others with the sources from which they take it. The bibliography, list of references, or list of works cited is one part of documentation.

To prevent the reader from having to look through the entire list of works cited every time she wants to check a point, however, a system of *citations* is always used. The purpose of these citations is to connect each specific bit of borrowed evidence with its exact location in the source from which it was taken. Researchers speak interchangeably of citing evidence or citing the sources for it.

Even if you feel you were well trained in the techniques of documentation in some previous class, you should still study carefully what is said in the paragraphs below. New versions of the most influential academic style sheets have recently adopted major modernizations of the time-honored system you probably learned in high school. This is particularly true if, like most students, you were trained to use the MLA system. For the changes explained here represent the most sweeping overhaul of

MLA documentation procedures in the history of the organization. The good news, however, is that the new MLA system is now as simple to learn and easy to use as the APA style.

Footnotes

In your reading for college work, you will find three ways of handling citations. They can be put in footnotes, endnotes, or parenthetical notes inserted into the text itself. A footnote, as the name indicates, is a brief note at the bottom of the page. Footnotes are numbered consecutively in a report. At the point where the citation is to be made, a raised number is inserted in the text to direct the reader to the proper footnote. There is no footnote at the bottom of this page, but just as a reminder we are inserting a sample number here.[1] Normally, the number is placed at the end of the sentence containing the material requiring support or comment. Exceptions are necessary, however, when several parts of the same sentence require separate references or comment. In such cases, the practice is to place the number at the end of the clause or phrase, as necessary, where it will cause the least interruption for the reader.

Earlier in this century, footnotes were the accepted means of citation for almost all academic disciplines. Now, however, the picture has changed. It is expensive to publish papers with notes at the bottom of the page. It is tedious to type manuscripts with several footnotes to be fitted onto each page. And with the explosion of knowledge and the consequent higher standards of scholarship, many more citations are now required. A better system was clearly necessary.

Endnotes

One improvement that reduced cost and increased convenience for writers and publishers was to go to a system of *endnotes*. Actually, endnotes are nothing more than footnotes that have been moved from the bottoms of the pages in a report and put in a list, in numerical order, at the end of the text. Endnotes go after any appendices that the paper may have, but before its bibliography or list of works cited.

Endnotes are still used sometimes for citations. But as with footnotes, the trend is to save them for times when brief explanations, side comments or qualifying statements of substance are absolutely necessary at points where their inclusion in the report would seriously confuse or interrupt its logical flow. Despite the convenience of endnotes for writers, their use just to cite sources creates a constant vexation for readers. A reader who is not particularly interested in checking a reference must still take time to check the end of the report, to make sure she is not missing an important comment. If you are following the MLA style, be sure to find out from your instructor whether you are still permitted to use notes for routine citations. When you are, use endnotes unless you are specifically instructed to use footnotes.

Parenthetical Citations

For a long time now, scholars in the sciences have used a different system for citations. Called *parenthetical* documentation because it places the citations in parentheses, within the text itself, this system has several advantages. It does not tempt the reader to stop and search for what she hopes will be a helpful comment, to find only a routine citation. It also simplifies the preparation of citations because, as you will see later, it makes double use of the publication information in the bibliography.

Like other style sheets in the sciences, the *APA Manual* has depended on parenthetical documentation for some time. Not until the 1984 edition of the *MLA Handbook,* however, did publications in the humanities make specific provision for this option. Because this is a period of transition, today's students in art, literature, and philosophy may need to learn both parenthetical and endnote citation. The examples and exercises in this book will teach you parenthetical citation and familiarize you with the use of endnotes.

COMMON-SENSE DOCUMENTATION

Once you understand that the purpose of documentation is to warrant the truth of what you say, you soon see that most of its conventions are merely codified common sense. A research report is written much as you would write any other factual account. You are perhaps a little more careful in your reasoning, a little more certain of your organization, and a little more aware of the evidence on which you depend. But the fact that you are citing your sources should not distort your writing in any way.

Incorporating Sources

This means, among other things, that your citations should be smoothly worked into your text and clearly connected to the point you are making. When documentation works properly, it should not call attention to itself. Neither of the versions below is ideal, but one is clearly superior to the other. Which do you find more understandable? Why?

A.   Stuart Chase called man the talking animal (8). Jerome

Bruner says that we win membership in humanity with language

(6), and Miller, Pribram, and Gallanter have developed a theory that shows how people set goals, solve problems, and make plans. Their theory also relies heavily on the role of language (125–194). The awareness that we all take for granted is, according to one psychologist, a product of our language (Church 94). Indeed, we could not even control our bodies efficiently, according to an eminent Russian scientist, without talking to ourselves while we learn to do it (Luria 96), nor could we think straight when faced with complex tasks without relying on language (Klein 162). In "Social Structure, Language and Learning," in John P. DeCecco's new anthology The Psychology of Language, Thought, and Instruction, Basil Bernstein writes, "What is significant in his [the growing child's] environment is taken into himself to become the sub-stratum of his consciousness by means of linguistic processing" (93).

B.   We must remember that man is the talking animal (Chase 8). It is with language that we gain membership in humanity (Bruner 6), with language that we formulate human goals, solve human problems, and make human plans (Miller, Pribram, and Gallanter 125–194), and with language that we win human awareness (Church 94). Indeed, language enables man to regulate both his bodily behavior (Luria 96) and his cognitive performance (Klein 162). "What is significant in his [the growing child's] environment is taken into himself to become the sub-stratum of his consciousness by means of linguistic processing" (Bernstein qtd. in DeCecco 93).

For students unaccustomed to material with numerous citations, paragraph *B* is still fairly heavy going. Unless the exact findings of each study were important to this report, it would be preferable in this case to use a bibliographical endnote. If that choice were made, the entire paragraph could be reduced to one sentence, such as: "The importance of language to human thinking is well established.[1]" The accompanying note would then list all the sources, separating them with semicolons. (Even with a parenthetical system, endnotes are still used for such multiple citations.)

Of the two passages shown above, however, most readers agree that paragraph *A* is worse. This is true not because the wrong documentation techniques were used in *A,* but because of the way they were handled. All the citations in both versions are technically correct. On the whole, though, those in paragraph *A* call too much attention to themselves while those in *B* do a better job of keeping the emphasis where it belongs—on the writer's point.

The moral is that, in documentation, correctness is not enough. Citations should be made with sensitivity to the reader's needs. For instance, most students who have difficulty with version *B* report that the abrupt insertion of the quotation at the end of the paragraph causes part of their trouble. Paragraph *B* would have been clearer if the quotation had been shortened and introduced, in this manner:

```
The distinguished British sociologist Basil Bernstein recently

declared that what is significant in the environment of a

growing child is "taken into himself to become the sub-stratum

of his consciousness by means of linguistic processing" (qtd.

in DeCecco 91).
```

Notice that the change which improves *B,* that of introducing the citation within the wording of the text, uses the same technique that proved so distracting early in version *A.* This apparent contradiction simply shows that the effective use of citations, like most other elements of writing, depends on judgment and consideration of context as well as on "following the rules." Fortunately, however, that judgment is largely a matter of common sense. It develops naturally, if you just keep in mind the goals and basic principles of documentation.

WHAT, WHEN, AND HOW TO CITE

What You Cite

In general, you cite sources for whatever you borrow. This means, at the least, that you provide documentation for each of the following:

1. any word-for-word quotations you take from source material;
2. any sustained sequence of ideas or information that you take from another writer, even if you have rephrased the original version in your own words;
3. any opinion, judgment, or theory formulated, expressed, or asserted in one of your sources;

4. any fact not generally known or certain to be confirmed by a quick check in any appropriate reference book.

The first three of these guidelines derive from the same underlying principle: that the fruits of a scholar's thinking belong to the scholar. You will recall from the earlier discussion of plagiarism that it is against the law to take somebody else's wording and pass it off as original. There are stiff penalties for plagiarism if the stolen material is published. In college, plagiarism is a serious academic offense. Most schools have regulations under which it can be severely punished.

If you use the exact words of another writer, you must treat them according to the conventions explained below for handling direct and indirect quotations. This shows exactly what you are borrowing and what is original with you. Of course, you must also name your source and give the exact location from which you took the borrowed material.

There is, incidentally, another good reason for citing sources when you introduce statements of opinion or judgment based on your research. Opinions worth citing are usually those of acknowledged experts in the field. Providing the necessary documentation, therefore, is a way of gaining additional credibility. Readers are less likely to question the judgment of a recognized scholar.

What NOT To Cite

There are of course times when common sense tells us that it is obviously unnecessary to cite borrowed material. Old sayings, well-known biblical scriptures, and quotations that are familiar to everybody need not be cited. Considering the purpose of documentation in research, it would seem pretentious to provide full, formal citations for borrowings like these:

1. A stitch in time saves nine.

   [*The saying is so familiar that nobody is likely to assume that you are claiming originality for it.*]

2. Forgive them; for they know not what they do.

   [*These last words of Christ are so well known to most Americans that they require no citation; however, in a report for readers from non-Christian societies a citation should perhaps be made.*]

3. . . . government of the people, by the people, and for the people. . . .

   [*Lincoln's words are so famous in our country that every reader is sure to recognize them. Again, though, a citation would be used in a paper addressed to readers from a different culture.*]

It is sometimes a little harder to decide which specific facts require documentation. A good rule of thumb is that you can properly leave undocumented facts which you can *safely* assume that "everybody knows" or which, if looked up in any standard reference, will check out exactly as you represent them. It would be pointless, for instance, to cite evidence that President Kennedy was assassinated. That fact is common knowledge. It is unnecessary to cite evidence when giving the date of the assassination. All reputable reference books are in agreement on that, and any interested reader can easily find a source to check.

On the other hand, if you need to assert in a documented report that a ship going through the Panama Canal from the Pacific to the Atlantic is, at one point in the journey, actually travelling *southwest,* you should expect to cite your source. This curious fact is not widely known and would be very difficult to look up. Most books and articles on the Panama Canal have no occasion to mention it.

A different need for documentation arises when you mention, say, the population of Vietnam. Though this fact can be quickly looked up in a great many standard sources, their estimates vary greatly. Such variation, by the way, is usual with statistical information. Yet no researcher's conclusions are better than the facts he or she depends on. So whenever the experts differ in their views of the facts, be sure to cite the source of the version you choose to accept.

While you are learning, a good practice is to check with an experienced researcher in your field when you suspect that you may be documenting the obvious. If that is not possible, remember that it is safer to cite a source you do not really need to cite than to omit a citation that should have been included. The first is an understandable beginner's mistake. The latter may appear to be something more serious.

EXERCISE 5.2:   Getting Clear on What To Cite

1. Define the following terms. Take particular care to distinguish differences in meaning among them.

   A. Documentation
   B. Bibliography
   C. Citation
   D. "Reference" or
      "Works Cited" List
   E. Endnotes
   F. Footnotes
   G. Parenthetical Citation

2. Why is it important for students who were well schooled in footnote use in high school to study carefully the material in this chapter?

3. Decide which of the following selections should be accompanied by a citation if you were to include it in a research report. Unless an item is preceded by an asterisk (*), assume that what you read here is what you found in your source and that you plan to rephrase it for your paper. For the items

marked with asterisks (*), follow the special instructions given in brackets below them.

a. A totally inactive substance with no medical value is called a *placebo*.

b. Arthur Shapiro, a prominent medical historian, estimates that until about 100 years ago, almost all medical practice was actually treatment by placebo.

c. On December 7, 1941, the Japanese attacked Pearl Harbor, and suddenly the United States was plunged into World War II.

d. Theodore Roosevelt was born on October 27, 1858.

e. To most of us nothing is so invisible as an unpleasant truth. Though it is held before our eyes, pushed under our noses, rammed down our throats—we know it not.

f. *"The meaningful word," said L. S. Vygotsky, "is the microcosm of human consciousness."

[*Assume that this is the exact sentence you plan to include in your paper, but that the quoted words appear in Vygotsky's book* Thought and Language.]

g. *I have read that nations that expect to go to war usually do. The process is said to work like this: such nations, because they do expect war, unintentionally communicate their expectations to potential enemies. Those countries, in turn, feel it "necessary" to prepare for war too. These preparations are then taken by the first country as confirmation of its expectation. So feedback loops are set up on both sides, and the two countries drift into war simply because, at the outset, one of them began to expect it.

[*This is your paraphrase of an argument by Gordon Allport that you learned in your sociology course.*]

4. Go back to that sample paper in exercise 5.1. Study the relationship of what is said in the paper to the citations. What signs do you see that the writer was not responsible in his documentation? What impression would it make on you if you found such sloppiness in the documentation of a research report that you had commissioned on a subject of importance to your business?

Where and How to Use Citations

The general rule is to cite the source as close to the point of reference and as unobtrusively as possible. Because these two requirements often conflict, however, style sheets differ in their detailed applications of the rule. Follow the instructions below for the style sheet you are using.

Citations in the MLA Style. MLA style uses a "name-page" system of reference. This means that the author's last name is cited, followed by a space (*no* punctuation) and the number(s) of the page(s) on which the cited information is found. The citation is made in parentheses at the end of the sentence and *before* the end punctuation. For example:

```
There is on record a case in which a famous diagnostician

apparently cured a patient by pronouncing him "moribundus,"

which is Latin for "dying" (Allport 9).
```

If the author's name can be gracefully mentioned in the text, only the page number need be cited parenthetically.

```
Innes gives us what is certainly our best short discussion of

the beta fish (404-407).
```

When citing a whole work, rather than specific pages of it, the simplest and usually the best solution is to name the author (and possibly the work) in the text and get rid of the parentheses altogether.

```
In The Reader, the Text, the Poem, Louise Rosenblatt undermines

virtually every belief of the so-called New Critics.
```

or simply

```
Rosenblatt offers a different view of the literary response.
```

Essentially the same rules are followed when quotations are used and—in most cases—when more than one author is involved.

Quotation with Single Author:
```
"The most difficult thing in the world is to change minds in

directions which conflict with the attitudes deeply embedded in

the nuclear self" (Brown 222).
```

Quotation (or Other Citation) with Two Authors:
```
There is considerable evidence, in fact, that even findings

of carefully controlled experiments tend most of the time to

confirm the expectation of the experimenter (Rosenthal and

Jacobson 21-30).
```

However, if the work cited has more than three authors, you do not name them all. You name the first author, skip a space (no punctuation), and add the abbreviation "et al." (for "and others"), followed by a space and, unless the whole work is cited, the page number(s).

```
A different view appears in one of the classic works of literary

history (Baugh et al. 1210-1213).
```

Citations in the APA Style. APA style uses a "name-date" system of reference. This means the author's last name is cited, followed by a comma and the year in which the source work was published. Only if the reference contains a quotation is a page number cited. In this case a comma follows the date and one space later comes the abbreviation "p." (for "page"), another space, and the page number. The citation is made in parentheses at the point in the text where the first clear reference is made to the source. If it happens to fall at the end of a sentence, it is placed *before* the end punctuation. For example:

```
There is on record a case in which a famous diagnostician

apparently cured a patient by pronouncing him "moribundus,"

which is Latin for "dying" (Allport, 1964).
```

If the author's name can be gracefully mentioned in the text, only the date need be cited parenthetically.

```
Innes (1966) gives us what is certainly our best short

discussion of the beta fish.
```

If both the author's name and the date can be gracefully mentioned in the text, no parenthetical information need be added.

```
In 1964 Allport noted that a famous diagnostician apparently

cured a patient by pronouncing him "moribundus," which is Latin

for dying.
```

Essentially the same rules are followed when quotations are used except that the abbreviation "p." is added one space after the date and followed by the page number from which the quote is taken.

```
"The most difficult thing in the world is to change minds in

directions which conflict with the attitudes deeply embedded in

the nuclear self" (Brown, 1963, p. 222).
```

If the work cited has two authors, both authors are named each time the reference occurs in the text.

```
There is considerable evidence, in fact, that even findings

of carefully controlled experiments tend most of the time to

confirm the expectation of the experimenter (Rosenthal &

Jacobson, 1968).
```

Notice that the author's names are joined by an ampersand (&) in the citation. If this reference had been made in the wording of the report itself, however, the ampersand or "and" sign would not have been used. In that case the word *and* would always be spelled out.

```
Rosenthal and Jacobson (1968) noted that there is considerable

evidence, in fact, that even findings of the most carefully

controlled experiments tend most of the time to confirm the

expectation of the experimenter.
```

If a work has between two and six authors, cite all authors the *first* time a reference is made. In subsequent references, cite only the first author followed by "et al." (for "and others"), followed by a space and the date. Note that a period comes after "al." but *not* after "et."

First Reference:

> Recently, researchers developed more reliable methods of
>
> collecting data on sleepwalking (Abe, Amatomi, & Oda, 1984).

Subsequent Reference:

> Our own inquiries need more of the creative data collecting that
>
> has recently been shown by the psychologists investigating
>
> sleepwalking (Abe et al., 1984).

If the work has six or more authors, list only the first author's name, the abbreviation "et al.", followed by a comma and the date. If you refer to several works that have been written by the same author in the same year, identify them by using the suffixes *a, b, c* and so forth.

> Several marine studies have been conducted along these lines
>
> (Ginsberg, 1958a, 1958b).

These suffixes are based upon the articles' alphabetical order (by title in the reference list).

MORE COMPLEX QUESTIONS ABOUT CITATIONS

The above examples cover only the most common cases, but if you learn these well, you will easily recognize the exceptions covered in appendices A and B for the common-sense adaptations they are. When referring to those appendices and when returning to this one later to look up specific points, be very sure that you are reading sections that pertain to the style sheet you are using. The passages read very much alike; so it would be easy for a hurried student to consult the wrong section without noticing.

How Citations Are Used

When citations are properly handled, casual readers can easily skip over them; however, readers who want to examine the sources can turn to the list of works cited and know exactly where to go from there. That is what we mean by saying that the citations "connect" the text to the reference list.

PROPER USE OF NOTES
WITH PARENTHETICAL CITATION

Even with the modern systems of parenthetical citation described in this chapter, there are still uses for footnotes and endnotes. Unless special circumstances compel the use of footnotes, endnotes are always preferable. They are regularly used in both the MLA and APA systems for the following purposes:

1. *To offer important side comment, explanation, or additional information* that cannot or should not be included in the text.

   EXAMPLE:

To make sure his readers knew that he was aware of an exception to something he said about a book he was reviewing, Richard Fulkerson added this endnote:

> [7]Actually when he treats literary discourse, Kinneavy
>
> abandons the triad of organization, logic, and style, and
>
> treats organization and style as one matter in "The Logic of
>
> Literature: The Primacy of Structure," 343 ff.

This lets his readers know that the comment in the text where the raised number seven appears is not intended to apply to page 343 and those immediately following. So Fulkerson's discussion goes forward without the distraction that would occur if this awkward but necessary explanation were injected into the wording of his critique.

Other similar uses for footnotes or endnotes include providing relevant information about the author (some publications require this at the beginning of the report), indicating that unpublished evidential material is available and explaining how to get it, and expressing acknowledgments to copyright holders' for permission to reprint their material.

2. *To cite several sources at once, especially when evaluative commentary is necessary* to sort out a confusing array of positions or approaches by different researchers.

   EXAMPLE:

To support his observation that the book he was reviewing had served as the basis for several modern textbooks, Fulkerson used this endnote:

> [2] New textbooks based explicitly on Kinneavy's formulations
>
> include Janice Lauer, Gene Montague, Andrea Lunsford, and Janet
>
> Emig, Four Worlds of Writing (New York: Harper, 1981); John J.
>
> Ruszkiewicz, Well-Bound Words; A Rhetoric (Glenview, Illinois:

Scott, 1981); and Gregory and Elizabeth Cowan, Writing (New
York: John Wiley & Sons, 1979). The Cowan text does not show
any direct influence of Kinneavy, but the teacher's manual
acknowledges the connection and explains it at some length.

Parenthetical citation of this many sources in one place would be awkward
at best. Moreover, it would leave unexplained why Fulkerson chose to include the last work cited, despite its failure to mention the book he is reviewing. The endnote allows for that necessary explanation and provides
a much more convenient way to cite multiple sources. In situations like
this, a note is the best solution. Incidentally, Fulkerson wrote this before
the new MLA style changes were in effect. The present handbook calls
for using shortened names for all standard publishers (for instance, Wiley
for the publisher named above). The approved shortened forms are listed
in chapter 6.

CHOOSING HOW TO HANDLE YOUR CITATIONS

You have several options to choose from when you cite a source:

1. *Often the easiest and best way is to mention the source naturally and proceed with your discussion.* Do this with the least use of parentheses and notes that you can manage and still make your references clear.

   EXAMPLES:
   MLA: In the first chapter of The Ethics of Rhetoric, Richard

   Weaver takes a different view of the Phaedrus.

   [*No parenthetical page reference is necessary because the entire first chapter is given over to the* Phaedrus, *and all the other information is given in the text. So no inter- ruption occurs unless a reader decides to get the page number for the whole chapter from the Weaver entry in the "Works Cited" list.*]

   or

   Weaver takes a different view of the Phaedrus (3–26).

   [*This simplifies reading for those who know the name of Weaver's book, though it requires those who do not to check the "Works Cited" list.*]

2. *When more extended use of a reference is necessary, you should normally paraphrase it,* i.e., put it into your own words, selecting only those points that are important to your research and providing page refer- ences in parentheses at appropriate points in the text.

   EXAMPLE:
   MLA: Gardner then turns his attention to medical cults (98–

   115). Sparing none that the average layman is likely to

   have heard of, he begins with homeopathy, the oldest (99–

```
103). Then he takes on naturopathy, ancient and modern

(103-111). And from there he goes on to lace into

osteopathy, (111 ff.) and chiropractic, which, he says,

is the greatest of medical follies (113-115). Probably

his most inspired criticism, though, is his cutting

analysis of Bernarr Macfadden's work on naturopathy. He

points out with obvious glee that, for cancer, Macfadden

suggested almost every conceivable remedy except calling

a physician (104).
```

[*Though no quotations are included, this summarized and paraphrased version has page citations at key points and can easily be checked against the original.*]

3. *Short passages of borrowed material may also be introduced through the use of* indirect *quotations.* Unlike the direct quotations that most students study in high school, indirect quotations do not reproduce the *exact* wording of the original. They must, however, follow the exact *meaning* of the original. The only allowable changes in wording are conventional adjustments in tense, case, and so on which signal to all native speakers of the language that indirect quotation is being used. Though seldom discussed in English textbooks, indirect quotation is common in everyday conversation and frequent in journalistic writing. While perfectly correct in report writing, it should be used only for short quotations where it is easy to make clear which words are quoted exactly.

Example:

Original:

When Debs' heart began to falter, the "doctors" administered a nature remedy—totally worthless—made from cactus.

(From Martin Gardner's *Fads and Fallacies in the Name of Science.* New York: Ballantine, 1957, 109)

Indirect Quotation:

```
Gardner says that when Debs' heart had begun to falter, the

"doctors" administered a nature remedy--totally worthless--made

from cactus.
```

[*Notice that, except for the underlined words, the indirect quotation is faithful to the wording of the original. The emphasized words illustrate two of the three common signals of indirect quotation: the use of the relative* that *to introduce the quotation and the change of verb tense one step further into the past. At times, pronoun shifts are also necessary when indirect quotations are used, but there is no need to discuss them here. These adjustments come naturally to every native speaker of English.*]

What is important is that you recognize that these passages *are* a form of quotation. So when you use them you are actually under three obligations. You must respect the rest of the original wording. You must cite the source, just as you would for a direct quotation. And if you are intermixing indirect quotation with paraphrase, you must make clear where you are following the original wording and where you depart from it.

4. *Finally, citations can take the form of direct word-for-word quotations and be placed in the usual quotation marks.*

TO QUOTE OR NOT TO QUOTE

As a rule of thumb, you should consider your options for handling citations in the order in which they are listed above. If a referenced mention of your source is all you really need for your report, then waste no more of your readers' time with it. If a summary or paraphrase is needed but the exact wording of the source is unimportant, then word the important points yourself so that they fit well into *your* report.

Quotations, either direct or indirect ones, are like fine silver and china. There is no substitute for them; they add a great deal to life. But they should be saved for special occasions, not cheapened and rendered meaningless by constant use. A good guideline is to quote only when doing so lends some obvious advantage. Direct quotations, especially, should be used sparingly. In most kinds of research writing, only a very small fraction of the total words in the paper should be quoted.

When To Quote

Occasionally, you will find that another author has said just the thing you want to say and has phrased it so memorably that a word-for-word quotation will add immeasurably to the power of your own argument. Or if you are quoting an expert whom you know to be esteemed by your readers, using a quotation instead of a paraphrase may be a subtle but effective way to make the most of the credibility of your source. Quoting makes clear that you could not possibly have misunderstood the expert. There are also times when you must make more liberal use of quotations simply because they are the best evidence available. Historical documents, trial transcripts, and literary works are often themselves the subject of study and research. When the wording and the reasons for that choice of words are the very questions under study, an examination of the phrasing is essential. For that, there is no substitute for direct quotations. Quotations also make good, attention-getting openings and closings and, occasionally, good summary statements to drive home the conclusion to a key line of reasoning in your paper.

How To Quote

Once you have decided to use a quotation, be sure to use it correctly. Following these guidelines will help you avoid the more common mistakes:

1. *Introduce your quotations.* Readers are irritated and distressed suddenly to find themselves reading quotations with no obvious connection to the report. Make sure that your handling makes clear not only who is being quoted but how you expect the quotation to contribute to your argument.

2. *Quote accurately.* Nothing destroys the credibility of a researcher more quickly than careless mistakes in quoted material. You owe your sources the courtesy of an accurate representation.

3. *Enclose all quoted material but none of your own words in quotation marks.* If a few of your own words are absolutely necessary to make the meaning clear, enclose your words in square brackets, to signal that they are not the words of your source.

> Example:
>
> *Original:*
> What is significant in his environment is taken into himself to become the sub-stratum of his consciousness by means of linguistic processing.
> [*The unexplained reference to "himself" keeps the quotation from fitting perfectly into the researcher's report. He needs an unobtrusive way of explaining that pronoun.*]
>
> *Incorrect:*
> "What is significant in the growing child's environment is taken
>
> into himself. . ."
> [*The original did not say "the growing child's." The researcher incorrectly substituted words of his own within the quotation marks.*]
>
> *Correct:*
> "What is significant in his [the growing child's] environment is
>
> taken into himself. . ."
> [*By placing his own words within brackets and leaving the original wording intact, the researcher. makes the quotation clear without misrepresenting it.*]

4. *Follow the rules of your style sheet for handling long quotations.* The use of quotation marks over long stretches often creates cumbersome problems. So virtually all style sheets prescribe special ways of handling long quotes. Moreover, what is considered a "long" quotation varies from one style sheet to another. Anything longer than forty words is long to the APA;

yet the MLA does not count a quotation long until it exceeds "four typed lines." The usual way of handling long quotations is to (1) omit the quotation marks, (2) indent the entire quotation, and (3) write it in block form within the text. On this point, the only difference between APA and MLA style is the amount of indentation.

EXAMPLES:

MLA: Emerson saw an audience not as something "out there," already given and determined by the circumstances, but as a swirling collection of human potential, ready to take its direction and character through its interaction with the speaker.

Notice that the quoted material is indented *ten* spaces from the left margin of the report itself.

There are many audiences in any public assembly, each one of which rules in turn. If anything comic or coarse is spoken, you shall see the emergence of the boys and rowdies, so loud and vivacious that you might think the house was filled with them. If new topics are started, graver and higher, these roisterers recede; a more chaste and wise attention takes place. You would think the boys slept and that the men have any degree of profoundness. . . . There is also something excellent in every audience,—the capacity of virtue. They are ready to be beatified. They know so much more than the orator,—and are so just (250–251)!

APA: The unreliability of both the lie detector and the confession have been established by

Brown (1963), who points out that the only
people from whom police really have difficulty extracting confessions are the career
criminals. He quotes from a police manual to
show how interrogators go about getting confessions from people who are, relatively
speaking at least, innocent.

> Suggest that there was good reason for
> his having committed the deed, that he
> has too much intelligence to have done
> it without rhyme or reason. In the case
> of sex crimes, explain that sex hunger
> is one of the strongest instincts moti-
> vating our lives. In the case of theft,
> suggest that the subject may have been
> hungry, or deprived of the necessaries
> of life; or in homicide, that the victim
> had done him a great wrong and probably
> had it coming to him. Be friendly and
> sympathetic and encourage him to write
> out or relate the whole story--to clean
> up and start afresh (p. 251).

Notice that the quoted
material is indented
five spaces from the
left margin of the
manuscript.

According to the *MLA Handbook*, quotations of more than three lines of
poetry should also be blocked in this way. Those of more than one line
may either be presented in quotation marks, like any other short quotation (with / marks used to separate poetic lines), or they may be inset. APA
style makes no special provisions for quotations of poetry.

5. *If you need to place special emphasis on key words in your quotation, underline those words and insert an explanatory note.* MLA style calls for the use of
the words "emphasis added" in parentheses, after the closing quotation
mark and just before the end punctuation. APA style inserts the words
"italics added" in square brackets immediately after the underlined material.

EXAMPLES:

MLA: "Even when no weak spot exists in a suspect's testimony, a
policeman who expects to find one will <u>create one</u>, to his

own satisfaction, at least" (emphasis added).

APA: "Truth and falsehood become hopelessly entangled in the

minds of <u>both the policeman and the suspect</u> [italics

added] when such methods are used."

6. *To make the best use of direct quotes, omit irrelevant parts of the original and signal that you have done so by use of the ellipsis mark (three spaced periods: . . .).* If the ellipsis happens to fall at the end of a sentence, it is used *along with* the normal period.

EXAMPLES (From Emerson's "Eloquence"):
"Eloquence must be grounded on the plainest narrative. . . . The

orator . . . keeps his feet ever on a fact. Thus only is he

invincible."

7. *If a quotation begins in the middle of your sentence, do not start it with a capital, even if the quote begins at what was, in the original, the start of a sentence.* The only exception to this occurs when you give the quotation special emphasis by introducing it formally and using a colon.

EXAMPLES:
Original (From Emerson's "Compensation"):
Things refuse to be mismanaged long.

Incorrect:
Emerson wrote that "Things refuse to be mismanaged long."
[*Though the first word in the quote was capitalized in the original, it should not be capitalized here, in the middle of your sentence.*]

Correct:
Emerson wrote that "things refuse to be mismanaged long."

Also Correct:
Emerson wrote this: "Things refuse to be mismanaged long."
[*The formal introduction, marked by the colon, makes the capital appropriate.*]

8. *Be sure to punctuate quotations properly.* Your quotations are key parts of your report. Don't weaken their force by making mechanical mistakes when you introduce them.

EXERCISE 5.3: Practicing with Quotations and Citations

Choose the paragraph below that matches the style sheet you are following. Edit it carefully, looking for all kinds of mistakes. Depending on how you count, each paragraph contains approximately ten mistakes.

MLA: Writing is not a matter of casually delivering

information, as shippers deliver freight. Modern

rhetoricians remind us that writers always have audiences
to consider (Ong, 53-80; Kroll, CCC May '84, 172-185;
Long, CE 221-226; Ede, 140-154; Ede and Lundsford, 155-
171). And Yancey argues convincingly that there are many
audiences to be considered. The situation is further
complicated, she says (p. 121),[1] "by the fact that, in
addition to the many audiences "out there", the writer
must also satisfy the demands of a clamor of competing
'audiences' within herself. (121) At least one other
expert (Stewart 67-74) has called attention to the
influence of the reader inside every writer. But according
to Yancey, Stewart said that "he had barely begun to
explain the complexity of the problem to my colleagues."

APA: It takes a competent professional to use hypnotism safely.
The very fact, as mental health experts often warn, that
hypnosis is so easy to induce makes it all the more
dangerous and subject to abuse (Gerschman, Reade, and
Burrows, 1980, pp. 472-476). The problem is that laymen
who induce hypnosis[1] have no understanding of the
personality, or psychic make-up of their hypnotic
subjects. Reports abound of neurosis and even complete
mental breakdowns which developed as accidental side
effects of misused hypnosis (Burrows and Dennerstein,
1980, pp. 100-200). Orne and Hammer point out that just
using hypnotism to relieve headaches can be dangerous,
even fatal, if the patient has a brain tumor. (1974) One
well-documented case exists of suicide that was caused by
the use of hypnosis. But in law enforcement particularly
the so called "forensic" use of hypnosis is "rife with
dangers and often abused by well meaning but poorly
trained police officers (J. Brody, 1980)."

WRITING ASSIGNMENT: A Short Report
Using Multiple Sources

The purpose of this assignment is to give you practice in integrating materials from several sources into your own theme and correctly crediting the authors you have borrowed from. Your assignment is to write two or three paragraphs of documented prose on one of the subjects listed below.

1. If you are far enough along in the exploratory reading for your major research report and if your instructor agrees, you may choose to take just one point that you expect to develop in that paper and make that the subject of these paragraphs. Concentrate on writing these paragraphs so that they put your sources to work for you in making that point.

2. Listed below are several questions around which discussions of *fairness* frequently take place. Choose one of these questions and read five–seven appropriate articles in periodicals, books, or standard reference works. Then use what you have learned from your reading to explain your views on some aspect of the question.

   a. Does the recent increase in the frequency of malpractice suits indicate more or less fairness to patients? To doctors?

   b. Are the tax laws (or the procedures of the IRS) really fair?

   c. Are some provisions of the laws concerning employment, marriage, divorce, or child custody unfair to women? To men?

   d. Can professional boxing possibly be fair to the (mostly uneducated, minority) athletes who make careers of it?

   e. Do poor people and white-collar criminals receive equal punishment for crimes, i.e., are the police and courts fair?

   f. Is the required use of standardized psychological tests and/or lie detectors as a basis of decision in the selection, retention, and termination of employees fair?

As your short report begins to take shape, use the following checklist to remind yourself of points to which you should give special attention. (It would be a good idea, also, to keep this checklist in mind so that you can use it when you are polishing future reports both in and out of school.)

Checklist for Evaluating a Documented Report

1. Are my citations correctly placed and in the correct style?

2. Are the central ideas in this paper my own?

3. Is there an appropriate balance between the material in my own words and that which I have quoted directly or indirectly from my sources?

4. Does the report meet the requirements of the assignment? In this case, did it make one of *my* points and did it draw upon several different passages in my sources?

5. Is all the source material cited in this paper there to do *my* work for me?

6. Do I quote directly only where there is good reason to do so?
7. Did I use good judgment in deciding what to paraphrase?
8. Are my paraphrases clear and purposeful?
9. Do I take advantage of the credibility of my expert sources where this is appropriate?
10. Have I excluded everything that is irrelevant to my point?

EXERCISE 5.4: Studying Citations at Work in a Student Paper

Directions: The following paper was written by a better-than-average writer. But he was—when he wrote this paper—struggling with the same decisions about documentation that you will be facing in your writing. Read it as a good example of how citations can be made to give support and force to one's own thoughts. Then sharpen your understanding of the kinds of judgments necessary for this common-sense documentation by answering the questions that follow.

```
Elmer R. Thomas

Professor Gaston

English 102

8 May 1984



                    The Way Is One


    "The way is one; the winds blow together." So goes an

old Chinese proverb. Somehow the memory of those words

hovers over today's battle between our would-be liberators

of women and our self-appointed protectors of ladies. It

haunts us as we watch almost any exchange between Phyllis

Schlafly and Bella Abzug on the network news and see how

quickly such disputes come to center around peoples' as-

sumptions regarding the one central mystery: are men and

women essentially, psychologically, different; or is gender

merely a superficial physiological difference with nothing

more than biological importance? On one side of the ques-

tion we have Schlafly defending the status quo against the
```

Equal Rights Amendment by merely echoing what D. H. Lawrence said about women many years ago.

> It isn't that she hasn't got a mind--she has.
> She's got everything that man has. The only dif-
> ference is that she asks for a pattern. Give me
> a pattern to follow! That will always be woman's
> cry. . . . Women are not fools. They have their
> own logic, even if it's not the masculine sort.
> Women have the logic of emotion, men have the
> logic of reason. The two are complementary and
> mostly in opposition. But the woman's logic of
> emotion is no less real and inexorable than the
> man's logic of reason. It only works differently.
> (196-197)

We shall see presently that Schlafly accepts the difference and celebrates it as real and good and beautiful and true. So naturally she ridicules what she sees as an effort to make men and women identical by constitutional amendment. Quite content to cuddle up to a male-imposed stereotype, like a sleepy kitten nestling in the lap of a trusted master, she raises the banner for every establishment housewife. "This kitten is warm, well-fed, and happy. Everything is A-OK. Do not disturb."

Schlafly may well be correct in claiming that her views are those of most women today. But it is highly questionable whether she speaks for the best women among us. Evidence is everywhere that we have for some time succeeded all too well at making our most talented women frustrated and miserable. Virginia Woolf once described how she had to struggle at the beginning to bring herself to write truly and powerfully. There was within her, she said, the stereotypical woman, "the Angel in the House," always tempting her to say whatever gentlemen would think it proper for a lady to say, rather than to tell the truth

she saw as she knew it should be told (236–238). Such a
confession seems both more important and less self-
serving than Schlafly's warning that women seeking equality
may lose their alimony and gain the risk of being drafted.
What is wrong with a society that so tempts women of genius
to stifle their genius just because they are women? Cynthia Ozick, not long ago, expressed in unforgettable and
unmistakable terms the rage of helpless indignation that
engulfed her when she was confronted socially by a physician who explained with arrogant self-assurance the biochemical basis of woman's inherent irrationality, using
"scientific" jargon to rationalize exempting women from
full participation in "standard" humanity (40–44). To
prostitute science in order to excuse chauvinist bigotry is
to leave today's intelligent woman powerless and without
hope of acceptance within conventional society.

When a woman as competent and intelligent as Marya Mannes, for instance, can seriously ponder the advantages of
establishing promiscuity as an alternative to marriage, we
have a measure of just how miserable Schlafly's cozy domes-
tic role must be for women with special gifts and talents
(65). Mannes says bluntly that men "will have to wake up
to the fact that for many women the need for a separate
identity is as important to them as their identity as wife
and mother." Such women are determined to break out of the
doll's house, even if they must awaken sleeping kittens to
do it. Clearly, the winds are not now blowing together,
despite the fact that all of us, male and female, know full
well that our way must ultimately be one.

Works Cited

"Issues and Answers." Interview with Phyllis Schlafly.

American Broadcasting Company. 10 July 1978.

Lawrence, D. H. "Give Her a Pattern." Phoenix II: Uncol-

lected Papers of D. H. Lawrence. Ed. Warren Roberts

and Harry T. Moore. New York: Viking, n.d.

Mannes, Marya. But Will It Sell? New York: Lippincott,

1964.

Ozick, Cynthia. "We Are the Crazy Lady and Other Feisty

Feminist Fables." Ms. Magazine Spring 1972: 40–44.

Steinem, Gloria. "What It Would Be Like If Women Win."

Time. 31 Aug. 1970: 22–25.

Woolf, Virginia. The Death of the Moth and Other Essays.

New York: Harcourt, 1942.

Discussion Questions

1. This passage was written to be the opening of a much longer paper. Did you notice that? What clues did you find? What clues can you find now that you overlooked before?
2. Why is the initial quotation not cited? What about the quotation at the very end of the first paragraph?
3. At the time this paper was written, Phyllis Schlafly was regularly appearing on TV news programs speaking against the Equal Rights Amendment, and Bella Abzug was a congresswoman who was much in the news and whose opinions on women's rights were well known. If this paper were being prepared for release now, do you think they should be identified more fully? Should this be done by rewording the text or by adding an explanatory note? Why?
4. Notice that the date of the D. H. Lawrence quote was unobtainable, even after extensive searching. Could this ever be important enought to force a writer to leave out material she had planned to use? When?
5. What do the four dots signify in the Lawrence quotation? What would three dots signify?
6. Why did the writer quote Virginia Woolf *indirectly* in paragraph two but quote Mannes directly in the last paragraph?
7. In the last paragraph an allusion to Ibsen's play *A Doll's House* is not footnoted. Should it have been? Why? What does this say about the importance of audience analysis in documentation?
8. Use the checklist on pp. 133–134 to evaluate the documentation in this paper.

6

Closing In On Your Topic

As you pursue your reading, you will quickly become more knowledgeable about your topic. However, you may also find yourself developing an uneasy feeling that at times approaches anxiety. Scientists Jones and Smith, you find, are emphatic in declaring that cigarette smoking causes heart disease. Scientists Williams and Thompson, with equally impressive credentials, say, just as emphatically, that it does not. How are you to decide? Confronted with such confusing contradictions, beginning researchers are sometimes overwhelmed by the very information they are working to assemble. It is not uncommon for such students to attempt to escape their uncertainty by "trying harder."

Finding themselves unable to write intelligently about what they have learned, some even go back to the library to gather still more "information." Possibly they feel that, if they just come up with enough facts, the true meaning of their data will suddenly jump out at them. Instead, they usually find that adding undigested facts to undigested facts only makes matters worse.

Other students, in desperation, decide to write up "what they have." So they plunge ahead, spilling unorganized data onto the page in a report about nothing addressed to no one in particular for no recognizable purpose. Or worse, they select from their data only facts supporting one oversimplified view of the subject. Then, ignoring important evidence against that view, they argue vehemently for it. This gives them a well-organized report with an apparent purpose, but it reduces the student's uncertainty at a very high price. Such reports represent the very opposite of research. Instead of taking a step towards new knowledge, they suppress relevant information that is available and thus distort the meaning of the information they do report.

Beginners who stumble into these pitfalls do not do so because they enjoy writing nonsense or want to mislead their readers. Usually they are taking the only sure way they know to escape the mental chaos caused by their "information overload." Fortunately, however, there are better ways to deal with that feeling of ambiguity and uncertainty so essential to much worthwhile research. Treasure it. Learn to manage it. Make it work for you.

These constructive responses require only that you recognize your uncertainty for what it is: an expression of your need to make sense of the world. It is a doubt born of the recognition that your information is running ahead of your understanding. This is an important recognition, and this kind of self-doubt, painful as it is, is healthy for a researcher.

Let it keep you humble, but do not let it intimidate you. You will be less likely to latch onto some incomplete or erroneous "solution" as long as that doubt is with you. Accept it as a challenge to keep a mental inventory of what you do and do not know about your topic and a proof that you have not yet found your best ways of thinking about it. For when those misgivings begin to arise, the researcher in you is warning that enough time has been spent on preliminary browsing. It is time to begin thinking like a researcher.

TURNING NOTIONS INTO QUESTIONS

Instead of becoming more anxious, what you need at this point is a relaxed, almost playful attitude towards your data. Fortunately the best way to prevent counterproductive anxiety and frustration is also the best way to play creatively with the facts at your disposal. Tilt your head a little and try looking at your data differently. Instead of looking to it for The Answer, give it a chance to suggest more and better questions.

If you did not begin reading with a specific question in mind, it is time to ask yourself what you really want to find out. If you had a question in mind, you should reexamine it. Why, exactly, can you not answer it with the information you developed? Did you lose sight of your original topic and spend time on reading that is only loosely related to it? If so, does this mean that you stumbled onto a more interesting topic? Or did you allow momentary interests to lead you away from the assigned subject? Possibly the information needed to answer your question was not available in the libraries near you. In any case, taking stock in this way is the first step to getting your research back on track.

As soon as you recognize one of these problems, the solution is apparent. If your reading led you into a more interesting aspect of the subject and you are free to change topics, consider doing so. If you are not free to change or if your real interest is still in your first choice, you may indeed have to go back to the library with a clearer, more conscious view of the reading to be done. If you are trying to investigate a subject beyond the scope of the available library holdings, you must either choose another topic or arrange to use an adequate library.

Chances are, however, that these are not the troubles besetting you at this point. By far the most common difficulty—for experienced researchers as well as beginners—is confusion over the exact question to be investigated. No research is better than the questions it answers.

Whenever you sense that you may be losing your bearings, therefore, look first to your questions. A general interest in the Lindbergh kidnapping or in social attitudes towards deformity or in the nature of hypnosis is plenty to get you started on your preliminary reading. But such vague, diffuse notions are not themselves topics for research. They are only green lights, encouraging you to continue searching in the direction you have chosen.

In research, as in driving, you will occasionally luck into green lights all the way home. You start out reading about witchcraft and become fascinated by the Salem witch trials. Then, as the world of puritan New England comes alive for you and you get to know the participants in that historical drama, you find yourself puzzled and intrigued by the actions and motivations of Giles Cory. This simple, stubborn farmer chose to die a slow, agonizing death as church leaders piled stone after stone on him until he was crushed. Why? You have followed your interests, intuitively, to your research question: Why did this man, who could have saved himself completely early in his ordeal and could have won a death that was relatively free of pain by simply pleading "not guilty" at his own trial, choose instead to martyr himself in this way? Why, in short, did Giles Cory make the decisions he did?

Notice that your vague sense that witchcraft was "something worth writing about" has gradually transformed itself into a well-defined question. In this case, your instincts have served you well. You know exactly what to look for in your data and where to direct your further reading in order to write an intelligent and informative report. It is Giles Cory that you will focus on as you study your notes and ponder your reading. Usually, though, researchers have to wrestle their way through a good deal of uncertainty and confusion before they arrive at a satisfactory formulation of their research questions. This requires close attention to investigative technique—but the most important part of that technique is almost always the framing of the question or questions to be addressed.

Phrasing Researchable Questions

As you learned in chapter 1, research is only one approach to truth. For that reason, not all questions can be answered by research. Moreover, of those which research could answer, many are not important enough to justify the effort. It is important for the beginning researcher to learn to shape answerable questions and to estimate whether they will develop enough new knowledge to justify the time, effort, and expense of investigating them. What, then, are the features of good research questions?

By far the most important requirement is that the question be clear. To a researcher's eye, many questions that seem clear enough in casual conversation appear to be floating in intellectual quicksand. "Does Computronics Corporation make a good computer?" "Does the mountaineer's quaint use of language affect the way he thinks?" "Are we nearing a cure for cancer?" At first glance, such questions seem clear, but only until they are measured by the standards appropriate for research questions.

A good way to determine whether a given question is precisely phrased is to subject it to the following test questions:

1. *Is this question ANSWERABLE?*

Many questions simply cannot be answered on the basis of obtainable information. Some are unanswerable because they refer to imagined rather than real subjects. "Which room would Zeus choose, if he stayed at Elmer's Shady Rest Motel?" There being no Zeus and no such motel, the question is unanswerable. Questions may also be unanswerable because the information they ask for is unspecified, inconceivable, or unavailable. A child asks, "How many stars are there?" and we are stymied. All we can say in reply is, "Sorry, dear. Information unavailable."

The general principle, for the researcher, is that a question is answerable *only when its wording suggests the observations needed to answer it satisfactorily and when those observations can in fact be made.* For most beginning students, "making research observations" is nothing more than reading the right passages in the right books. But in the experimental sciences elaborate procedures are sometimes necessary so that exactly the right observations can be made. And natural scientists like astronomers and meteorologists must sometimes wait for years for a natural event that will enable them to make the observations needed to answer their questions. What is common to all research, however, is that it is the question under investigation that determines what observations must be made.

Unless a question gives this kind of guidance, it is not really answerable. "Is it correct English to say 'hadn't ought to'?" No linguist would touch a question worded like that. Unlike the rest of us, linguists cannot dodge the question by appealing to authority. They can't look it up in a book because they are the people who write the dictionaries and usage manuals that the rest of us depend on. Before they help us, though, they first must understand the complexities of language usage for themselves.

To do that, they cannot work with unanswerable questions about what is "correct English." Such questions do not suggest where and how they might look for answers. So they ask instead, "How frequently is the construction 'hadn't ought to' used in the speech of college-educated people in the East Midland area of the United States?" "How often does it appear in the writing found in American magazines?" "What percentage of professional writers and editors report, when asked, that they consider it incorrect?" These reformulations of the question do suggest observations that a researcher could make to answer them. They are answerable.

2. *Is this really ONE QUESTION?*

Sometimes what seems to be a straightforward question contains hidden premises or biases that need to be considered separately. One example appeared above: "Does the mountaineer's quaint use of language affect the way he thinks?" The question *assumes* that mountaineers use language differently, "quaintly." But until it was demonstrated that mountaineers do something different from the rest of us with their dialects, it would be premature to try to show that their language affected their thought in some unique way. The first question to examine is, "Do mountaineers use language differently from the way it is used by a cross-section of other Americans?" This question, though hidden, is very much a part of the one about whether their language influences their thought.

Often these hidden questions express biases that tend to keep us from considering our subject objectively. Good researchers know that they cannot get ahead of themselves. If several questions must be answered to complete a project, they keep those questions separate and evaluate each systematically, according to the evidence relevant to it.

3. *Can every term in this question be DEFINED OPERATIONALLY?*

Researchable questions must be phrased so that there is no room for confusion about what they refer to. In research, "a thing is what it does." So the best definition of an object or concept is one that tells what it does or what we do to identify it. "Does Computronics Corporation make a good computer?" Until we know the definition of "a good computer," the question is unanswerable. Give us an operational definition of a good computer; tell us what a good computer must be able to *do*. Then we can easily tell you what you want to know about Computronics products.

The researcher does not ask herself, "are we nearing a cure for cancer?" She knows that experts have identified over thirty kinds of cancer and that the word "near" means quite different things to a biology student, a drug manufacturer, and a cancer patient. She knows too that the word *cure* is beset by ambiguity. What percentage of patients at what stage of disease must be restored to what degree of health by a drug before it is deemed a cure?

Instead of talking about whether a "cure" for "cancer" is "near," an informed researcher would prefer to estimate the chances that a medicine will be developed within five years that will induce remission in 75 percent or more of patients suffering with Stage IV ovarian cancer. Such unusual precision may seem tedious, but it is absolutely essential to the intellectual work of the researcher. Until we know exactly what a question means, we cannot be sure where to look for its answer.

4. *Does the question NEED ANSWERING?*

It is hard work to subject information to the kind of rigorous thought we are recommending here. Unless the new knowledge to be developed is likely to be a stepping stone to some further intellectual or practical goal, the question may not be worth that much time and effort. "What medication was prescribed for President Lyndon Johnson during his recuperation from his appendectomy?" We could probably find out, but what would be the point? What would we possibly understand better or do differently if we knew? Notice, though, that there is nothing wrong with the question itself. It is one, answerable question made up entirely of clearly defined terms.

In a different context such a question might indeed add to our understanding. Given the scientific advances since George Washington's day, it makes sense for medical historians to ask what treatment was prescribed during his last illness. It happens that—according to the accepted medical theory of the day—Washington was deliberately bled three times on the last day of his life. Today's doctors suspect that this treatment was in fact the cause of his death. So trivial points are worth researching when there is reason to believe that they might add significantly to our fund of knowledge. Medical historians need to know how frequently it happened, two centuries ago, that doctors unwittingly killed their own patients. In most cases, though, pursuing narrow issues with pat, factual answers is a little like counting the earthworms in your back yard. A lot of digging will get you an answer that is very definite, very reliable—and very likely to be useless.

EXERCISE 6.1: Shaping Questions and Discovering Answers

PART ONE: JUDGING RESEARCH QUESTIONS

Directions: Evaluate the following questions by the standards recommended in this chapter. Be prepared to tell whether the question is clear and, if not, which of the four tests listed above it fails to meet.

1. Was Gerald Ford a good president?
2. Should your state retain (or adopt) the death penalty?
3. Can apes talk?
4. Are dolphins smarter than people?
5. What was the position of the American Civil Liberties Union when the American Nazi Party attempted to stage marches in the Jewish neighborhood of Skokie, Illinois in 1977?

PART TWO: FINDING MEANING IN YOUR DATA

In looking through some old copies of a French newspaper to check on its coverage of Napoleon, you have made the following notes. Study them, rearrange them as necessary, and see whether you can find in these announcements a pattern of significance.

March 18, 1815	"The usurper has ventured to approach to within 60 hours' march of the capital."
March 9	"The monster has escaped from his place of banishment."
March 20	"Napoleon will arrive under the walls of Paris tomorrow."
March 22	"Yesterday evening His Majesty the Emperor made his public entry and arrived at Tuileries. Nothing can exceed the universal joy."
March 11	"The tiger has shown himself at Gap. The troops are advancing on all sides to arrest his progress. He will conclude his miserable adventure by becoming a wanderer among the mountains. . . ."
March 19	"Bonaparte is advancing by forced marches, but it is impossible he can reach Paris."
March 10	"The Corsican ogre has landed at Cape Juan."
March 21	"The Emperor Napoleon is at Fontainebleau."
March 13	"The tyrant is now at Lyon. Fear and terror seized all at his appearance."
March 12	"The monster has actually advanced as far as Grenoble."

PART THREE: ASKING WORKABLE QUESTIONS

  1. Go back to the questions listed in part one. Reword each question that needs it so that you end up with a question on the same general topic that *is* researchable.

PURPOSEFUL READING

Once you have developed a researchable question, your reading becomes more purposeful and more efficient. After browsing for a couple of weeks among books and articles on hypnosis, one bright pre-med student was struck by an irony. He had chosen that topic because he had heard all the usual tales about hypnotism and wondered how much if any of what he had heard was true. Half-convinced that it was "all a fake," he began his reading.

He had heard, for instance, that some hypnotists put subjects into trances and are unable to wake them. He had heard that hypnotists can easily make entranced subjects do things that are contrary to their deep-seated religious or moral values. His first few readings had convinced him that those so-called dangers were more apparent than real. Doctors and psychologists, he found, have long used hypnotism as both a therapy in itself and as a supplement to other conventional treatments. But he found no cases of zombies who never woke up or Svengalis who stole the will-power from helpless young girls.

While immersed in this background reading, he was thinking vaguely of doing a paper on the question of whether hypnotism really existed. But he soon realized that such a paper would have little point. The answer was obvious. Yes, hypnotism did exist. So what? Even dubious lay readers would find such a trivial conclusion to be poor justification for wading through a documented research report. He toyed briefly with the idea of trying to answer the question, "What, exactly, is hypnosis?" But he found so much division of opinion among the experts that, in the time available, he could not hope to learn enough to do justice to such a complex question. It was while he was casting about in this way, looking for his research question, that the irony struck him: hypnotism *was* dangerous *but not for the reasons most people imagine.*

Precisely because so many people do not believe in hypnosis, they do not take it seriously. They permit its use by anyone at all, for parlor entertainment, in carnival sideshows, or even in unlicensed "treatment clinics," for all manner of complaints. Already he had found in his reading enough case histories to know that this was at times really dangerous. Here, then, was a research question worth dealing with. "When and how is hypnosis dangerous?" The fact that hypnosis can be dangerous, in itself, would not be new knowledge for many readers, but the *reasons* it is dangerous, the nature of the danger, and the data he could offer to explain the dangers could change their thinking in important ways and possibly even dissuade some of them from taking foolish risks.

Once his research question was clear, the student's reading took on purpose and direction. He knew immediately that many of the titles he had taken down for possible use would be of no help; so he scratched them off his list. On the other hand, he realized that some of the material he had not considered seriously in his casual exploration would be more important than he realized. He would have to go back and make notes on those cases involving misuse of hypnosis and instances of psychological harm to subjects. And he would have to focus his further reading on finding more such cases and locating authoritative discussions of this aspect of hypnosis.

COMPLETING YOUR BIBLIOGRAPHY

When you have reached this point in your own work, your research is truly under way. Your first task is to put your notes on your preliminary reading in order. Discard all material, no matter how interesting, that is not logically connected with the question you have chosen. A certain amount of background information may be necessary to enable you to state the question clearly and explain its importance, but put everything else aside.

You should also go through your bibliography cards, sorting them into three piles: those listing works unlikely to contain information on your questions, those naming sources you will read for background, and those with titles that sound like they bear directly on your question. Then go through your "discard" pile again, reconsidering each title. If you are fairly sure that a work will contain nothing on your subject, go ahead and put the card aside. But if you are just guessing wildly, you may want to take a quick look at the work itself to be sure. This is particularly true in the case of books containing general treatments of your subject. A quick check of the index will soon tell you whether a book mentions enough topics related to your question to merit further attention.

You will, of course, prepare reference cards on all works selected for your actual research. At this point, you will probably have to return to some of the bibliographical source books you learned about in chapters 3 and 4. Some titles that you overlooked in your initial browsing may turn out to be important references now that you have a definite question in mind. Make cards on those new leads too. Then, as you begin your systemic reading, remember the principle of the pyramid. Let one good source lead you to several others.

ESTABLISHING A RECORD

Note Cards

A well-formulated research question also makes your note-taking easier and more efficient. The important thing, though, is to begin making systematic notes as soon as your question is clear in your mind. Most researchers soon develop individual styles of note taking that seem to work best for them, but for your first effort, we suggest that you follow the procedure outlined here.

1. *Use large cards and write only on one side.* We recommend 5" × 8" file cards or half-sheets of typing paper. Paper that has been used on one side is actually preferable to new paper, because notes on the backs of cards are often overlooked when the paper is being written. Avoid this common error by training yourself from the outset to make notes on only one side.

2. *Use a separate card for each source.* It is imperative that you know what information came from what source and that you be free to rearrange notes for your convenience as you work. If notes from two or more sources are on the same card, you are much more likely to make mistakes in your citations. You may also need to separate the notes for use in separate sections of your report. Plan for this by using a separate card for each book or article you use.

3. *Identify the source adequately on each note card.* If the notes you make on any one source are very extensive, they may not fit on one card. You need not take time to put all the publication information on every card, but do be sure to use an adequate system for marking all note cards so that they can easily be matched with the card that fully identifies the source. Once your "Works Cited" list is complete, you can simply number the entries there and copy the number of an entry onto each note card from that source. If your bibliography is still growing, however, you must work out a different system. One way is to put at the top of the first note card the same information that goes in the parenthetical citation in your paper, i.e., the author's last name, the page number, and, if necessary, a short version of the title. Then, using a separate letter for each set of notes that requires more than one card, you can adopt an alphabetical coding system. In a lower corner you can mark each card in the first set "A-1," "A-2," "A-3," etc. The next set would be marked "B-1," "B-2," etc. This enables you to move these cards around freely as you compose your report, and still keep your sources straight so that your citations will be accurate.

4. *Keep track of page numbers.* An easy way to do this, when your notes span several pages from the same source, is to put a heavy diagonal line on your note card at each page break, with the number of the new page right after it. If you like, you can indicate where you skip one or more pages by using a double slash.

5. *Use summary notes, unless you have good reason to copy the wording of the original.* You should be reading primarily for meaning; so capture the meaning as concisely as possible in your own words. Only when the wording is itself important to your research, as it is in questions of law or of definition, for example, or when the expression of an idea is so fitting that you want to quote it directly, should you copy the wording of the original. When you do copy, be sure to put the copied material in quotation marks so that, later, you do not forget and treat borrowed material as if it were your own.

6. *Evaluate each reading as you make notes on it.* Approach your note taking in two phases: (1) getting down the substance you need from your source and (2) evaluating the worth of the source and the data you are taking down. One good way to do this is to draw a line under the notes you use to record data and factual content. Then, while your impressions are still fresh in your mind, *characterize* your source and the information you have taken from it *as you see them in connection with your research question.* For example: "Admits he is only authority to hold this view. Book well-documented, but presented in argumentative style. Not objective." Such reminders help you keep similar works from blurring in your memory and, properly phrased, may even find a place in your paper.

Study the sample note cards in Figure 6-1 to see how the recommendations listed above are applied in practice. Then do the following exercise to test your understanding.

EXERCISE 6.2:   Efficient Note Taking

1. The selection below appeared in a collection of descriptive materials about mountain folkways. The collection was titled *The Foxfire Book*, edited by Eliot Wigginton, and published in 1972 by Anchor Press at Garden City, New York. Make a "Works Cited" card for it. Then on one or two separate cards make enough notes to enable you to discuss the article intelligently without looking back at it.

MOONSHINING AS A FINE ART

The manufacture of illicit whiskey in the mountains is not dead. Far from it. As long as the operation of a still remains so financially rewarding, it will never die. There will always be men ready to take their chances against the law for such an attractive profit, and willing to take their punishment when they are caught.

Moonshining as a fine art, however, effectively disappeared some time ago. There were several reasons. One was the age of aspirin and modern medicine. As home doctoring lost its stature, the demand for pure corn whiskey as an essential ingredient of many home remedies vanished along with those remedies. Increasing affluence was another reason. Young people, rather than follow in their parents' footsteps, decided that there were easier ways to make money; and they were right.

Third, and perhaps most influential of all, was the arrival, even in moonshining, of that peculiarly human disease known to most of us as greed. One fateful night, some force whispered in an unsuspecting moonshiner's ear, "Look. Add this gadget to your still and you'll double your production. Double your production, and you can double your profits."

Soon the small operators were being forced out of business, and moonshining, like most other manufacturing enterprises, was quickly taken over by a breed of men bent on making money—and lots of it. Loss of pride in the product, and loss of time taken with the product increased in direct proportion to the desire for production; and thus moonshining as a fine art was buried in a quiet little ceremony attended only by those mourners who had once been the proud artists, known far and wide across the hills for the excellence of their product. Too old to continue making it themselves, and with no one following behind them, they were reduced to reminiscing about "the good old days when the whiskey that was made was *really* whiskey, and no questions asked."

We got interested in the subject one day when, far back in the hills whose streams build the Little Tennessee, we found the remains of a small stone furnace and a wooden box and barrel. On describing the location to several people, we were amazed to discover that they all knew whose still it had

FIGURE 6–1

Darton, p. 3

In 1778, Mesmer arrived in Paris, claiming that he had discovered a fluid which, though undetected by the human eye permeated all bodies /4 Sickness, according to Mesmer, resulted from obstacles which blocked the flow of the invisible fluid.

A-1

Darton, p. 4

Mesmer was even said to have cured blindness by inducing sleep-like states in his patients /18 Mesmer often made use of tubs filled with iron filings and mesmerized water. The patients "transmitted" the mesmerized fluid to the area of their sickness by means of an iron rod.

A-2

Britannica - Macro., p. 133

The term hypnosis was first coined by a Scottish physician named James Braid. It is taken from the Greek hypnos meaning "sleep."

Britannica is a good overview but doesn't contain enough specific information to make it useful for my report.

C-1

---

been. They all affirmed that from that still had come some of the "finest home brew these mountains ever saw. Nobody makes it like that any more," they said.

Suddenly moonshining fell into the same category as faith healing, planting by the signs, and all the other vanishing customs that were a part of a rugged, self-sufficient culture that is now disappearing. Our job being to record these things before they die, we tackled moonshining too. In the six months that followed, we interviewed close to a hundred people. Sheriffs, federal men, lawyers, retired practitioners of the old art, haulers, distributors, and men who make it today for a living; all became subjects for our questioning. Many were extremely reluctant to talk, but as our information slowly increased we were able to use it as a lever—"Here's what we know so far. What can you add?"

Finally we gained their faith, and they opened up. We promised not to print or reveal the names of those who wished to remain anonymous. They knew in advance, however, that we intended to print the information we gathered—all except that which we were specifically asked not to reveal. And here it is.

In The Beginning

According to Horace Kephart in *Our Southern Highlanders* (Macmillan, 1914), the story really begins with the traditional hatred of Britons for excise taxes. As an example, he quotes the poet Burns' response to an impost levied by the town of Edinburgh.

>Thae curst horse-leeches o' the Excise
>
>Wha mak the whiskey stills their prize!
>
>Haud up thy han', Deil! ance, twice, thrice!
>
>There, sieze the blinkers!
>
>An' bake them up in brunstane pies
>
>For poor d—n'd drinkers.

Especially hated were those laws which struck at the national drink which families had made in their own small stills for hundreds of years. Kephart explains that one of the reasons for the hatred of the excise officers was the fact that they were empowered by law to enter private houses and search at their own discretion.

As the laws got harsher, so too the amount of rebellion and the amount of under-the-table cooperation between local officials and the moonshiners. Kephart quotes a historian of that time:

>Not infrequently the gauger could have laid his hands upon a dozen stills within as many hours; but he had cogent reasons for avoiding discoveries unless absolutely forced to make them. [This over two hundred years ago.]

A hatred of the excise collectors was especially pronounced in Ireland where tiny stills dotted rocky mountain coves in true moonshining tradition. Kephart quotes the same historian:

>The very name [gauger, or government official] invariably aroused the worst passions. To kill a gauger was considered anything but a crime; wherever it could be done with comparative safety, he was hunted to death.

Scotchmen (now known as Scotch-Irish) exported to the three northern counties of Ireland quickly learned from the Irish how to make and defend stills. When they fell out with the British government, great numbers of them emigrated to western Pennsylvania and into the Appalachian Mountains which they opened up for our civilization. They brought with them, of course, their hatred of excise and their knowledge of moonshining, in effect transplanting it to America by the mid 1700s. Many of the mountaineers today are direct descendants of this stock.

These Scotch-Irish frontiersmen would hardly be called dishonorable people. In fact, they were Washington's favorite troops as the First Regiment of Foot of the Continental Army. Trouble began after Independence, however, with Hamilton's first excise tax in 1791. Whiskey was one of the few sources of cash income the mountaineers had for buying such goods as sugar, calico, and gunpowder from the pack trains which came through periodically. Excise taxes wiped out most of the cash profit. Kephart quotes Albert Gallatin:

> We have no means of bringing the produce of our lands to sale either in grain or meal. We are therefore distillers through necessity, not choice, that we may comprehend the greatest value in the smallest size and weight.

The same argument persists even today—battles raged around it through the Whiskey Insurrection of 1794, and over government taxes levied during the Civil War, Prohibition, and so on right to this moment.

The Law vs. The Blockader

The reasons for the continuous feud implied in this heading should be obvious by now. The government is losing money that it feels rightfully belongs to it. This has always been the case. In the report from the Commissioner of Internal Revenue for 1877–78, the following appeared:

> The illicit manufacture of spirits has been carried on for a number of years, and I am satisfied that the annual loss to the Government from this source has been very nearly, if not quite, equal to the annual appropriation for the collection of the internal revenue tax throughout the whole country. In [the southern Appalachian states from West Virginia through Georgia and including Alabama] there are known to exist 5,000 copper stills.

It's different now? Clearly not, as seen in an article in the May 3, 1968 Atlanta *Constitution* on the interim report of the Governor's Crime Commission. In October, 1967, there were around 750 illicit stills in Georgia, operating at a mash capacity of over 750,000 gallons. This amounts to approximately $52 million in annual federal excise tax fraud, and almost $19 million in state fraud. The article quotes the Commission, placing the blame for Georgia's ranking as the leading producer of moonshine in the United States on "corrupt officials, a misinformed and sometimes uninterested public, and the climate created by Georgia's 129 dry counties."

Originally arrests had been made by government officials ("Feds" or "Revenuers"), but during Prohibition much of the enforcement was left up to the local sheriffs. This put many of them in a peculiar position, for the moonshiners they were being told to arrest were, in many cases, people they had known all their lives. As it turned out, however, most of the lawbreakers were reserving their hostility for the federal agents and the volunteers (called "Revenue Dogs") who helped them. They had nothing against their sheriff friends who, they understood, were simply doing their jobs. The sheriffs, for their part, understood the economic plight of the moonshiners. For many of these people, making moonshine was the only way they had at the time of feeding their families. As one told us "I felt like I was making an honest dollar, and if it hadn't'a been for that stuff, we'd a had an empty table around here."

The situation resulted in a strange, friendly rivalry in most cases. As one moonshiner said, "I never gave an officer trouble except catchin' me. After I'uz caught, I'uz his pickaninny."

The same man told us of a time when he was caught by a local official who was as friendly a man as he had ever met. He wasn't treated like a criminal or an animal, but treated with respect as another man making a living for a large family—which he was. After it was all over, the local official had made a friend instead of an enemy, and the two are still fast friends today.

During the same period of time, there was another sheriff whom he often encountered on the streets of a little town in North Carolina. The sheriff would always come up to him, greet him, and ask him what he was up to down in Georgia. The other would usually reply, "Oh, not much goin' on down there." If, however, the sheriff had gotten a report about one of his stills, he would follow that reply with, "I hear you're farmin' in th' woods." The moonshiner would know that that was a warning for him to watch his step. Despite the warnings, the sheriff was able to catch him and cut down his stills on three separate occasions, but they remained fast friends.

We talked to several retired sheriffs (one of whom, Luther Rickman, was the first sheriff to raid a still in Rabun County), and they agreed completely. Most of the blockaders that they had encountered ran small operations, and the whiskey they made was in the best traditions of cleanliness. Besides, times were hard, and a man had to eat. Despite the fact that the sheriffs at that time were paid on the "fee system," and thus their entire salary depended on the number of arrests they made, they did not go out looking for stills. They made arrests only after reports had been turned in voluntarily by informers who, as we shall see later, usually had personal reasons for reporting the stills. They were never hired to do so.

Operating on the fee system, the local officials got $10 just for a still. If they were able to catch the operator also, they received between $40 and $60. Extra money was given them if they brought in witnesses who could help convict. For the blockader's car, they received approximately half the price the blockader had to pay to get it back which was usually the cash value of the car. And they were allowed to keep any money they could get from selling the copper out of which the still had been made.

Confiscated moonshine, beer, and the like were poured out. The sugar was often donated to an institution like a school or hospital.

The number of stills actually uncovered varied drastically from month to month. Some months, twenty or thirty would be caught and "cut down," but other months, none at all would be discovered. Hardest of all was catching the men actually making a run. In almost all cases they had lookouts who were armed with bells, horns, or rifles, and who invariably sounded the alarm at the first sign of danger. By the time the sheriff could get to the still, the men would have all fled into the surrounding hills. We were told about one man who was paid a hundred dollars a week just as a sentry. Another still was guarded by the operator's wife who simply sat in her home with a walkie-talkie that connected her with her huband while he was working. The still, which sat against a cliff behind the house, could only be reached by one route, and that route passed directly in front of the house. The operator was never caught at work. On those occasions when the sheriffs did manage to catch the men red-handed, they usually resigned themselves to the fact that they had been caught by a better man, and wound up laughing about it. On one raid, a sheriff caught four men single-handedly. There was no struggle. They helped the official cut their still apart; and when the job was done, everyone sat down and had lunch together. When they had finished, the sheriff told the men to come down to the courthouse within the next few days and post bond, and then he left.

The same sheriff told us that only rarely did he bring a man in. He almost always told them to show up at their convenience, and they always did. To run would simply have shown their lack of honor and integrity, and they would have ultimately lost face with their community and their customers. They simply paid their fines like men, and went on about their business.

It was a rivalry that often led to friendships that are maintained today. One of the sheriffs, for example, spent two evenings introducing us to retired moonshiners, some of whom he had arrested himself. It was obvious that they bore no grudges, and we spent some of the most entertaining evenings listening to a blockader tell a sheriff about the times he got away, and how; and naturally, about the times when he was not so lucky.

Today federal agents have largely taken over again, and so the character of the struggle has changed. The agents actively stalk their quarry, sometimes even resorting to light planes in which they fly over the hills, always watching. In the opinion of some people, this is just as it should be. One said, "The operations are so much bigger now, and sloppier. If the Feds can't get'em, the Pure Food and Drugs ought to try. That stuff they're makin' now'll kill a man." And another said, "People used to take great pride in their work, but the pride has left and the dollar's come in, by th'way."

2. Review the notes that you have already taken for your own research paper. Choose notes on some material you will need to use in your report. Transfer that material onto note cards using the techniques described above. If necessary, go back to the source to be sure that you have all the details you need to cite exact page numbers, etc.

3. Each of the note cards in Figure 6–2 (p. 154) violates one or more of the recommendations given above. Study the cards; identify the violation(s) in each, and explain the disadvantages and/or risks of taking notes in that way.

4. Figure 6–3 (p. 155) shows a group of note cards based on an unsigned article entitled "Intelligence: This Fish is a Smarty," in the July 4, 1960 issue of *Newsweek*. These notes are being used by a biology major for a report on animal intelligence. She plans to submit her paper for possible publication in *Horizons Unlimited*, a general science magazine distributed nationwide to high school science students. Study the cards, and answer the questions about them that appear below.

   A. According to the recommendations in the text, what is the purpose of the notation below the line on each card?

   B. Why does *each* card bear an abbreviated symbol identifying the source from which its notes were taken, i.e., *NW*, 7/4/60, p. 59?

FIGURE 6–2

Braid

"I feel quite confident we have acquired in this process [hypnosis] a valuable addition to our curative means; but I repudiate the idea of holding it up as a universal remedy; nor do I even pretend to understand, as yet, the whole range of diseases in which it may be useful."

Good source for Braid's initial research on hypnosis.

C – 3

"I consider it [hypnotism] to be merely a simple speedy and certain mode of throwing the nervous system into a new condition, which may be rendered eminently available in the cure of certain disorders"

Braid

FIGURE 6–3

NW, 7/4/60, p. 59 – cd 1

Bottle-nosed whale (dolphin)
studied since 1949. Navy
funding. Research by Dr. John
Lilly Claims dolphins may
be smarter than humans.

First record I found of
this claim.

NW, 7/4/60, p. 59 – cd 2

Lilly had dolphin brain tissue
analyzed by John Hopkins
University. Found cell counts
equal to human brains. First
class neural equipment and
40% larger than human brain.

Here Lilly seems to be exag-
gerating preliminary findings

NW, 7/4/60, p. 59 – cd 3

Dolphins have complicated
language of whistles and
squawks and buzzes. Can even
imitate English in a Donald
Duck voice.

Is this real talk? Do experts
agree Dolphins can use
human language?

NW, 7/4/60, p. 59 – cd 4

Comparing intelligence hard.
Lilly: "What are you going to
test"? Compared with me, a
dolphin is a genius in the
water, but he would be a moron
in the Library of Congress."

Possible title idea: "Morons
in the Classroom: Geniuses
in the Wild"

7

Putting Your Data in Order

As long as you keep your research question foremost in your mind, you can proceed with your reading and note taking knowing that you are on safe ground. Unfortunately, however, many beginning researchers find that this is easier said than done. One of the most important lessons to be learned from the guidance given to you in this book is the necessity for intellectual self-discipline. So monitor yourself carefully, to be sure that you do not allow momentary interests to lead you away from the question you are supposed to be investigating.

WORKING YOUR WAY TO A PURPOSE

Perhaps the best protection you can have against these temptations to fragment your work is a well-formed thesis or purpose statement backed up with a specific plan for your forthcoming report. For this reason, as soon as your reading has progressed to the point where you can recognize the answer to your research question, you should begin thinking about the overall structure of your report.

Phrasing Your Thesis or Purpose Statement

If you can give a definite answer to your research question, then you should summarize that answer in one straightforward *thesis*, or position statement. When you state your thesis in the paper itself, you may want to handle it more gracefully, but at this point—when you are using it primarily to guide your own work—use the simplest, bluntest, and sparsest

156

wording you can find. Most of the principles for phrasing researchable questions explained in chapter 6 also apply to wording thesis statements.

Sometimes, however, beginning writers make mistakes with thesis statements that do not show up in their research questions. The following guidelines will help you avoid these common pitfalls:

1. *Use a simple sentence whenever possible.* Dependent clauses may sometimes be necessary to label properly ideas that work as units in your larger thought. But use them sparingly and keep them as simple as possible. Sentences with numerous complicated clauses and modifying phrases almost always contain more than one major assertion. The purpose of the thesis statement is to help you identify and keep in mind the one central claim of your paper. Do not risk losing that central idea at the outset by burying it among a lot of unnecessary words. Those extra ideas you want to cram into your thesis statement probably are important. But usually they belong in the supporting argument you will present in your paper, not in the thesis itself.

2. *Always use a complete sentence.* To state a logical position adequately, two things are essential: (1) naming the topic under discussion and (2) asserting something about it. These two tasks, naming and asserting, are the proper functions of subjects and predicates in sentences. An adequate expression of your thesis, therefore, requires a complete sentence.

3. *Avoid figurative language.* While putting your report together, you require of your thesis the same clarity you needed earlier in your research question. Literal language that you can clearly define in operational terms is your best defense against sloppy thinking at this point. There is time enough to reword later, to give your paper style and freshness. Use your working thesis to be sure your thinking is in order.

If you see that your data will not support the kind of definite conclusion required of a thesis statement, you should begin to think about how you *can* go about making sense of what you have learned. If you are lucky enough to be dealing with a simple two-sided question, you may find it quite workable to organize your report around a pseudothesis that simply asserts your uncertainty. "Bruno Hauptmann's guilt in the Lindbergh kidnapping has neither been proven nor disproven." Notice that this statement names the topic under investigation, just as a thesis statement does. But instead of a definite predication about that topic, it merely says that no conclusion is possible. A paper built around this assertion might well be organized like this:

First part: Evidence for Hauptmann's guilt
Step one: Presentation of the evidence
Step two: Critical examination of the evidence

Second part:	Evidence for Hauptmann's innocence
Step one:	Presentation of this evidence
Step two:	Critical examination of this evidence
Third part:	Assessment of unresolved issues showing that neither case is conclusive

Most questions worth researching, however, will not reduce themselves to the kind of simple two-sided discussion that can be organized around such a pseudothesis. Suppose you are trying to find out what caused the huge arctic glaciers that once moved all the way down into the northern half of the United States. You will soon find that scientists have many theories but that they do not consider any theory satisfactory.

Faced with such confusion, about the best you can do is to classify your data in some sensible way and come up with a framework or purpose statement that makes clear your pattern of organization. "Theories about the cause of widespread glaciation fall naturally into three groups." Notice that such a purpose statement names the topic, as a thesis statement would, but that it neither takes a position nor asserts complete uncertainty. It contents itself with suggesting a way of thinking about the question. It says simply that the theories seem to fall into "three groups." A report built around this framework statement might be organized like this:

First group:	Theories holding that glaciation is caused by factors originating in outer space
Step one:	Brief explanation of some representative theories involving astronomical causes
Step two:	Critical examination of each of these theories, showing that they all fail to account for the known facts about glaciation
Second group:	Theories holding that glaciation is caused by factors originating in the atmosphere
Step one:	Brief explanation of some representative theories involving atmospheric causes
Step two:	Critical examination of each of these theories, demonstrating that they too fail to account for the known facts
Third group:	One theory holding that glaciation is caused by factors originating in the earth itself
Step one:	Brief explanation of the "volcanic dust" theory
Step two:	Demonstration that this theory also fails to account for all the relevant facts

You now have three choices to consider in phrasing a working version of the central idea of your report: (1) the thesis statement; (2) the pseudothesis, and (3) the framework statement. Use the form that best suits your data and your purposes. However, you want to begin thinking about this decision as soon as you know enough about your subject to decide whether you can qualify yourself to "take sides" in your report.

EXERCISE 7.1:   Thesis Statements, Pseudotheses, and Purpose Statements

1. Below are several efforts by students to word thesis and purpose statements for use in their research papers. Some are well constructed, and some violate one or more of the principles given in the text. Study the list, and answer the questions below.

   a. The American carnival developed from a merger of the circus with the museum and the traveling ride, so the modern carnival carries with it three major types of attractions.
   b. Whether or not the Loch Ness monster exists remains an open question.
   c. It is adherence by the South to the dogmas of tradition that has left it complacent with established ideas and unreceptive to modern conceptions so that even today, sixty years after the epic battle between fundamentalism and modernism, the South still remains ultraconservative, for reasons that can only be understood if we define the views of the contending schools of thought and trace their respective influences on the South over the past century-and-a-half.
   d. Pressure on the television networks to reduce the amount of violence in children's shows is coming mainly from four sources.
   e. The conduct of Tennessee's famous "Monkey Trial" showed legal incompetence at almost every point.
   f. The real battering of today's woman is that done daily to her self-respect by media stereotypes and male chauvinist attitudes.
   g. Television violence has an adverse effect upon children.

   ### Questions

   1. Which of the above entries is a good example of a pseudothesis?
   2. Which two entries contain too many complex clauses and phrases to put the necessary emphasis on one main point?
   3. Which entry is confused by figurative language?
   4. Which entry is a good example of a framework or purpose statement?
   5. Which two entries are good examples of straightforward thesis statements?

2. On a scratch sheet of paper, write five or six trial thesis statements for the paper you are working on.

3. Refer to the standards for good research questions listed in chapter 6 and to the guidelines for writing good thesis statements given in this chapter. Use these tips to help you evaluate your trial theses. Discard your worst candidates, but note any good features or ideas that you might want to retain. Then revise, compare, and combine phrases and ideas from the different versions until you arrive at a wording that meets all the requirements and

fits the content and organization you plan to use in your paper. Write your final version on a new sheet of paper and keep it for further use.

Matching Your Report to Your Audience

Researchers do not normally have a great deal of latitude in choosing the audiences for their on-the-job reports. If they are doing contract research, their project reports go to the sponsor of the project. Those working for private business usually address their reports to designated officers in the corporation, and those preparing reports for scholarly journals must necessarily write for the readership of the journal most likely to publish work on their subject.

This is one point at which the student may have an advantage over the professional. Unless your teacher has instructed you to write for a specific audience, you probably have some choice in the matter. In either case, now is the time to consider your audience. A thesis that is perfect for one audience may be totally inappropriate—even insulting—for another. People differ greatly in what they know, what they assume, and what they are prepared to believe. What is valuable new knowledge to one group can be either obvious or incomprehensible to another. For that reason, you can get valuable guidance, as you begin to organize your data, if you *work with your audience in mind.*

Only when he began to consider his subject from the perspective of a possible audience did the author of the paper on hypnotism succeed in finding the research question and thesis statement that led to his success. The minute he realized that the real dangers of hypnosis are not the ones that worry most people, he realized that his report would be properly directed to intelligent but uninformed laypersons. The facts that had surprised him and changed his thinking would probably be equally striking to them.

On the other hand, the same information would be wasted on an audience of psychologists and psychiatrists. They have long known everything he could say on the subject. To direct his argument to them might actually offend them, for it would suggest that the writer thought them uninformed in their own fields of expertise. Notice, though, that much of the same data could be used as evidence for a report addressed to these experts if the research question and thesis were changed somewhat. Suppose that writer changed his thesis to, "Laws are needed to prohibit the use of hypnosis by unqualified people." He might then speak modestly, as a concerned layperson, to persuade these mental health experts to join him in working for the passage of such laws. In such a paper, many of the same case histories and statistics could appear without the slightest chance of giving offense. This shows that, while the audience is one important factor, it must be considered along with all the other factors as you begin to put your data in order.

EXERCISE 7.2: Getting to Know Your Audience

Decide on a particular reader or group of readers who might be likely to read a research report of the kind that you are writing. Your selection will designate the audience to whom you will address your report. On a separate sheet of paper, answer the questions below according to the best information you have about that audience. Doing this now will help you judge how best to "put things" when you begin to write your report.

1. Name first the obvious things about your audience. How old are they? How much education and income are they likely to have? What occupations do they have? What voluntary memberships do they have in civic groups, social clubs, or hobbyists' associations that might help you better understand their interests and values, their likes and dislikes?

2. Consider now how much they know about your topic. Is your subject close to the areas they are familiar with, or will you have to provide extensive background information for each step in your discussion? Identify the areas of your topic that are likely to be easiest and hardest for them to understand, based on your assessment of their present knowledge.

3. Think about how that audience is likely to regard you, in your role as writer on your chosen topic. What is your social and professional status, as they will perceive it? Will they see you as their superior, their subordinate, or their equal? Will they see themselves as more or less knowledgeable than you, on your chosen topic of research?

4. What judgments can you make about their beliefs, attitudes, and values that could give you guidance in the writing of your report? Does your information about their interests, knowledge, and group memberships give you any reason to believe that they might already be disposed either to favor or disapprove of the position you will take in your report? If so, can you find other values or beliefs of theirs that you can draw on to make your report more acceptable to them?

5. Look back over your answers to the preceding questions and draw from them as many tips as you can on how best to adapt your research report to your audience. Make a list of do's and don'ts that you should follow to make sure that your readers will take an interest in your report, accept its findings, and think well of you for writing it.

ORGANIZING YOUR NOTE CARDS

With your thesis statement in mind, thumb through your note cards asking yourself exactly how the information on each card is connected to your thesis. Do not settle for such general phrases as "example," "quotation from acknowledged expert," and "statistical support." Be sure that you can specify the points that will be supported by your examples, quotations, and statistics. "Example of harm done by trained hypnotist using hypnosis outside his field of expertise," "quote giving graphic description of burn injuries treated by hypnosis," "statistics on early uses of hypnosis as anesthesia"—these are the kind of labels you want to form in your mind. Such labels will help you decide where each bit of information should fit into your finished paper. Put abbreviated versions of them on cards as you proceed.

Gather your labelled cards into different groups, according to which points they deal with. The historical data in one pile, for instance, can all be used to establish the fact that hypnosis is a genuine phenomenon. The facts cited in a second pile help account for the widespread scepticism about hypnosis. The cards in a third pile give evidence that this scepticism itself is sometimes a source of danger.

At times you will probably need to set up subcategories. This large group of cards dealing with the medical uses of hypnotism today is further evidence for its reality. Obviously it should be placed alongside the notes on the historical material, giving you two subcategories of evidence in support of the same point. As you organize your data in this way, you have an excellent opportunity to see what it does and does not permit you to say about your subject. If your thesis depends on points that you cannot support with evidence already collected, you obviously have more research to do.

Your most important job at this point, however, is to get a perspective on your forthcoming report. You are grouping your notes so that you can organize your data and fit it into a coherent paper. So all the notes you plan to use must be assigned to categories. Then the groups of cards should be placed in the order you expect to use them as you write your report.

EXERCISE 7.3:   Labelling and Organizing Note Cards

1. Look back at the sample note cards in Figure 6–3 (p. 155). Those cards do not yet have category labels assigned to them. Where will those labels be written when they are assigned? What purpose will they serve?

2. Which of the following category labels would best identify the notes on card #1 of that group? (The notation "cd 1" after the page number designates card #1.)
   __ **a.** First claim for dolphin superiority
   __ **b.** Strongest claim for dolphin superiority
   __ **c.** Evidence
   __ **d.** Evidence for importance of study of animal intelligence

3. Which of the following would be the best category label for card #2?
  — **a.** Evidence
  — **b.** Further evidence—dolphin intelligence
  — **c.** Tissue and size evidence
  — **d.** Good quote

4. Which of the following would be the best category label for card #3?
  — **a.** Irrelevant (card to be discarded)
  — **b.** Whistle languages
  — **c.** Further evidence—dolphin intelligence
  — **d.** Good quote on dolphin IQ

5. Pick the best category label for card #4.
  — **a.** Quote showing difficulty of research question
  — **b.** Impressive quote
  — **c.** Further evidence—dolphin intelligence
  — **d.** Support for Lilly's findings

WRITING A PROSPECTUS

As soon as you can see the overall pattern of your argument, an excellent strategy is to write a prospectus. A prospectus is a planning document in which you describe in general terms the purpose, organization, content, and conclusions of the paper you will write. Writing a prospectus is a good way to make sure you have not wandered away from your original purpose, and to think through the various options available to you in presenting the fruits of your research. Your research is usually incomplete when you write your prospectus; so you cannot summarize your paper in detail. But sketching your argument in broad outline helps you see how your data are fitting together, and enables you to pinpoint the information you still need to gather in order to answer your research question.

A prospectus is adequate only if someone who knows nothing about your topic can read it and come away with an accurate understanding of what the topic is, why it is important, and how you intend to approach your discussion of it. There is no set format for prospectuses. The earlier you write yours, the more general and incomplete it will have to be. Yet the more useful it will be in helping you keep your research on track. On the other hand, the further along your reading is when you write your prospectus, the more complete it can be and the more guidance it will give when you write your report.

One good way to write a prospectus is to address, in order, as many of the following questions as you can on the basis of the work you have already done.

1. *What is your topic and why is it worthy of discussion?* What situation in

the real world or what findings in previous research on the topic justify your research undertaking?

2. *What background information is necessary in order to understand why your
research begins and proceeds as it does?*

3. *What is your thesis or purpose statement, and exactly what does it mean?*
What do the key terms in your thesis statement mean to you?

4. *What plan of investigation will you follow to develop the information still
needed to support that thesis?* What, exactly, is the information you
need, and how will you go about getting it?

5. *What points will you make in support of your thesis, and what is the nature
of the evidence you will introduce in support of these points?*

Notice how these questions are dealt with in this sample prospectus:

The Real Dangers of Hypnosis

Mistaken notions about hypnosis are
widespread. Most people doubt its reality or consider it a harmless amusement.
Even those who recognize its potential

What is the topic, and
why is it important?

danger usually fear it for the wrong reasons. Consequently, much harm is done by
unqualified hypnotists dabbling with hypnosis out of curiosity or presenting it
for entertainment.

The problem cannot be taken seriously
by those who doubt the reality of hypnosis. Moreover, it is likely to escape
the notice of most other laypersons who

What background
information is
necessary in order
to explain why you
approached the topic
as you did?

see professional hypnotists only occasionally on the stage or in night clubs and
who are only moderately curious about the
numerous unlicensed hypnotic "clinics"
that have sprung up recently in many

states. But the problem is real, and the
public should be informed.

The thesis of this paper is that hypnosis is properly used only when a qualified professional acts within his or her
field of competence for the benefit of
the hypnotic subject. By a qualified professional, I mean, most often, a licensed
and properly trained physician or psychologist. Under certain conditions, however, other health-related specialists
may be qualified to use hypnosis for a
limited range of applications within
their own specialties.

Most of the information necessary to
support this thesis is already in my
notes; however, I will have to go back to
some sources and get complete details on
some case studies that I skipped over in
my preliminary reading. I also need to
look at the literature on hypnotic susceptibility, to see whether it provides usable evidence that people with certain
personality traits should not be hypnotized at all.

This thesis will be established in
four steps: First, I will show that skepticism and apathy are natural results of
the distorted and sensationalized views
of hypnosis presented in the mass media.
In the second step, I will cite authoritative evidence from both historical and
contemporary sources in order to demon-

What, exactly, is your
thesis?

How do you plan to
get the information
you need to complete
your argument?

strate that the reality of hypnosis has been scientifically established beyond reasonable doubt. If hypnosis is real, it can have real consequences. So the third step in the argument will be to dem-onstrate that those consequences are of-ten extremely harmful. Authentic case histories and authoritative scientific evidence will support this assertion. I will then move to my fourth and final step: stating and explaining the thesis set forth above. The paper will close with the observation that the preponder-ance of evidence suggests that some ele-ment of danger is present whenever hypno-sis is used. It seems clear, therefore, that a person cannot be hypnotized ethi-cally except by someone trained to mini-mize the risk and competent to use hypno-sis for the subject's own benefit.

What points will you make in support of your thesis, and what kind of evidence will you use to support those points?

EXERCISE 7.4:   Analyzing a Prospectus

Study the following prospectus. Does it answer all the suggested questions? Put notes along the left margin to identify the passages that deal with each question. Then consider the prospectus as a whole. Does it enable you to understand what the student will say in her paper? Do you think this prospectus provided useful guidance to her when she wrote the paper? Why?

Why?

Since time began, there have been people with abnormal physical features, "freaks" as they are popularly called. Such extreme deviations from normality could hardly pass unnoticed in any human community. The unexpected appearance of a giant, a midget, a hunchback, or a monster requires explanation, adaptation, and unique decisions not only by relatives and friends of the family but by the community at large. The subject of my research, therefore, is how such deformed people have been regarded in different societies throughout history. Any common patterns for dealing with these strange people would seem to imply something basic about the nature of humanity itself. It is hard to imagine a better way to learn the truth about ordinary people than to study their reactions to and treatment of the human oddities among them.

With physical abnormality, interestingly enough, there is no single body of scientific research comparable to that found in the literature on abnormal psychology. Except for occasional mention in medical books, one finds little authoritative discussion of deformity and physical abnormality. Those accounts that are found in scientific writings usually emphasize descriptions of the afflicted individuals, paying little or no attention to other people's reactions to them. Consequently, this study must rely chiefly on popular accounts by biographers, literary critics, and journalists. Fortunately, such accounts do exist, and they give the kind of information I need about people with a wide range of abnormalities from a wide variety of historical periods and geographical areas.

My conclusion is that the treatment given to people with physical abnormalities has no rational basis and is therefore unpredictable. One can say that such people are almost always given some exceptional treatment, that this seems to be true at every level of society, everywhere, and that it seems always to have been true. It is easy to demonstrate that their treatment is special, that it is often unrestrained and excessive. But it is impossible to explain why the excess is sometimes in the direction of indulgence and generosity and other times at the opposite extreme of bestiality and cruelty. The three popular books on freaks that I have already read are comprehensive enough to assure me that no evidence will turn up which significantly alters the position stated above. However, I still need to locate biographies of several famous people whom those books identified as deformed so that I can learn more about how they were treated as a result of their abnormality. Anne Boleyn, Alexander Pope, and Cyrano De Bergerac require further investigation. I also need to find a biography of Charlemagne to learn more about why he chose to disinherit his hunchback son.

I believe that I can support my thesis by presenting evidence for five points: (1) Abnormal people have always and everywhere been given special treatment; (2) sometimes they were shown special favor; (3) sometimes they were punished with special hardships; (4) at times, unimaginable cruelty was inflicted on them; (5) whether a particular person was helped or punished because of his abnormality seems to be governed solely by whether the key people happened to be educated or superstitious, compassionate or callous.

EXERCISE 7.5:   Writing Your Prospectus

1. *Drafting Your Prospectus.* With your note cards at hand, study the list of planning questions on pp. 163–164. If you feel that questions should be added, deleted, or reworded to make the list more appropriate for your topic or your audience, make those modifications. Then decide on the best order to address those questions in your prospectus, and write out your answers.

2. *Finishing Up Your Prospectus.* Read over the answers you have written to be sure the meaning flows smoothly as the reader moves through your draft. Add any connectives and transitions that seem to be needed. Compare your prospectus to the samples above and make improvements where necessary. Then make a clean copy of your revised draft.

DEVELOPING AN OUTLINE

After your prospectus is written and you have finished whatever reading and note taking is necessary to complete your research, you are ready to go on to the next step. What that step should be depends on several factors: (1) your teacher's instructions; (2) any schedule of "turn-in" dates that has been announced; (3) the length and complexity of your research project; and (4) your own composing style.

Often your teacher will ask you, at this point, to outline your forthcoming paper or will schedule a date, well in advance of the deadline for the paper, on which you are to turn in an outline. Pay particular attention to those instructions. They should determine how you apply what you learn in the rest of this chapter. If you are given no special instructions, however, you can decide for yourself how to proceed, just as you would if you were a professional researcher.

Deciding When To Outline

In making that decision, you should be aware of at least three things. First, know that many audiences of research reports expect to find them preceded by an outline of some kind. Often the outline is used, with accompanying page numbers, as the table of contents. In any case, the chances are that you will be expected to do an outline at some point in the preparation of your paper.

The second thing to consider is the length and complexity of the research you are reporting on. If you know in advance that the presentation of your findings will follow a simple plan and present no problems, then you have a clear choice. If you prefer, you can probably write your first draft directly from your prospectus, without the help of an outline. If, on the other hand, the plan of development in your prospectus is tentative and vague in your own mind, it often helps to prepare a formal outline at this point. Most people find that a good outline helps keep their thinking straight while they are groping for the best way to express the complex ideas and relationships that go into good research. This is especially true when the report is long or the subject complicated.

The last thing to be aware of, as you consider whether to outline now or later, is your personal composing style. Some people seem naturally more inclined to plan than others. "Think before you speak," is their motto, and they cannot comfortably express an idea without mentally running ahead of it to check out its implications. Such people often prefer to outline in advance, where other writers would just plunge in, composing in their heads as they wrote. These planners value the sense of order, method, and efficiency that they get from following a well-conceived outline.

Other people seem to work best when they are allowed to find their meanings as they write. Often these students report that they can only write outlines *after* finishing their papers. They may work their way through several messy drafts before finding the pattern they are looking for. But this does not bother them. The outline, after all, is merely a tool for demonstrating a pattern of organization. There is nothing inherently wrong with organizing first and outlining later *so long as the organization is sound and is accurately represented by the outline.* Planners rightly point out that those who use this "backwards" approach deny themselves the guidance of their outlines while they are writing. To this, the pencil and paper "explorers" reply that it makes little difference whether a confused and disoriented writer is working on a draft or an outline. At one point or the other, the researcher has to come to grips with his or her confusion.

So whether you use your outline to help you put your thinking in order or to test an order you arrive at by other means, you will need to construct one. To give you a complete understanding of the process for doing this, we will assume that you are doing your outline after writing your prospectus but before beginning your first draft. Some of the steps described, therefore, will be omitted when you are outlining a finished composition.

What Is an Outline?

An outline is, essentially, a picture of the logical structure of your report. It employs special conventions to use numbers, letters, and indentations to show the logical relations among ideas. Figure 7–1 summarizes the most important of these conventions. You may want to refer to it while preparing your own outline. It gives you a convenient way to refresh your memory on the mechanical details.

FIGURE 7–1
Outline demonstrating conventions of labelling and indentation used in sentence and topic outlines.

The Conventions of Outlining

Thesis: Outlines use a conventional system for labelling
         and placing ideas according to their relative im-
         portance.

I.   The word "thesis" or "purpose," followed by a colon,
     appears at the left margin to identify the central
     idea of the paper, as shown above.

II. The main points of support or explanation are marked
     by capital roman numerals, flush with the left margin,
     as shown in this entry and the one just before it.

     A. Normally, the points named in the "plan of develop-
        ment" section of the prospectus are given capital
        roman numerals and treated as main points in the
        outline.

     B. When other main points must be introduced to com-
        plete the argument or explanation of the report,
        that should be done.

III. Important statements of support for the main points
     are indented beneath them and marked with capital
     letters.

     A. This sentence and the two just below provide three
        examples of how to treat this first rank of sup-
        porting material.

     B. Two other examples appear in the sentences marked A
        and B under main point II above.

     C. Still other examples can be found below, in the two
        divisions under main point IV.

IV. When further subdivisions are necessary, letters and numbers are alternated and each successive subordination is indented further.

A. The subdivision begins with large Roman numerals and capital letters, as shown in this entry and the one just above it.

   1. The next level of subordination is marked by Arabic numbers, as is done with this sentence.

    (a) Further subdivision is usually unnecessary.

    (b) However, the conventions allow the process to continue indefinitely.

      (i) For example, small Roman numerals can be used at the next level of subdivision.

        A. Small capitals, without parentheses, can then be used, as has been done with this sentence.

        B. This would be followed, if necessary, by capital Roman numerals without parentheses.

      (ii) These alternations of numbers, letters, size and punctuation of the identifying characters allow for indefinite continuation.

B. The outline ends when the last idea is correctly placed according to this scheme; no special ending is necessary.

Getting Started on Your Outline

Perhaps the most efficient way of drafting an outline is to continue working with your note cards. The sorting and labelling you did prior to writing your prospectus gives you a good start on your outline. So get all your note cards together; be sure you have plenty of blank cards; put a full-sized pad or notebook within easy reach; and you are ready to begin.

1. *Double-check to be sure all your note cards are sorted and labelled properly.* Notes made on the research you have done since writing your prospectus may not have been sorted with the same care you used earlier. Be sure to classify and label all the data you plan to use. If your latest research has caused you to modify your thesis or redefine your purpose, be sure to put aside your notes on any data that are no longer needed. But all the data that will go into your paper should now be organized as explained on pp. 161–162.

2. *Take a new card; write the word "Thesis" on it; and copy your working thesis, just as it will appear at the beginning of your outline.* (See Figure 7–1 for an example.) Place this card to one side. It is the first of a stack that you will gather and rearrange as necessary to create your outline.

3. *Take several more new cards; on each one, write one of the main points that you identified in your prospectus.* If any other main points have been added as a result of your further research, put those on cards too.

4. *Study the points on these cards and put them in the order in which they should be taken up in your report.* Be sure to put first things first, so that your reader will be prepared to understand your discussion of each successive point as you come to it. Feel free to shuffle the cards around as necessary while you are thinking about this. But when you are sure that you have arrived at the right sequence, number the cards with capital Roman numerals as shown with the major divisions in Figure 7–1.

5. *Take the note cards pertaining to your first main point and arrange them in the order in which their information will appear in your report.* Try not to get caught up in the wording now present on your note cards. Think ahead to how you will be "putting things" in your final discussion. Remember that most of what you take from your notes will be recast drastically and rearranged according to the needs of your report. So keep those needs in mind as you sequence your cards.

6. *Group the cards just arranged into logical categories, according to the nature of the information on them.* Look through the stack and find the natural breaks, where your labels suggest that the information on the following cards deals with a different point or a different kind of support.

7. *Write summarizing sentences for each of these groups.* Study each subset of notes to see if you can find a phrase or sentence on one of the cards which summarizes accurately the exact claim that body of evidence enables you to make in support of your first main point. If you find such a summarizing sentence, copy it onto a new card, revising and condensing it as necessary. If you do not find one, write one now. Often your category labels will start you in the right direction. When finished, be sure the summarizing cards are in the right order, and mark each one with a capital letter followed by a period, as shown in Figure 7–1.

8. *Repeat steps 5–7 with your note cards for each of your main points.* If you get lost at any point, stop and copy all of your summarizing sentences onto the full-sized pad, placing them as shown in Figure 7–1. This will enable you to see the overall organization of your paper as it is emerging in your outline and to make any changes you find necessary.

9. *If your instructor requires a more detailed outline, simply repeat the above process.* Take the cards for each summarizing statement in turn, subdivide them, and on new cards write more detailed summarizing statements for each subdivision, marking each of the new statements with an appropriate Arabic number, as is done in the third-level subdivisions in Figure 7–1.

10. *Put all your summary statements in order behind your thesis card, and copy them onto full-sized paper, using indentation to signal the logical relationships among them, as shown in Figure 7–1.* You should now have a satisfactory sentence outline of your report. It is good practice at this point to put your sorted note cards into the stack of "outline" cards so that your notes on each bit of data are behind the card bearing the outline or summary statement that it supports.

Below you will find a sentence outline for a paper based on the sample prospectus on pp. 164–166. Compare the outline to the prospectus and to the step-by-step description just given for writing an outline.

The Real Dangers of Hypnotism

Thesis: Hypnosis should only be used by qualified profes-
         sionals acting within their fields of competence
         for the benefit of their hypnotized subjects.

I.   Widespread ignorance causes many people to doubt the
      existence of hypnosis or to take it so lightly that
      they do not worry about its misuse.

      A. As children, most Americans are exposed to media
         which present a distorted view of hypnosis.

      B. As adults, they find the misuse of hypnotism for
         entertainment so common that they take it for
         granted and consider it of little importance.

    C. Exposure to such misinformation causes many intelligent people even to doubt the existence of hypnotism.

II. The reality of hypnosis is established beyond reasonable question.

    A. Almost two centuries of scientific evidence attests to its authenticity.

      1. Since the early 1800s, surgeons have used hypnosis as an anesthetic.

      2. Since Freud, psychiatrists have used hypnosis to help patients identify and resolve hidden conflicts.

    B. Within the past thirty years, health professionals have begun to find many more uses for hypnotism.

      1. It is now frequently used in the management of chronic pain.

      2. It is sometimes used in burn cases to lessen tissue damage and speed healing.

      3. It is used to rid surgical patients of debilitating fears and thus to decrease the actual risk of the surgery.

III. Because hypnosis is real, its misuse can result in real harm.

    A. The widespread skepticism about the reality of hypnotism prompts volunteer "debunkers" to endanger subjects when hypnosis is used for informal entertainment.

    B. Carelessness in making or cancelling suggestions made to the subject during hypnosis can cause serious and prolonged distress.

    C. People with certain kinds of personality problems cannot be hypnotized safely.

IV. Hypnosis can properly be used only by qualified pro-

fessionals acting within their areas of expertise for
the benefit of their hypnotic subjects.

A. The training of qualified professionals gives them
many important advantages.

   1. They can often recognize subtle signs of personality problems that make hypnosis inadvisable.

   2. They can assess a person's resistance and judge
   whether it should eliminate him as a candidate
   for hypnotism.

   3. They are likely to recognize the need for a
   safe, controlled setting.

   4. They are competent to recognize and deal with
   unexpected developments before serious harm is
   done.

B. Case studies show that tragedies have resulted when
even qualified professionals used hypnotism outside
their areas of competence.

C. Because some risk is always present when hypnosis
is used, even qualified professionals cannot ethi-
cally use it except for the benefit of the subject
himself.

Topic Outlines

Some instructors do not require the kind of fully developed outline
shown above, in which every entry is a complete sentence. You may be
asked instead to submit a *topic outline*. Topic outlines use the same conventions of indentation and follow the same principles of organization that
sentence outlines do. But the only complete sentence in a topic outline is
the thesis statement at the beginning. All the other entries are brief
phrases that simply serve to identify the kind of information that will go
in each section of the report.

Here is a topic outline of the hypnosis paper.

The Real Dangers of Hypnotism

Thesis: Hypnosis should only be used by qualified profes-
         sionals acting within their fields of competence
         for the benefit of their hypnotized subjects.

I.   Widespread Ignorance of Subject

     A. Distortions by Media

     B. Common Misuses for Entertainment

     C. Uninformed Skepticism

II. The Reality of Hypnotism

     A. Classical Scientific Uses
        1. Anesthetic

        2. Psychotherapy

     B. Recent Scientific Uses

        1. Pain Management

        2. Burn Treatment

        3. Mental Preparation for Surgery

III. Real Dangers of Hypnosis

     A. Misinformed "Debunkers"

     B. Mismanagement of Hypnotic Suggestion

     C. Personality Types at Special Risk

IV. Proper Use of Hypnosis

     A. Advantages of Qualified Professionals

        1. Recognizing Personality Problems

        2. Evaluating Resistance

        3. Controlling the Setting

        4. Dealing with the Unexpected

     B. Reason for Confining Use to Area of Professional
        Expertise

     C. Reason for Requiring that Hypnosis Be Used Only for
        Benefit of Subject

EXERCISE 7.6: Preparing an Outline

1. Listed below in their correct order are the sentences required for an outline for the paper described in the prospectus on pp. 166–168. Copy them onto a sheet of paper, placing them properly and putting the proper numbers and symbols in front of them. You may refer to Figure 7–1 and to the sample outlines in this chapter for guidance.

Why?

The exceptional treatment generally given to people with physical deformities has no rational basis.

It is a fact that deformed people have almost always been given special treatment.

This was true almost everywhere.

It was true of the Orient, where Siamese twins were considered such a risk to public safety that they were killed at birth.

It was true of the United States, where P. T. Barnum made a fortune and won himself respectability and political power with his renowned freak shows.

It was true of England, where Joseph Merrick, the so-called "elephant man," knew almost every extremity imaginable during his short, tragic life.

It was true of Europe, where royalty used to keep dwarfs at court for the good luck that they supposedly brought.

This seems to be true of almost all social classes.

Even the great Charlemagne disinherited his own son because, being a hunchback, the son seemed to carry on his body a sign of God's disfavor.

Yet it was the common people who flocked to Barnum's American exhibits and paid admission in England when Merrick was on public display.

As the examples cited above show, special treatment seems to have been given to deformed people throughout history.

Sometimes deformed people were accorded special favor.

Dwarfs were given great latitude in the castles and courts of Europe.

Charles Stratton, better known as the midget Tom Thumb, became an international personality.

Sometimes unreasonable hardships were imposed on them.

In the Middle Ages, European giants were considered evil; they were ostracized, and barely allowed the means to live.

Because of her six fingers, Anne Boleyn, the second wife of Henry VIII, was the subject of special attention, alternatively taken by the populace to be a seductive witch and an unfortunate victim of a rapacious king.

The French soldier, Cyrano De Bergerac, was forced to fight over 1000 duels to avenge offenses given because of his huge, unsightly nose.

At times, the most inhumane cruelty was inflicted on them.

The quick death of the Siamese twins mentioned above was mild compared to the lives of abject poverty and the brutality inflicted on certain other people with deformities.

Merrick was abandoned by his father and stepmother and forced into a side show, where he was so badly abused that, when he was finally rescued by a noted surgeon, he was taken for an idiot.

The unpredictability and variance noted in the treatment of deformed people demonstrates its lack of rational basis.

Tom Thumb's lifelong prosperity was due as much to Barnum's early favor as to his own talents.

Merrick, who was brutalized and treated like an idiot, proved to be of superior intelligence, with a gift for poetic expression.

2. Prepare a topic outline based on the information given in question 1. You can do this either by reducing the sentence outline you produced in your answer to question 1 or by starting fresh and creating appropriate topic entries for the sentences listed above.

3. Use the procedures described in this chapter to write an outline for your own research report. Before beginning, make sure you know whether your instructor requires a sentence outline or a topic outline.

8

Drafting the Research Report

Now that your research is finished, your prospectus written, and possibly your outline already prepared, you have an excellent start on the body of your report. The intellectual content of your paper is fairly well established. However, the ultimate success of your report may well depend on the thought and effort you put into the work ahead. Except for revising and proofreading, some of which obviously must come last, the tasks listed below can be accomplished in any order. But all of them must be attended to before your paper is turned in.

1. *Choosing a Title.* If you have not already thought of a title for your paper, you must begin thinking about one now.

2. *Writing an Introduction.* At some point you will have to consider what you can do to make sure that your report is read by the right people in the right frame of mind. To a large extent this is determined by your introduction.

3. *Producing a Draft.* The overall plan you developed in your outline or prospectus must still be turned into effective prose and the documentation put in place.

4. *Writing a Conclusion.* The end of a report is of special importance. The conclusion shapes the impression that will be left in the mind of the reader when she puts your report aside.

5. *Revising Your Drafts.* Nobody can run through this entire process without a few missteps and false starts. The important thing is to keep revising until the report does justice to your research. Keep reading over your draft from the beginning, trying to see it through your readers' eyes. Try to remain ready to make any changes required or even to scrap what you have done and start over if you discover a better approach.

6. *Proofreading.* Proofreading means rechecking details of spelling and sentence structure, along with those of punctuation, capitalization, and all the other mechanical aspects of correct written English. Do not make this a primary concern until you are sure that the organization is in its final form and that your wording has, for the most part, done justice to your meaning. But once you feel ready to begin your final draft, you will want to proofread rigorously.

7. *Packaging Your Final Draft.* Readers expect research reports to follow well-established conventions of format and arrangement. So the last thing you will do before turning in your report is to make sure that it is properly "showcased," i.e., that it meets your instructor's expectations as to cover sheets, title page, outline, list of works cited, and so on.

Chapters 8, 9 and 11 explain the best way to go about this remaining work.

"WHERE DO I START?"

You can begin almost anywhere and know that you are making progress, so long as you keep in mind how the work at hand will fit into the overall project. If your instructor asks you to proceed in some particular order, you should of course follow her instructions. Otherwise, take the direction that seems best to you.

For most students, the choice quickly reduces itself to two options. Some students prefer to start on the introduction so that they can see their papers from the outset as their readers will see them. Others do better if they draft the body of the report first, so that when they go back to write the opening paragraphs, they know definitely what commitments they can make to their readers. In this chapter, we will assume that you are developing the body of your paper first.

FLESHING OUT YOUR PROSPECTUS

Ideally you will have both an outline and a prospectus to work from at this point. If not, take whichever one you do have and put it with the set of note cards that you organized and labelled as instructed in chapter 7. Have all this material at hand when you begin your first draft.

Before You Write

Read over the prospectus and outline once more to be sure that the overall structure is fresh in your mind as you write. If you have not yet prepared an outline, it is even more important that you work with an awareness of the preliminary planning you did in your prospectus. While writing, you will be thinking about the best way to express your meaning. It is all too easy, at this stage, to drift away from the line of thought your research commits you to. Your prospectus and outline are your two best protections from the tendency to wander. So begin with them clearly in mind, and return to them to reorient yourself any time that you feel uncertain.

As You Write

Before placing your outline and prospectus aside, study carefully what you planned to assert as your first main point. Then review the evidence on the note cards you selected for your discussion of that point. With this clearly in mind, you are ready to start writing.

Plan to Revise. Think of this draft as a worksheet. If you are very lucky, you may later find that you can use whole sections of it more or less as written. Ironically, though, that is more likely to happen if you do not demand too much of yourself at this point. For now, concentrate on getting words on paper that approximate your meaning as you see it at this point.

Use Your Prospectus and Outline for Casual Reference. Do *not* copy your plan word for word. Your planning documents, both your outline and prospectus, were addressed to yourself. Your report must be addressed to the audience you have chosen. So refer to your plan when you are momentarily lost, but put it aside again as soon as you get your bearings.

Write with Your Audience in Mind. Assess everything you know about the values, attitudes, backgrounds, and potential of the people who will read your report. This will help you decide how best to appeal to their present interests and how to make the new and difficult information in your report clearer to them. Like everyone else, you have been adapting oral messages to your listeners in conversations, interviews, and conferences all your life. The same intuitive sense of how to "put things" that taught you to use one tone with your friends, another with your parents, and still another with your high school principal will guide you in drafting your report, if you just let it. So get a vivid picture of your audience in mind and keep thinking of your readers as you write.

Try to Write Rapidly All the Way to the End. Your main goal at this point is to shape your paper at the higher levels of organization. If the right information is going into the right sections in the right sequence, you are doing fine. You can perfect the sentence structure and mechanics later. Try, at this point, to keep writing—as long as you can do so with a sense of purpose and direction. Only if you find it absolutely necessary should you stop and revise extensively at this point.

Make Good Use of New Ideas. One advantage of rapid writing on the first draft is the sense of freedom most writers feel when they try it. They often report that good ideas pop into their heads as if from nowhere. Sometimes these ideas just give them better ways of expressing or explaining points that they had already planned to include. Sometimes, though, they see connections between bodies of data or points of significance that they had overlooked before. If this happens to you, make the most of it. Even if you have to go back to the library and do more research, revise your report as necessary to make it reflect your latest and best thinking.

Reread Frequently from the Beginning. Every time you come back to your work after a long break, or find yourself uncertain about what to write next, or interrupt your work to write a long footnote, it is a good idea to read your draft over from the beginning. Studies show that good writers spend much more of their time at this than mediocre writers. Rereading makes it easier to keep your purpose and your audience clearly in mind, and that, in turn, makes it easier to judge how best to move forward according to your plan.

HOW TO HANDLE DOCUMENTATION IN YOUR FIRST DRAFT

As you learned in chapter 5, you have two alternatives for handling your responsibility for documentation.

Parenthetical Citations

Most of your references will normally be handled by parenthetical citation. It is usually fairly easy to insert parenthetical documentation as you write. If your notes are in good shape, you will have the page numbers at hand for any evidence you cite or quotations you introduce. Unless you have good reason not to, therefore, you should document your first draft. Students who find it a distraction to look up page numbers as they write should just insert parentheses and leave them empty, as markers for citations to be inserted later. Use the method that works best for you.

Notes

Endnotes and footnotes are a little harder to handle efficiently during the first stages of your composing. Normally, you will only use them for long citations in which you name and possibly comment on several sources at once or for side comments or explanations which, though too important to be omitted, would interrupt the orderly progress of your discussion.

How to Handle Endnotes. When your draft is far enough along to enable you to be pretty certain what will finally go where, the traditional way of handling endnotes works quite well (see Figure 8–1). This method requires only that you draw a special line across the page at the point where the note number is to be inserted.

Beneath the line, you write a preliminary draft of your note, just as you are doing for the rest of your report. When your endnote is finished, draw a similar line to indicate that the text of the report resumes at that point.

FIGURE 8–1

Titterman and Gister disagree about the characteristics which separate animal from plant in the marine environment.

Janice Titterman, *Uncertain Animals in the World Ocean* (New York: Pnyn, 1982) 4, qtd. in McGuffy, 116: Theodore Gister, *Marine Plants and Their Properties* (Boston: Honbert, 1981) 27, qtd. in McGuffy, 119–20.

Both authors agree, however, that the dividing line between plant and animal is not as clear as we have been led to believe.

EXERCISE 8.1:   Turning Your Plan into Prose

1. Begin now on the first draft of the body of your paper. Try consciously to organize your work as described in this chapter, but if you find after a fair trial that you can do better work by adapting these procedures to your composing style, do not hesitate to do so. If your report is too long to finish in one or two sittings and if your instructor has not told you otherwise, go on to the rest of this chapter, while you are finishing your draft.

2. If you have not already completed your outline, you may find it helpful to prepare a tentative draft of it as you work on this preliminary version of the body of your paper. Some students find it helpful to alternate between writing and outlining. Whenever they are lost momentarily, they put a few entries on their scratch outline, enough to guide them for the next few paragraphs. As soon as they are sure they have their bearings, they go back to writing. When finished, they go back and revise as necessary to make sure the outline matches the paper.

THE TWO FUNCTIONS OF THE INTRODUCTION

The introduction to a research report serves two functions: (1) getting the report read and (2) preparing the reader. Both functions are important, but in any given situation either one may be more important than the other. For instance, an unsolicited report by an unknown subordinate with little status which arrives at the desk of a busy executive certainly has, for its first and most important purpose, catching the executive's attention. The introduction to such a report challenges its writer to make a dignified but effective bid for attention.

On the other hand, a report by a consulting firm hired by the government to make recommendations for disposing of toxic waste would benefit more from a conventional opening. The function of such an introduction is to give readers an overview of the report so that they can read each successive part with a perspective on the whole. Thus the introduction makes it easier for readers to read and appreciate complex arguments and technical information that, otherwise, might leave them lost. Providing this advance organization for the reader is almost *always* necessary in a report. At times, in fact, it is all that need be done in an introduction.

In the case of the toxic waste report, for instance, it can be taken for granted that the people who sought expert guidance are going to read the report. Any obvious attempt to capture attention, in this case, might well backfire. It would seem undignified, if not actually offensive. When an audience is assembled and waiting, it is pretentious for a spokesman to clamor for attention.

When and How To Catch Your Readers' Attention

When it is clear that a writer must compete for a reader's attention, it is usually appropriate for him or her to use special techniques for capturing interest. Not all the attention-getting devices explained below are equally suited for every report. But some of them can be used to advantage for reports written under the following circumstances:

1. When the subject of the report is outside the reader's normal range of interests and responsibilities;
2. When the intended audience has no special obligation to read the report;
3. When the writer is unknown or is subordinate to the reader to some significant degree;
4. When the writer is initiating a report without assignment or invitation, solely on his or her own authority;
5. When spokespeople for competing views are also trying to reach the same audience.

Titles

If possible, find out what kinds of titles are generally used by others who address reports to your audience, and study the examples that show the most originality. This will give you an idea of how far you can go without risk of seeming eccentric.

Most of the attention-getting devices described below in the section on interesting openings can easily be adapted to wording titles. Perhaps the best way to assess all the possibilities is to study titles of articles in popular magazines. Writers for those publications *must* get read, if they hope to continue publishing there.

Reader's Digest offers a particularly good way to learn how well-worded titles can spark interest. Each month the front cover lists all the articles in that issue. Look over the lists for six or eight issues, and you are sure to find examples of all the devices listed below. You will also notice some arresting stylistic tricks that work better in titles than in running prose. Alliteration, for instance, must be used sparingly in report writing. But it produces such excellent titles as "Hullabaloo over Hearing Aids" and "Homemade Hocus-pocus."

Interesting Openings

When the situation warrants an open bid for your readers' attention, consider the following possibilities:

1. *Quotations and Allusions.* An allusion is a mention that refers, or *alludes,* to a well-known event, literary work, or famous quotation. Famous quotations are effective attention getters, whether or not they are introduced by allusions. The first example below combines allusion and quotation. The second begins more abruptly, with a quotation devoid of any introduction.

EXAMPLES:

[*From a paper on early medical missionaries*]
Twelve years after Kipling wrote that "East is East and West is West, and never the twain shall meet," an American doctor arrived in China to begin, as he said, "building bridges" between the two cultures.

[*From a report assessing the effectiveness of President Johnson's "War on Poverty"*]
"The poor," according to the Bible, "you have always with you." But to the majority of Americans, committed as they are to the ideal of an equal-opportunity nation, that prophecy seems less than glorious.

2. *Striking Statements.* By singling out significant aspects of your topic that readers are likely to find surprising or shocking, you can arouse their curiosity. They will usually read on to reassure themselves that their sense of the way things are or should be is not wrong.

EXAMPLES:

[*From a report on the internal security system of the U.S. Postal Service*]
Americans who assume that hidden doorways and secret passages went out with the Middle Ages had better check up on where their tax money is going. Last year the government spent an estimated 22 million dollars designing such structures into public buildings, and the chances are good that any given citizen will stand within twenty feet of one the next time he mails a letter.

[*From a paper on Oriental glassblowing*]
While Roman armies marched victorious throughout the known world and Christ walked barefoot on Babylon's dirt paths, healing the sick and preaching to multitudes, Japanese glassblowers created fine glassware for royal tables with techniques almost identical

to those used today at the Tokushu glass factory near Fukuoka, Japan.

3. *Challenging Questions.* If your topic can be introduced to readers in a cogent question that will dramatize its relevance, you have an excellent opportunity to seize their attention.

EXAMPLES:

[*From a paper investigating a scandal in military procurement*]
What can be said, finally, about the Sergeant York, the miracle machine that was supposed to shield American infantrymen behind the most devastating curtain of firepower ever unleashed on a battlefield? Why was it scrapped? Was it the product of honest mistake, colossal stupidity, or a billion dollar boondoggle?

[*From a report suggesting that an injustice was done in a famous trial*]
Did Bruno Hauptmann really kill the Lindbergh baby, or was he the helpless victim of a rapacious prosecuting attorney? An objective view of the evidence suggests the latter.

4. *Short Narrative.* From early childhood, we learn to enjoy stories and to value those which illustrate truths worth remembering. A short anecdote, appropriately related to the subject, will often bring willing readers to a report that might otherwise go unread.

EXAMPLES:

[*From a report on physical therapy as a career*]
A bolt, three nuts, two marbles, and a wad of tinfoil tumbled out of the glass and clattered to rest on the table. Slowly, awkwardly, uncertainly, a partially bandaged hand groped for one of the nuts. One-by-one the hand picked up the objects and dropped them back into the glass.

"I still have trouble," said William Schaefer, owner of the hand and patient in the physical therapy program at Flint, Michigan's Anaphan clinic. "But my control is better every time I come here."

Schaefer is one of approximately . . .

[*From a paper on the duties of the headquarters security platoon for a combat infantry division*]

Two men on a lonely guard patrol walked along a rocky Korean road. They walked silently, accompanied only by a full moon, the roar of a nearby river, and their own thoughts.

Both saw it at the same time . . . a light, about three-quarters of the way up the side of a nearby hill.

"There is not supposed to be anybody up there," said one of the men. But his partner was already talking to platoon headquarters on the walkie-talkie. . . .

5. *Direct Address.* It is not always appropriate to address the reader directly, using the pronoun *you,* in a research paper. Reports that are to be considered impersonally in more or less formal situations cannot properly take such a casual tone. But reports addressed to equals or near-equals with whom you have a good, informal working relationship may even be better received if they are lightened by a casual tone. Using direct address in your opening is one excellent way to spark interest and gain readers. Notice how much more intriguing the first example below is, now that direct address has been added to the version used above as an example of the striking statement.

Examples:

[*From a paper on the internal security system of the U.S. Postal Service*]

If you thought that hidden doorways and secret passages went out with the Middle Ages, you had better check up on where your tax money is going. Last year the government spent an estimated 22 million dollars designing such structures into public buildings, and the chances are good that you stood within twenty feet of one the last time you mailed a letter.

[*Signals of direct address are underlined to make it easier to recognize how this revision differs from the earlier version.*]

[*From a research report on the psychology of magical entertainment*]

If you are like most people, you believe that the hand is quicker than the eye. The truth, however, is that nobody's hand is quicker than anybody's eye. It is misdirection, not speed, that enables the sleight-of-hand artist to fool his audiences.

It is important to remember that the opening must never overshadow the serious purpose of the report. Always keep it as short as possible and move quickly and smoothly into the announcement of your subject and an explanation of why that subject is important. Some time-tested ways of handling that presentation are explained in the next few pages.

EXERCISE 8.2:   Sharpening Your Ability to Catch Readers' Attention

1. List on a blank sheet of paper five different audiences (i.e., five types or groups of readers) who might conceivably read a report on your research topic.

2. On separate sheets of paper, write five different openings for reports on your research topic. Use as many of the attention-getting techniques as you can, and address at least some of these practice efforts to audiences other than the one for which you are writing your actual report.

3. Pick your best two or three openings and continue to work with them, cutting out excess words, tightening the wording to give them as much "punch" as you can, and adding appropriate phrasing to bridge quickly to the announcement of your topic. If one of your best first efforts happens to be slanted to an audience other than the one you are writing for, study it carefully before discarding it. Try to find a way to adapt it or imitate it in some way that would be appropriate for your audience.

4. Let some time lapse after you have completed step 3. Then consider your three drafts carefully. Choose the one that—all things considered—would be best for the report you are preparing. Do a final draft that would actually fit into the introduction to your report. (Do this as a learning experience, even if you do not want to use a novel opening in the report that you submit.)

When and How to Use a "Routine" Opening

In some situations, the use of special attention-getting openers is unnecessary and possibly damaging to the credibility of the writer. A more conventional introduction should usually be considered for reports written under the following conditions:

1. When the readers addressed have special expertise or interests that make the report of compelling relevance to them;

2. When the report has been commissioned or requested by those to whom it is addressed;

3. When the audience has professional responsibilities that obligate them to read the report;

4. When the writer is a recognized authority or holds rank or status superior to that of the readers addressed; and

5. When the writer is sure that the audience is inclined to read and accept the views expressed in the report over those of any competing spokesperson.

If your report is addressed to readers like these, you probably have most of the information you need for your introduction in your prospectus. Remember the first three questions you answered in writing your prospectus?

1. What is the topic, and why is it important?
2. What background information is necessary in order to explain why you approached the topic as you did?
3. What, exactly, is your thesis or purpose?

These are the questions you must answer for your readers at the outset of your report. Usually, what you wrote for your own guidance about the importance of your topic can easily be reworded so that it is clear and convincing to your readers.

However, your prospectus may only give you a start towards what you need to say in your introduction concerning questions 2 and 3. You probably know a good deal more helpful background information than you needed in your prospectus. And the chances are that the thesis will need fuller clarification than you could give it at that time. Fortunately, report writers have developed more or less standard ways of presenting this important information.

Thesis Paragraphs

In practice, the thesis paragraph may not be a single paragraph at all. We refer to it as a paragraph only because in short reports one paragraph is often sufficient and because most students find it easier to remember the basic formula if they think of it as the plan for a single paragraph.

Not all the following points will have to be addressed in every report. But those that do need attention should be dealt with at the outset. Think of them as potential functions of your thesis paragraph.

1. *State the central point or purpose of the report.* This must always be done. Studies show that readers who are given a general idea of the information in a passage will read it faster, understand it better, and remember it longer. So always state your thesis clearly—and unless you have a compelling reason to do otherwise, state it early in the report.

2. *Define any terms that may cause confusion.* Key terms in the thesis or purpose statement should be defined at the outset. One student's research led him to a fascinating thesis: "Slang serves some of the same functions within a social group that popular music and poetry serve for the culture as a whole." Unfortunately, however, he forgot that to many people *slang* means profanity, obscenity, and incorrect English was well as the brash but innocent word play he had in mind. Because he failed to define what *slang* meant to him, the classmates to whom he addressed his report failed to understand his point.

3. *Restrict and clarify the thesis.* Sometimes it is as important to stipulate what you are *not* asserting as to state what you do claim. "It is important to realize," said a psychologist in a report to schoolteachers, "that when I say learning theory can help you teach students to avoid 'errors of writing,' I am not saying that learning theory will help with all errors that *can possibly* be made in writing. For instance, I am not saying that it will help with style, word choice, tone, or even organization. But notice that misjudgments of these kinds, while possible in writing, can also be made in speech. The errors that my research deals with can *only* be made in writing. It is to these errors—of spelling, punctuation, and capitalization—and only to these errors that the following discussion is directed."

4. *Give a brief overview of the report.* If your report runs longer than a page or two, readers will benefit from a brief summary in which you outline in a sentence or two the important steps in the discussion that follows. This gives the reader a sense of direction and equips him or her to recognize the milestones as your discussion moves to each successive step. Usually, the plan you sketched in your prospectus can be easily adapted for inclusion in your thesis paragraph.

Notice how all four of these goals are achieved in the following purpose statement from a short psychology report.

Thesis stated

The thesis of this paper is that Eric Weiss, who became world famous as the magician Harry Houdini, was deeply neurotic. The evidence shows that his case was almost a textbook example of

Phrasing suggests enough about meaning of term *Oedipus complex* to enable reader to follow

an Oedipus complex and that the extraordinary closeness he shared with his mother continued to blight his life to the end of his days, even when she was long since dead. This is not to say that Houdini himself ever recognized his problem; it is doubtful

Thesis restricted and clarified

that he did. If anything, his neurosis was made more debilitating by his lack of insight. The discussion that

Overview of report
presented (Note that
provision is made for a
more adequate
definition of the term
Oedipus complex as
the first step in the
discussion.)

follows will first define the term
Oedipus complex, as it is used in
psychoanalysis. Then it will summarize
pertinent facts about Houdini's life as
they were recorded by the mystery man
himself, by his wife, and by several
close friends and business associates.
It will be seen that the biographical
facts reported reflect a personality
disorder that meets in every particular
the definition of an Oedipus complex.

Review of the Literature

Often it is necessary to accompany the thesis paragraph with a summary of previous research on the same topic. This makes it easier to explain how the question under investigation fits into the larger picture and why the question was approached as it was. The conventional name for this background information, which should always be fully documented, is "Review of the Literature" or sometimes, "Summary of Previous Research."

Notice how the opening paragraphs from the scholarly report below present a review of the literature and move to a thesis paragraph. Notice that, in this case, it actually takes several paragraphs to cover all the points in our "thesis paragraph" formula. One paragraph presents the statement of purpose and provides an overview of the report. The next qualifies and limits the task described in the purpose statement, admitting the possibility of distortion due to personal bias or subjectivity. The remaining paragraphs (plus three more not quoted) are all devoted to defining the term *carnival* and emphasizing the important distinction between carnivals and circuses, with which they are often confused.

Towards an Ethnography of the
Carnival Social System*

PATRICK C. EASTO & MARCELLO TRUZZI

Recent studies in anthropology and sociology have called growing attention to what Erving Goffman (1961:4) called *total institutions*. These refer to

*Extracted from *Journal of Popular Culture* 6 (1973):550–552.

institutions whose "encompassing or total character is symbolized by a barrier to social intercourse with the outside and to departure that is often built right into the physical plant" (Goffman 1961:4). Several varieties of such institutions were distinguished, one of which consisted of those "purportedly established the better to pursue some workmanlike task and justifying themselves only on those institutional grounds" (Goffman 1961:5). One such total institution which has received a minimum of attention by sociologists and anthropologists is the American carnival. Like the American circus, which it strongly resembles along some dimensions (Truzzi 1968, 1966; Gerson 1969), but with which it is too often confused by many people, the carnival is a highly integrated social and cultural system with strong boundaries maintained between itself and the community in which it is temporarily stationed while operating. Like a ship (Zurcher 1965), the carnival is largely self-contained, has its own distinctive culture, and maintains a separate social structure.

Good data on carnivals are not readily available. Bibliography on the carnival is diffuse and often unreliable. Sociological investigations have been both scant and limited (Krassowski 1954; Cuber 1939; Easto 1970; Bryant 1970). The major source of information on the American carnival is to be found in the carnival "bible," the magazine *Amusement Business* (formerly called *Billboard* and still thus referred to by many if not most carnival workers), especially in its recent special 75th Anniversary Issue (Billboard Publications 1969). There are several relevant historical works (Braithwaite 1968; McKechnie 1932; Frost 1881), the best of which is by William F. Mangels (1952). Several autobiographical works are informative (Dadswell 1946; Holtzman and Lewiston 1969; Mannix 1951) as are several exposé works (Anonymous 1949; Scarne 1961; Gibson 1946; Doc and the Professor 1939; Carrington 1913) and the occasional book written for the carnival insider (Boles 1967). Finally, there are journalistic books (Lewis 1970; Gresham 1953) and articles (Gresham 1960, 1948; Klein 1969; Mannix 1969, 1964, 1958, 1961, 1948; Jones 1947; Millstein 1952; Poling 1953; *Time* 1956, 1958; Zinsser 1967). This last category of works is the most unreliable, for the journalist is still viewed as an outsider (except as with Mannix, who is an ex-carnival worker), and carnival informants are very much aware of their public image. Thus, most of these accounts merely relate the folklore of the carnival world, often exaggerated if not mythological stories, and stress the way the carnival has been "cleaned up" into an honest "Sunday school" show for the whole family. As with the folklore of the circus (Truzzi 1966: 300), the carnival informant usually gives the inquiring reporter what he thinks the reporter and his audience want to hear and what he wants them to hear. In short, these accounts present us with a highly glamorized image of the carnival. Even when the author of these articles is not "taken in" by his informants, he is usually aware of what constitutes a "good story," and that is what he strives to write. Therefore, these journalistic accounts are valuable but usually distorted in their presentation of carnival life.

The purposes of this paper are modest; we wish here merely to introduce the carnival to the social scientist, and in so doing, we would suggest that one of the better testing grounds for notions we have about subcultures and total institutions might be found here. Beginning with a definition and succinct history of the carnival, we will attempt to describe the prestige hierarchy and social structure of the carnival. We will then look at the function of carnival language as a boundary maintaining device. Finally, we will look at some of the special problems involved in investigating the carnival world.

Although our review which follows will rely heavily upon the bibliographic materials cited and upon numerous interviews with carnival workers, the bulk of our data relies upon participant observation. It must be noted, however, that the ratio of participation to observation has been weighted heavily on the side of participation. As with Nels Anderson in his now classic work on homeless men (1923), our scholarly interest in the carnival developed after spending several years of involvement in that milieu. We draw, therefore, upon our experiences and our memories after they have been formed through our participation. Though we do not feel that this seriously distorts our perspective, it does mean that many things might have been observed which were not thought to be important. Thus, data are still unavailable to us on many important aspects of the carnival world.

A precise definition of the carnival is not a simple task. A typical dictionary definition is: "an entertainment with side shows, rides, games and refreshments, usually operated as a commercial enterprise." Yet, at any one time, any one of these elements can be missing. It is far easier to define a carnival by example. The three major features of a carnival are (1) riding devices, (2) shows or exhibits, and (3) concessions. Riding devices include the familiar merry-go-round (considered by some to be a necessary element in the definition of a carnival), the ferris wheel, the Tilt-a-Whirl, and many others which constitute the major rides. In addition to these major rides, there are the "punk rides" which cater to small children, the boat rides, miniature train, tank ride, etc.

There are a wide variety of shows and exhibits. These include presentations of performers (as in girl shows, freak shows, etc.), animals (wild life, rare or "freak" animals, etc.), or interesting objects (wax figures, historical objects, even dead people as in the case of preserved freak embryos like a two-headed baby). Almost without exception, however, the largest show on the carnival midway is the freak show or "ten-in-one."

Concessions include a wide variety of both games and refreshment operations. There are two major types of games: "flat-stores" and "hanky-panks." The flat-store or joint refers to those concessions which are strictly gambling operations where the probability of winning is rarely on the side of the patron. Examples would include the "Swinger," a game where the customer swings a small bowling ball in such a fashion as to knock over a small bowling pin; the "Roll-down," where the customer spills a number of marbles down a runway filled with numbered depressions; or the "Six-cat" where the object is to toss three baseballs and knock over two large cat-like dolls. The other type of game, the hanky-pank, typically rewards its patron with a prize each time he plays. Typical hanky-panks are the fish-pond, the ring-toss, and dart throwing games. The crucial distinction between the flat-store and the hanky-pank is whether or not the customer is rewarded each time he plays.

In the minds of many of the public, carnivals are equated with circuses. Though a limited degree of intersection between the carnival and circus worlds exists (that is, there are a few people in the carnival world who have worked on circuses and vice-versa), they are very separate and very different social and cultural worlds. Within the outdoor amusement industry itself, circus personnel are generally ranked higher in the overall stratification system. Circus people often "look down" upon carnival people. The circus has been defined as "a traveling and organized display of animals and skilled performances within one or more circular stages known as rings before an audience encircling these activities" (Truzzi 1968: 315). Thus, the circus is perceived as an extension of theater by its members. The carnival is perceived by carnival and circus people as having very different origins and connections: from street fairs and the world of gambling. The circus is primarily a display whereas the carnival is primarily an entertainment which seeks the participation of the customer. The carnival seeks, in general, an active customer in contrast to the more passive viewer of the circus.

Secondly, carnivals differ from circuses in terms of the economic relationship between the management and workers. . . .

EXERCISE 8.3:   Sharpening Your Handling of the Standard Opening

Refer as necessary to your prospectus, your outline, and as much of your preliminary draft as you have finished to help you answer the following questions.

1. List on a sheet of scrap paper any technical terms or words in your thesis that have meanings for you which may not be known to your audience. After each one, give the shortest definition you can that is completely adequate to explain the meaning given to that term in your report.

2. Consider any existing knowledge, beliefs, prejudices, and habits that may cause your readers to misunderstand your use of the terms named above or to miss the significance of any other key concepts or lines of reasoning in your report. After each entry, make a note of the feature in your paper that might create a problem for readers with those characteristics.

    For example, the notes of a student who addressed a report opposing capital punishment to the congregation of her rural church looked like this:

Rural people, practical interests. Do not read much.

Thesis will confuse any who happen not to know that "capital punishment" means "execution."

Deeply religious. Strong sense of justice includes emphasis on guilt, contrition, and redemption.

May feel that execution is necessary for criminals to make amends for crime so that they deserve mercy. Will find it hard to focus on my argument that capital punishment is unjust because irretrievable.

3. Write a "thesis paragraph" for your report. Define any troublesome terms and add any clarifying comments necessary to make clear exactly what you do and do not intend to demonstrate (or, in the case of a purpose statement, what you do and do not expect to accomplish) in your report. Do not forget to include a brief overview of your paper, similar to the one included in your prospectus.

4. Write a brief review of the literature, in which you report on the readings you relied on when you formulated your research question or purpose. Simply explain what past work has been done on your topic, citing sources as you mention them, and show how that work fits together to make your question a logical one to raise. Try assuming that the review of the literature will go in your paper after the statement of the thesis and overview of the paper.

If you find that the thesis cannot be understood unless the review comes first, assume the placement that works best for you.

5. Look over the drafts you did for questions 3 and 4 above and make the changes necessary to meld them into one smooth opening. Try, if possible, to begin with your thesis paragraph and introduce your review of the literature afterward. However, if a different arrangement or more extensive revision is necessary to give you a smooth, effective opening, make the necessary adjustments now. When finished, you should have a series of paragraphs which, by themselves, could serve as a conventional opening for your paper and which—if preceded by any of the attention-getting openings described earlier in this chapter—would prepare readers for the substantial part of your report.

CONCLUSIONS FOR RESEARCH REPORTS

It should not be surprising that many students find it hard to "think of good endings" for research reports. Despite their extraordinary importance in everyday business and professional activity, reports are almost never read by young people.

Since most of us acquire a good deal of what we know about writing from incidental observations during our reading, the research report presents a problem. It is the one important form of writing that you are expected to learn to do before you have a chance to read much of it. For some students, this poses special problems in deciding what constitutes an acceptable ending.

The Importance of the Conclusion

The truth is that library research reports—unlike certain technical reports sometimes used in business and industry—can end in almost any way that would be appropriate for any other essay. Although this gives the writer a great deal of latitude, it by no means suggests that the ending is not important.

Some Techniques for Effective Closings

Finding a workable ending, fortunately, is not difficult at all, if you just keep in mind a few basic principles and commonly used techniques.

The most important principle is to *alert your reader ahead of time that the end is near.* Nothing is more disconcerting to a reader than to zip up to the end of a sentence, expecting more, possibly even turning the page looking for a continuation, only to find that the writer just stopped abruptly. As often as not, such a shock is due not to any logical omission or incompleteness in the report but to a failure to remind the reader that the discussion was nearing completion.

Appropriate use of phrases like the following will smooth the way to your stopping point:

This *concludes* the discussion of . . . It *only remains* to . . .
What, *finally,* does all this mean?
In *drawing to a close,*
In summary . . . [or] In conclusion . . .

The second principle for handling conclusions is to *make it obvious that the ending IS the ending.* There are several conventional ways of doing this. One of the simplest is to turn the discussion back to something mentioned in your opening. "It is now clear that the question posed at the beginning of this paper is not the question we most need to address." Such a reference suggests that your redefinition of the question is your contribution, and that your report is therefore almost complete.

Another signal is to change the tone or the time orientation of the language. For instance, if the language becomes a little more formal or if a report devoted to summarizing findings of research done in the past suddenly turns to a consideration of what lies in the future, most readers will sense that the report is drawing to a close.

Each of the closing techniques explained below provides additional signals to prepare your reader and enhance the effectiveness of your ending.

1. *Summary.* Unless there is a special reason not to include it, a summary should always be part of your closing. The summary need not be long and certainly should not be detailed. But it should reiterate your thesis and remind readers how well you have supported it.

EXAMPLES:

[*From a literary critic's study of a poem*]
It is now clear that the evidence in the poem itself, the
evidence available from published sources, and the evidence
found in the private correspondence of the three principal
parties is all consistent with the thesis advanced. We may
never know for sure why Wordsworth interrupted his work for so
long, but the fact is that he did. Only the first four stanzas
of the "Intimations Ode" were written in 1802.

[*From a report on the private slang of carnival workers*]
Taken together, these special words provide a good insight into
the carny's value system. The first group of words shows that he

prizes action, movement, power, dominance, and--above all--

freedom. The second set shows with equal clarity that he

despises whatever is routinized, constrained, and predictable.

In short, he loves the carnival and despises the humdrum

existence that is taken for success on every Main Street in

America.

2. *Striking Statement.* Properly handled, most of the devices for arresting attention at the opening can also be used in the conclusion to focus interest and leave a greater impression in the reader's memory. The striking statement, for instance, works as well as an ending as it does for an opener. In fact, a particularly good technique for closing any kind of persuasive or argumentative paper is simply to restate the thesis in vivid, concrete, and dramatic wording.

EXAMPLES:

[*From a report advocating the reorganization and expansion of the youth centers in a slum neighborhood*]

It is no exaggeration to refer to the conditions described in

this report as social dynamite. But the evidence shows that if

the recommended changes are begun immediately, the calamity can

yet be avoided and, what is more, that a year from now everyone

concerned, taxpayers and teenagers alike, will walk the streets

of Thistown, happier people and better citizens.

[*From a historical report on the origin of the Western romance*]

Whether the Western will ever again dominate popular literature

as it did in the first half of the twentieth century is a matter

of conjecture. Nobody who considers the facts mentioned in these

pages, however, can be in doubt about where the Western began.

It began with Owen Wister's <u>Virginian.</u>

3. *Call for Action.* The findings of most research reports point the way to further research. Sometimes this is the most important contribution a researcher can make. At other times, the social or political implications of the research are so clear that action is obviously called for. When a responsible call for further research or practical action can be made on the basis of what you have learned, closing with an appropriate plea for action is a good way of emphasizing the importance of what you have covered in your report.

EXAMPLES:

[From a report on the nuclear arms race]

What is at issue is, quite simply, the survival of humanity.
Such an issue is too important to leave to the experts, for on
the worth of life every person is an expert. The technicians are
failing us. The politicians are failing us. But the power of an
informed people has yet to be felt. If it is to make a
difference, however, the will of the people must be heard soon.
The nuclear clock is ticking away; and when the alarm finally
goes off, it will be too late then to put aside petty
differences and demand that our leaders rise above politics to
statesmanship.

[From a report urging doctors to go on record in favor of outlawing boxing]

American physicians have rightly appointed themselves advisors
to the public on matters of health and safety. They have a
tradition of speaking out in opposition to quackery and in
support of reason. How then, faced with statistics like these,
can they keep silent while hundreds of young men risk
irreversible brain damage in the name of sport?

Every doctor should take responsibility for warning his
patients of the dangers of boxing. And every professional group
of doctors should begin immediately to promote legislation to
declare this so-called sport illegal.

4. *Quotation.* A fitting quotation, with or without additional comment by
the writer, often provides a way of making the ending sharper and easier
to remember.

EXAMPLES:

[From a report by a psycholinguist to a group of educational administrators and English teachers]

By now it is obvious that the research in psycholinguistics
summarized in this report strongly suggests that the mental
processes used in English composition are of crucial importance
not only in writing but in all higher order thinking. So the
answer is now clear to a question posed over a century ago by

the great English essayist Thomas Carlyle. "What," he asked, "can we teach a student after we have taught him to read?" The answer is that we still can, and must, teach him to write.

[*From an explication of a Renaissance play by a literary critic*]
Faustus is so rich in meaning and so powerful in imagination that the question becomes ever more insistent. Which of its many themes should be regarded as the most important, most central one? On that point, the view taken in this paper admits but one answer. Marlowe wrote Faustus to say in 1593 exactly what Maurice Maeterlink said less artistically but more concisely in 1903: "All our knowledge merely helps us to die a more painful death than the animals that know nothing."

EXERCISE 8.4: Shaping the Conclusion of Your Report

1. Draft a conclusion for your report in which you summarize your major points concisely in fresh language. End with the most vivid and striking re-wording of your thesis that you can come up with.
2. Study the draft you just completed, and make whatever changes you need, to be sure that it will be recognized and accepted by *your readers* as a satisfying ending.
3. Put aside, for now, the conclusion you have just written. Choose some of the other closing techniques that appeal to you, and draft at least three other endings using those techniques. Allow yourself time to play around with the possibilities, and keep working until you have shaped at least one of these efforts into a clean, finished draft.
4. Go back to the summary conclusion you prepared in steps 1 and 2. Consider this version in the context of your complete report. If you use it in its present form, will it do justice to your report? Or would your purpose or your readers be better served if you combined the summary conclusion with one of the other endings you experimented with? If so, pick your most promising effort and add it to your summary. Reword and revise until this complete ending reads just the way you want it to.

9

Revising and Editing the Report

Once your draft is complete, you are ready to start transforming it into a competent professional document that will be taken seriously by qualified readers and reflect well on its author. Alexander Pope, the famous eighteenth-century writer, is said to have sent nothing to press that he had not scrutinized for two years. In return for his care, Pope earned a reputation as a stylist that is still secure two centuries later. But life progressed more slowly in Pope's day. Today, neither college students nor working professionals have the luxury of going over the same manuscript hundreds of times.

Still, there is a lesson to be learned from Pope. His dedication to revision, though extreme by today's standards, is by no means unusual among professional writers. J. R. R. Tolkien took over ten years to write his *Lord of the Rings* trilogy, agonizing over each chapter and paragraph and finally submitting it for publication only after he had retyped the entire manuscript three times because of his numerous revisions. We mention this because beginners tend to believe that the need for revision fades as writers gain experience. Nothing could be further from the truth.

There are, however, some simple techniques that will help you work systematically towards the best possible version of your paper, even under tight deadlines. Essentially, revision is just a matter of managing your work so that you are always looking for the right things at the right time.

WHEN TO REVISE

Try to allow some "cooling off" time between completion of your first draft and the beginning of your revision. Revising immediately makes it difficult to evaluate your own work objectively. So budget your time to allow yourself at least a day or two to stop thinking like a writer and begin thinking like a reader. Good revising requires you to see your paper through your reader's eyes. If you start too soon, you will find it harder to avoid seeing what you meant to put on the page instead of what is actually there.

WHAT TO LOOK FOR

Always look for the big problems first. Start by reviewing the organization of your paper to make sure that you have ordered the information and examples in the strongest possible fashion. Review your outline, if you worked from one, to make sure that it shows the strongest and most logical sequence for your material. When you are sure that it does, compare your outline with the paper. If there are discrepancies, make the changes needed to ensure that your paper has the clearest and most effective pattern of development you can conceive of.

If major revisions are required, now is the time to make them. No amount of superficial tampering can make an acceptable research paper out of a badly organized hodge-podge. Ask yourself whether your points are properly supported with well-chosen examples and evidence and, if so, whether everything is properly placed in a pattern that will be apparent to the reader.

Checking for Unity

Glance over the whole paper to see how the paragraphs are fitting together. Check to be sure that each paragraph advances the thesis of your paper. Then examine the paragraphs individually. Make sure that all the sentences in each paragraph support its central point.

Checking for Coherence

Next, check to see whether connections between paragraphs are clearly signalled. Does the flow of information in each paragraph follow from that in the last? If not, what kind of transition signals are needed? Are there paragraphs which should be combined or divided, to increase the coherence of the whole?

Within paragraphs, read to be sure that each sentence connects smoothly and clearly with what has gone before. Make sure that every pronoun refers clearly to something actually named in the surrounding text. Watch for abrupt shifts that may suggest to readers that your thought is taking a new direction. Unless your thought *is* taking a new direction necessary to make your point, do not abruptly change numbers of nouns, tenses of verbs, or person of pronouns within the paragraph.

Checking for Completeness

This is also the time to make sure that every point has appropriate support. Occasionally, you will find that you failed to support an assertion because you were so close to the work that you assumed it to be self-evident. In revising, your job is to be a sceptical reader of your own work. Prove everything to yourself. Check to make sure that you have included all of the relevant points, that all points which require substantiation have been addressed, and that, where appropriate, you have addressed both sides of controversial issues.

Checking for Clarity

Is everything understandable? At this point it is particularly important that you keep the audience of your paper firmly in mind. Check one last time to be sure that you have defined every key term clearly. With your audience in mind, look also for any word choices that might disrupt clear communication.

Checking for Style and Correctness

Finally, read through the paper checking for stylistic flaws and grammatical mistakes. Sharpen your editorial pencil and make sure that the paper follows all the rules and conventions of standard English. We recommend that you read through your draft several times, concentrating each time on a different aspect of your revision. Few people can revise successfully on all these levels at the same time.

GETTING EVERYTHING INTO SHAPE

Once you have carefully edited and revised your paper, it is time to consider its format. Always consult your style manual at this point. This chapter will guide you through the correct MLA and APA procedures. If your instructor has asked or allowed you to follow any other manual, you should adapt what you learn in the following pages to the directions in that manual.

Though there are variations, most style guides require the following components in this order:

A title page.

An abstract, outline, or table of contents.

The body of the paper.

Endnotes (if any).

Works cited list, reference list, or bibliography.

DOING A GOOD ABSTRACT

While not every style sheet requires that you include an abstract as part of your paper, chances are that sooner or later, you will have to write one or read one. In either case, you should know what an abstract is and what it is supposed to do.

Essentially, there are two kinds of abstracts: descriptive and informative. The descriptive abstract is a concise description of the contents of the paper. It does not detail the conclusions, or summarize the main points. Its main function is to provide the prospective reader with just enough information about the content to enable him to decide whether or not to read the article. An informative abstract, on the other hand, must summarize all of the main points in the paper. Each part of the abstract is roughly proportional to the portion of the original it summarizes. Thus if 30 percent of the paper deals with the history of mental disorders, then about 30 percent of the abstract must also deal with the history of mental disorders. The overall length of an abstract should not normally exceed 10 percent of the length of the paper. Abstracts of long works will represent a much lower percentage of the original.

Paraphrase your points rather than quoting them from the text. Each sentence should be concise and specific. Summarize the paper, leaving out personal comments or evaluations, so that the finished abstract digests the original in readable, connected prose, not a hodgepodge of points and reactions.

EXERCISE 9.1:   Getting Straight on Abstracts

Read the two abstracts below, both of which were written from the "hypnosis" paper for which you saw the prospectus in chapter 7. Then answer the questions that follow.

A.   Hypnosis Is No Parlor Trick

    In two hundred years of scientific experimentation, hypno-

tism has proven useful to doctors, dentists, and psychiatrists,

as an anesthetic, an aid to psychotherapy, a means of pain control, and an adjunct therapy in the treatment of surgical and
burn patients.

Despite these facts, the public is badly misinformed about
hypnosis. Stage entertainers, inaccurate books, and distorted
presentations in the media cause laypersons to view it either
too sceptically or too superstitiously, leaving them even more
susceptible to real dangers that they never suspect.

Case histories show that many serious physical and mental
injuries have resulted from the misuse of hypnosis. Untrained
hypnotists are known to have triggered psychosomatic illnesses,
nervous breakdowns, and even suicides in subjects whose unusual
psychic needs went unrecognized in normal activity.

For these reasons, only competent professionals, acting
within the scope of their expertise, should be allowed to practice hypnosis, and then only for the benefit of the hypnotized
subject. Only such a professional can reliably determine who
should and should not be hypnotized, can evaluate resistance to
hypnosis and resolve it if possible, and if not can withhold
hypnosis from subjects who might be at risk.

The evidence shows that even with their advantages, trained
professionals sometimes misjudge. They are, however, qualified
to deal with the unexpected problems that arise in such cases
and to minimize the subject's distress. The possibility of such
distress suggests that the proper use of hypnosis is comparable
to the proper use of anesthesia. Only qualified people should
ever be allowed to use it at all—and not even they, unless
their doing so is for the benefit of the hypnotized subject.

B.   Hypnosis Is No Parlor Trick

Scientific history shows the reality of hypnosis to be established beyond doubt by its successful use in medicine, den-

```
tistry and psychiatry. Yet the public, being ignorant of this,

fails to recognize dangers in today's widespread abuse of hypno-

tism. Evidence is presented to demonstrate that this is a seri-

ous problem, and the conclusion is reached that hypnosis can

properly be used only by a qualified professional working within

his or her area of expertise to perform services for the benefit

of the hypnotized subject.
```

1. Which of the abstracts is informative? How well does it follow the standards set forth in the text for informative abstracts? Is it self-contained? Does it emphasize points in approximately the same proportion as the original? About how long should the finished paper be that matches this abstract? How can you tell? Can you suggest changes that would make this abstract better, or do you find it quite satisfactory as it is?

2. Which abstract is descriptive? How did you recognize that it has a different purpose? What is that purpose? How well does this abstract accomplish its purpose? Do you have improvements to suggest, or do you find this version satisfactory?

3. Refer to your assignment or consult your instructor to find out whether you will be expected to submit an abstract of the research paper you are working on. If so, learn whether yours is to be an informative or a descriptive abstract, and write it now, making sure that it meets the standards described above.

ENDNOTES AND CITATIONS

Examine your notes and citations to be sure that they are arranged and punctuated exactly as the style manual directs. Check the appropriate examples and instructions in this book or, if you are not using the APA or MLA format, in your own manual.

If you are having someone else do the final typing, do not rely on that person to catch your errors in style and format. Remember that, as the author, you, not your typists, are responsible for the appearance and accuracy of the final product.

EXERCISE 9.2: Proofreading Works Cited and References

Directions: Choose the part of this exercise that corresponds to the style manual you are using for your report. Carefully proofread the citations in that part, correcting all errors in format, grammar, spelling, or punctuation. If information necessary for a correct citation is missing, make up appropriate names, etc., and complete the entry in a manner that is technically correct, according to your style manual.

PART ONE: MLA FORMAT

```
McGill, Ormond. The encyclopedia of stage hypnotisim. N.p.:
     Abbott Magic Company, n.d., Colon, Michigan.
Miller, Michael M.. Therapeutic Hypnosis. New York: Human
     Sciences Press, 1979.
Orne, Martin T., and Hammer, Gordon A. "Hypnosis."
No author given. Encyclopaedia Britannica: Macropaedia.
     1974.
```

PART TWO: APA FORMAT

```
Angier, B. (1972) Survival With Style. Harrisburg: Stack
     Pole Books.
Tacoma Mountain Rescue Unit. Outdoor living: problems, sol-
     utions, guidelins. Tacoma, 1970.
Miller, Michael M.. Theraputic Hypnosis. New York: Human
     Sciences Press, 1979.
The Handbook of Hypnotism and Psychosematic Medicine. 1980.
```

ATTENDING TO THE LITTLE THINGS

Make sure that your printer wheel or typewriter keys are clean and functioning properly. Start with a new ribbon, and use a high quality bond paper, preferably one that is at least 25 percent cotton. *Do not* use "erasable" bond papers. They smear and smudge too easily.

Avoid typewriters or printers with ornate or unusual type faces. They only make the document harder to read. Double space all text, including the title, quotations, notes, works cited list, and abstract, if you have one. You may use triple or quadruple spacing in special situations to improve the readability of your text, but do not use single or fractional spacing unless the style manual you are using specifically requires it. Neither the MLA nor the APA does.

Copies

Always be sure that you keep at least one copy of the paper. In school, this is excellent protection against the occasional loss or accidental destruction of the paper before your grade has been recorded. In future research, your file copy is evidence of your claim to priority in case someone else later submits a report on similar work. Moreover, your past papers constitute valuable bibliographical references whenever you are doing further studies on related research questions.

Paragraph Indentations

Indent the first line of every paragraph and every note five spaces. The exception to this is the abstract page in the APA format, which is typed in block format.

MLA Formatting

The MLA system does not make use of a cover sheet or title sheet. Instead the author's name, followed by a double space, the name of the professor, double space, the course abbreviation, double space, and the date should be typed in the left-hand corner of the paper (see Figure 9–1) one inch in from the left of the paper and one inch down from the top.

This is followed by a double space and the title of the paper, centered. Then leave four spaces and begin the paper.

The MLA manual does not require an abstract or an outline. If your

FIGURE 9–1

```
                    ↓
                    1"
                    ↓
←1"→  Sam Knight

      Professor Smith

      IND 221

      12 May 1986

                    Lost Souls at Sea


      Elmer Krugg has suggested that the so-called

      modern man and woman are really much more primitive in

      their views of the need for art than. . . .
```

instructor asks you to provide one, be sure to check further. You will probably need to prepare a title page also.

Pagination. Beginning with page 2, number every page, as shown in Figure 9–2. The page number should be preceded by the last name of the author and placed ½″ down in the upper right hand corner of the paper. Number all pages consecutively throughout the paper.

Margins. With the exception of the space above page numbers, all margins should be one inch from the edge of the paper. The first word of each paragraph should be indented five spaces from the left margin. Quotations longer than four lines should be set off from the text and indented ten spaces from the left margin (see Figure 9–3). Shorter quotations should be incorporated into the text.

Notes. If you have used endnotes in your paper, you will need to include a note page. The note page follows immediately after the text, before the works cited page. Begin your note page on a new sheet of paper. Center the title "Notes" one inch down from the top of the page. Double space and begin the notes. Indent each note five spaces, begin with the

FIGURE 9–2

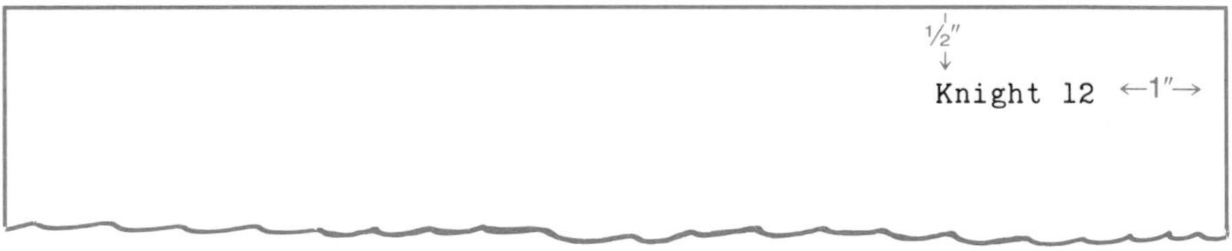

½″
↓
Knight 12   ←1″→

FIGURE 9–3
Handling long quotations in the MLA format

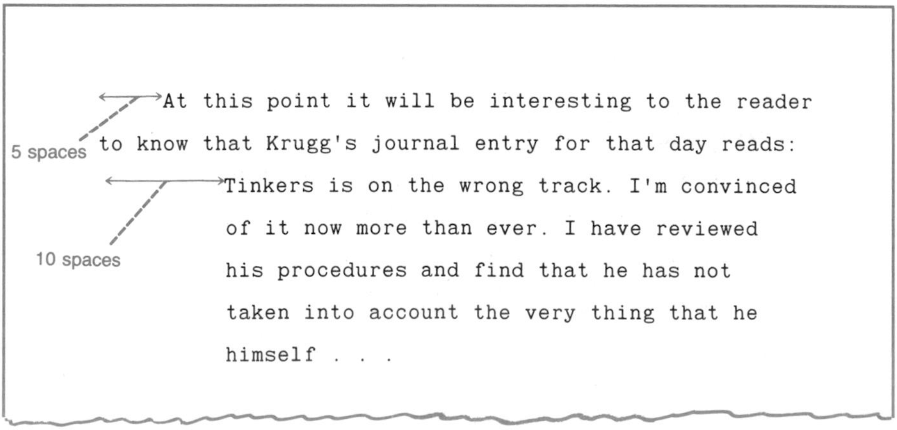

```
          ┌──────→At this point it will be interesting to the reader
5 spaces   to know that Krugg's journal entry for that day reads:

          ┌──────→Tinkers is on the wrong track. I'm convinced

                   of it now more than ever. I have reviewed
  10 spaces
                   his procedures and find that he has not

                   taken into account the very thing that he

                   himself . . .
```

note number, raised above the line as shown in Figure 9–4, and double space throughout the note. It is important that the notes be numbered in the order of their occurrence in the text and typed in proper order.

Works Cited. Like notes, lists of works cited begin on a new page. The title "Works Cited" should appear one inch down from the top of the page, centered. After the title, double space and begin listing entries in alphabetical order by authors' last names, according to the instructions in chapter 5. Remember to indent every line *except the first line of each entry* by five spaces (see Figure 9–5).

FIGURE 9–4
Sample portion of a note page in the MLA format.

½"

1"

Sanders 16

Notes

1 Janice Titterman, Uncertain Animals in the World Ocean (New York: Pnyn, 1982) 4, qtd. in McGuffy, 116; Theodore Glister, Marine Plants and Their Properties (Boston: Humbert, 1981) 27, qtd. in McGuffy, 119–20.

FIGURE 9–5
Sample portion of a works cited page in the MLA format

½"

1"

Brown 19

Works Cited

Blythe, Peter. Hypnotism: Its Power and Practice. New York: Taplinger Publishing Company, 1971.

Burrows, Graham D., and Lorraine Dennerstein. Handbook of Hypnosis and Psychosomatic Medicine. New York: Elsevier/North–Holland Biomedical Press, 1980.

Cheek, David B., and Leslie M. LeCron. Clinical Hypnotherapy. New York: Grune and Stratton, 1968.

Tables and Illustrations. A table is a compilation of data in columns and rows so that a great deal of information can be summarized in a short space. The columns and rows usually have headings to indicate their data and may be accompanied by totals and percentage calculations to make the data easier to interpret. An illustration is any other kind of visual that might be included in a report: a graph, photo, or drawing, for example. Tables and illustrations are numbered *separately* in the order of their appearance.

Both should be placed as close as possible to the part of the text that they illustrate. Generally, a table should be labeled "Table," and assigned the appropriate Arabic numeral. "Table" should appear flush with the left-hand margin. After it, double space and add a caption, also flush with the left margin. The caption is a heading explaining in as few words as possible what information is summarized in the table. It appears just above the table, and the source from which the information is taken should appear directly below the table (see Figure 9–6).

FIGURE 9–6
MLA table format

Table 1

Birth Defects in Irradiated Frogs

Group	c	1	2	3
Male				
With	81	59	54	48
Without	19	41	46	52
Female				
With	78	56	50	42
Without	22	44	50	58

Source: "Frogs' ability to withstand radiation" by B. F. Short, Radiation Experiments, 23, p. 432.

APA Formatting

Title Page. APA does not require a blank cover page but it *does* require a title page. On it should appear a title, describing the paper's contents as accurately as possible, and the author's name and school or institutional affiliation.

Type the title in upper- and lower-case letters. Center it on the page as shown in Figure 9–7. If the title is more than one line long, double space between lines. Then double space after the title, type the name of the author(s), centered, double space again, and type the institutional affiliation, centered. At the bottom of the page, type the "running head," the abbreviated title that will be at the top of each page when the article is printed (see Figure 9–7).

FIGURE 9–7
APA title page

Cargo Cults   ←1½″→

1″

1

Cultural Change in Cargo Cults

as a Response to External Stimuli

Kathy Eaton

Martin University

Running head: CULTURAL CHANGE IN CARGO CULTS

Pagination. All pages, with the exception of figures, should be numbered consecutively. The pages should be arranged in the following manner*:

title page (numbered page 1)

abstract (new page, numbered 2)

text (including introduction, body, and conclusion) of the report (new page, numbered 3)

references (new page)

appendices (start a new page for each one)

footnotes (new page)

tables (each on a separate sheet)

figure captions (each on a separate page)

figures (each on a separate page)

Page numbers should be placed in the upper right hand corner, approximately one inch down from the top and 1½ inches in from the right side. An abbreviated form of the title should appear two lines above the page number, ending 1½ inches in from the right margin. This version of the title is located here as a convenience to the editors who will work with the manuscript; it does not have to be the same as the running head (see Figure 9–8).

Abstract. Always include a descriptive abstract. APA suggests a maximum length of 100–150 words. To make it easier for other researchers to locate your report, the abstract should make use of key words from the paper that can be used as indexing guides. The abstract should be typed on its own page, in block (unindented) paragraphing format. A short title of the paper should appear in the upper right hand corner, along with the page number. The title "Abstract" should appear 1½ inches down in the center of the page, as shown in Figure 9–9.

FIGURE 9–8
APA page heading

```
                                          1"   Cargo Cults ←——1½"——→
                                                     10
```

---

*The manuscript is arranged in this manner for ease of editing. APA assumes that the publisher will then put the elements in the necessary order. Some instructors may prefer that students arrange their manuscripts in the more normal order, with tables and figures interspersed with the text. Be sure to follow your teacher's instructions on this point.

FIGURE 9–9
APA abstract page

```
                                      Cargo Cults
              1½"
                                             2

                       Abstract
        Shortly after World War II, the arrival of

        Australian patrols in the remote areas of New

        Guinea resulted in the formation of cargo cults

        among the natives.
```

Margins. Margins should be a uniform 1½ inches on all sides of the manuscript (see Figure 9–10). Even if you are using an electronic printer, the right margin should be left ragged (unjustified). Do *not* divide words at the end of a line.

References. On a new page, type the word "References" in the center of the page, 1½ inches down from the top of the page. If there is only one reference, then the page should be titled "Reference." The first line of each entry should be typed flush with the left margin and subsequent lines should be indented three spaces, as shown in Figure 9–11.

Appendices. Appendices should be double spaced. Each appendix should begin on a new page. Type the word "Appendix" centered, 1½ inches down from the top of the page, followed by a capital letter indicating which appendix it is, the first being Appendix A, the second B, and so forth. With only one appendix, no identifying letter is necessary. After the appendix designation, double space and type a descriptive title, underlined (see Figure 9–12). Then double space, indent five spaces, and begin the body of the appendix. Appendices should appear in the order in which they are referred to in the text.

Author Identification Notes. Author identification notes are mandatory for published reports in APA format; however, your instructor will probably not expect you to use them in this introductory effort. Be sure you understand and follow your instructions on this point. In professional reports, such notes pertain to one of three things: (1) acknowledgement of the basis of the study (such as a grant, doctoral dissertation, etc.) or special assistance (either in conducting the study or preparing the manuscript); (2) elaboration of the author's affiliation, for instance, mentioning

FIGURE 9–10
APA margins at top, sides, and bottom of page

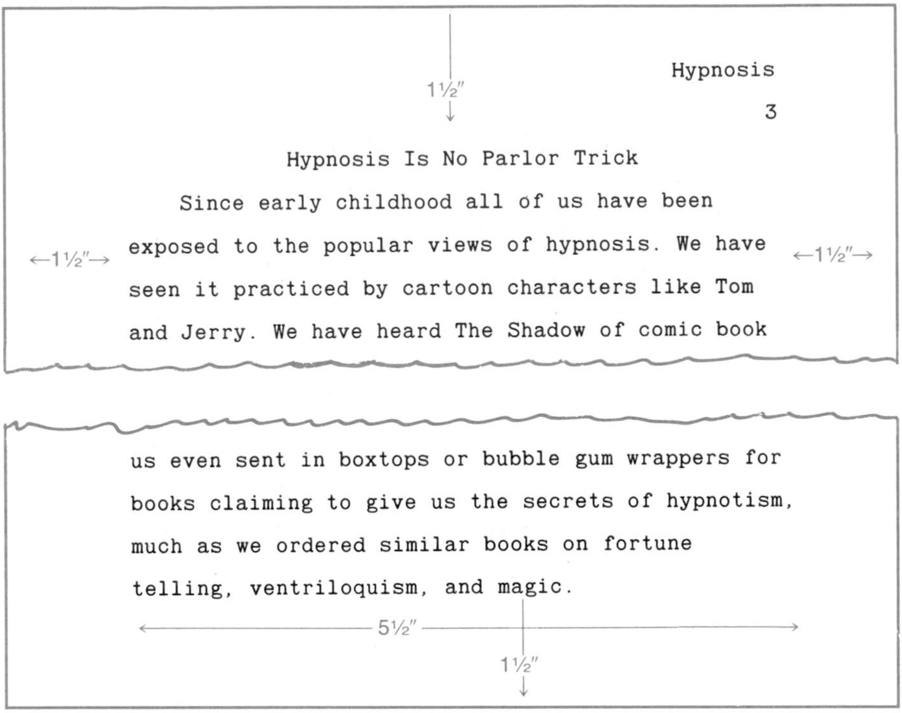

Hypnosis

3

1½″

Hypnosis Is No Parlor Trick

Since early childhood all of us have been

←1½″→ exposed to the popular views of hypnosis. We have ←1½″→

seen it practiced by cartoon characters like Tom

and Jerry. We have heard The Shadow of comic book

us even sent in boxtops or bubble gum wrappers for

books claiming to give us the secrets of hypnotism,

much as we ordered similar books on fortune

telling, ventriloquism, and magic.

←——————— 5½″ ———————→

1½″

FIGURE 9–11
APA references

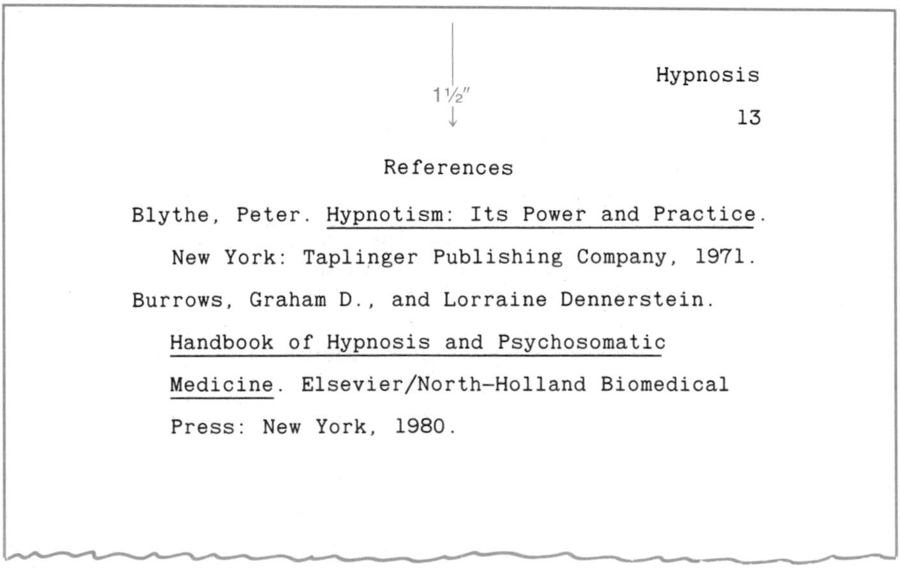

Hypnosis

13

1½″

References

Blythe, Peter. Hypnotism: Its Power and Practice.

New York: Taplinger Publishing Company, 1971.

Burrows, Graham D., and Lorraine Dennerstein.

Handbook of Hypnosis and Psychosomatic

Medicine. Elsevier/North–Holland Biomedical

Press: New York, 1980.

FIGURE 9–12
APA appendix page

```
                                    Captive Wolves
         1½"
                                         22

                        Appendix A
                Collection of Statistical Samples
              The following statistical samples were
        collected in May of 1985.
```

a change that may have taken place since the paper was written or the study conducted; and (3) providing an address to which readers may address requests for reprints or further information.

Author identification notes are not numbered or referred to in the text. On a separate page, center the words "Author Notes" 1½ inches down from the top of the page. Indent five spaces and if acknowledgements are to be included, start with those; then go to the information about the author. Author notes precede other footnotes in the manuscript.

Footnotes. Content footnotes are numbered consecutively, beginning on a new sheet of paper. Type the title "Footnotes" 1½ inches from the top of the page. Indent the first line of each note five spaces, put the note number a half space above the line, then begin immediately to type the wording of the note, double spaced (see Figure 9–13). An exception occurs with copyright permission notes for tables and figures. These are typed beneath the appropriate tables and kept with them, as explained below.

Tables. Tables are numbered consecutively according to the order in which they are introduced in the text. Indicate the position of the table in the text by typing a clear break and inserting the table number (see Figure 9–14). Each is identified by the word "Table," followed by its sequential number. Regardless of size or space limitations, begin each table on a separate page.

Double space the lines within each table, no matter how long it is. After the table number, double space and type the title of the table,

FIGURE 9–13
Footnotes page

```
                                        Captive Wolves
                        1½"
                                                22

                            Footnotes
              1
                Similar data have not yet been collected

           from observations of noncaptive wolves, so no

           correlation can be drawn at present.
```

FIGURE 9–14
Table reference

```
          ------------------------------------------

                    Insert Table 4 about here

          ------------------------------------------
```

underlined. If the title is longer than one line, double space between lines. Double space after the title, and begin the table, as shown in Figure 9–15.

Table Notes. All table notes should appear at the end of the table, double spaced. The first note should be begun flush left (see Figure 9–15).

Figure Captions. Each figure is captioned. However the captions are not to be listed with the figure. Instead, each figure caption is typed on a separate sheet. Type the heading "Figure Captions," centered, 1½ inches from the top of the page. Double space and begin the first and all subsequent captions flush left. Type "Figure," underlined, followed by the appropriate number (also underlined), and a period. Then, without underlining, type the title of the caption, capitalizing only the first word and proper names (see Figure 9–16).

FIGURE 9–15
APA style table

Irradiated Frogs

21

Table 11

Radiation Sensitivity of Frogs

Group	c	1	2	3
Male				
With	81	59	54	48
Without	19	41	46	52
Female				
With	78	56	50	42
Without	22	44	50	58

Note. From "Frogs' ability to withstand radiation" by B. F. Short, Radiation Experiments, 23,
p. 432. Copyright 1984 by Bezzel Publishing. Reprinted by permission.

FIGURE 9–16
Sample of figures page in APA format

1½″ Irradiated Frogs

23

Figure Captions

Figure 14. Defects in irradiated frogs.

Figures. Figures are indicated by the same kind of break and insertion note in the text that is used for the placement of tables (see Figure 9–14). Like tables, figures are numbered consecutively according to the order in which they are referred to in the text. They are then included at the end of the text, after the figure captions. Each figure should have a label on the back of the sheet giving a short version of the article title, the figure number, and an indication of how the figure is to be placed.

EXERCISE 9.3:   Bailing Out Your Boss

Directions: You are a package designer for a major food products manufacturer. Recently the vice president of research and design asked for a recommendation from your boss, who is responsible for package design. For the purposes of long-range planning, the vice president wanted some indication of the direction your company's packaging should take in the future. After assembling the necessary information, your boss suddenly became ill. Since the report is due tomorrow, the boss asked you to finish it for him. He stressed the importance of "doing it up right" since the vice president and his superiors are sticklers for detail.

Go through the information your boss has assembled. Proofread and edit as necessary to keep your boss out of trouble. Then assemble everything in proper research report form, with all matters of organization, spelling, capitalization, grammar, and formatting attended to.

Good title?

According to August 1985 issue of modern plastics, in an article entitled "A Modern Plasticts Special Report on Packaging" plastics may well become the leading packaging material in the next few years (page 41). Plastics are now being used to package everything from McCormick Vodka to yogert to cookies to barb.b.q sauce, and even Hormel Lasangna (information from the same article pages 42–52). Plastics have been used for several years in the beverage industry with a great deal of success. The rise in packaging non liquids using plastics is due partly to the fact that, in recent months, better adhesives for sealing plastic packages have been invented. These adhesives help keep the food fresh and, more importantly, they also help to prevent tampering.

In the past, we have used packages made from a variety of materials: wooden packages for our gourmet cheeses, "tin" packages for our Crackle Crackers line, coated paper for our Captain Bob's Crunchy cookies, and metal cans and coated paper boxes for our Heartland vegetables. Coated paper packages and metal cans could easily be replaced by a more economical and more flexible material. The cheese package could also be replaced by a cheaper one. In fact, according to Jack Bullock, our head of cost accounting, the wooden packages are our biggest liabilty, costing us and average of $.34 a unit, even though we're having them manufactured overseas (I talked to Jack last week on Tuesday).

If we were able to use similar materials in each of our packaging lines it would be easier to promote our company image by creating a family appearance between all of our products. According to Tom Kelly, our vice president of retail marketing, we only have two or three items that are commonly associated with our company (vegetables and crackers). He feels, based on the research he has done, that the rest of our products would benefit in sales if they were associated with our company. (I talked with Tom last Friday. He said that he would be sending me the marketing information. I wonder how I should attach it to the report.)

The cracker package is another problem. Many people, according to Tom (same conversation) purchase our crackers because they like the container, he has noticed however, that cracker sales are down 2% and feels that this is due to the $.24 per package difference between our crackers and those of our nearest competitor. This package falls into the catagory of dual- use packages. According to a leading packaging authority, Stanley Sacharow, dual-use packages are generally successful to the degree that people are able to perceive a clear secondary use for the package (Sacharow discusses this on page 66 of his book Packaging as a marketing tool).

On the same page, Sacharow also points out that the dual-use package can provide additional advertising in the form of product visiblty since the average consumer hesitates to discard a useful container. If the consumer cannot easily perceive a second use for the container he or she will usually purchase another brand of product, rather than paying extra for a container that is of no immediate use. I talked with Sue Seagren, in new product marketing last Thursday, and she informs me that we are planning to market a gourmet cracker line. Perhapse we should switch to a cheeper package for our regular line of crackers and use the tin type of packaging for our gourmet line.

In a recent memo Linda Freely informed me that most of the people who are buying our cracker containers are buying them because they want to have a more permanent cracker container or they plan to use the container to store flower or sugar in. Only about 32% of the people who purchase our crackers do so without a purpose in mind for the container (Linda is the head of consumer affairs. The memo was dated last Thursday). Linda and I both feel that We could increase sales in the cracker line if we developed a more useful container.

I recently had a chance to review some package design by a Japanese packaging firm and was impressed by their use of color and packaging graphics. Examples of these packages can be found in Katsu Kimura Package Direction by Rikuyosha. I feel, that in addition to using plastics as our primary packaging material, we should explore the use of color and graphics in our packages with the goal of developing more appealing packages.

Based on the material I have been able to amass over the last week, I recommend that we switch over as much of our packaging to plastics as possible. The exception of course being our cracker package which I recommend we use on the gourmet cracker line, switching over to plastic packaging for the regular cracker line.

My department is currently finishing up the packaging for our new zippy mint after dinner mints, and should be in a position to begin exploring the use of plastic packages in more detail by the first of the month.

Beck, Fonald D. (1980) <u>Plastic product design</u>, 2nd ed. New York: Van Nostrand Reinhold Company.

Burns, D. and S. Venit (Oct. 1985) "PC story board: Business graphics get moving." <u>PC.</u> pp. 163–166.

Sacharow, S. (1982) <u>The PacKage as a Marketing Tool.</u> Randor: Chilton Book Company.

STUDENT MODEL

On the pages that follow, you will find a sample research paper prepared according to both the MLA and APA formats. The paper in the MLA style follows on page 224; the paper in the APA style begins on page 235. Study the version that your instructor wants you to follow, and use it as a guide as you prepare your own report.

James Knight

Professor Gaston

ENGL 102

April 6, 1986

Hypnosis Is No Parlor Trick

Since early childhood all of us have been exposed to the popular views of hypnosis. We have seen it practiced by cartoon characters like Tom and Jerry. We have heard that "The Shadow" of comic book and pulp fiction fame attributed his invisibility to a "special form of hypnotic suggestion." Many of us even sent in boxtops or bubblegum wrappers for books claiming to give us the secrets of hypnotism, much as we ordered similar books on fortune telling, ventriloquism, and magic.

As adults, we may see hypnotism on the stage, in night clubs, and on TV. So it is not surprising that most of us tend, unconsciously, to think of hypnotism in much the same way that we regard the simple magic tricks we used to order from the backs of comic books when we were children—as a hoax that can be perpetrated by anyone who owns the right gimmicks and can repeat the right patter.

But hypnotizing a human being is quite different from picking coins out of the air or restoring cut ropes. Hypnosis is no parlor trick. In fact, almost two centuries of scientific evidence attests to the fact that hypnosis is a very real phenomenon. Though it is not yet fully understood, doctors, dentists, and psychologists have long used hypnotism as both a treatment in itself and an adjunct to other treatments.

In 1843, before chemical anesthesia was widely available, one English surgeon reported that he had performed many surgical operations using hypnosis as the sole pain killer (Hilgard 233). In India, at about the same time, a young Scotch surgeon named James Esdaile used hypnotism to control pain and surgical trauma in over three hundred major operations and thousands of minor ones (Miller 19). Only the development of ether, which was quicker, surer, and less dependent on the psychological makeup of individual patients, prevented hypnosis from becoming the nineteenth century surgeon's anesthetic of choice (Gorsky and Gorsky 25).

Psychiatrists from the days of Freud to the present have used hypnosis as a method of unlocking patients' subconscious minds so that they could help them identify and resolve hidden conflicts. In fact, it was Freud's opinion that in order for psychotherapy to become widespread it would be necessary to use hypnotism as a shortcut (Miller 23). And because the hypnotic state is so puzzling, psychologists continue to study it (Orne and Hammer 139–40).

As a result, an increasingly wide range of uses have been discovered for hypnosis within the past thirty years. Doctors are once again finding uses for hypnotism, especially in pain control and in the reduction of pre- and postsurgical trauma. Faced with

Knight 3

evidence that patients who fear surgery have a much
higher death rate than those who are calm, doctors are
increasingly turning to hypnosis as a means of ridding
patients of debilitating fears and unconscious
conflicts (Cheek and LeCron 153-57). In fact, for
some minor surgical procedures, hypnosis is once again
the only anesthesia used (Miller 199; Cheek and LeCron
156).

An especially fruitful application of hypnosis
has been in teaching patients to cope with chronic or
long-term pain. With guidance, patients with cancer
and similar illnesses can be taught to use self-
hypnosis in the management of their pain. This
significantly reduces the amount of medication they
need and thus increases their clarity of mind, their
sense of control, and their ability to maintain the
integrity of personality and the dignity which
contribute to making life desirable.

Hypnosis is also being used to treat burn
victims. One surgeon reports that, if it is used soon
after the burn occurs, hypnotism can actually limit
the severity of the injury, decrease healing time, and
increase resistance to infection. As evidence, he
cites the case of a 28-year-old man

> whose leg was immersed in molten aluminum at
> 950 degrees Centigrade; he was hypnotized
> within 30 minutes, developed only a second
> degree burn, and although antibiotics were
> not used, had no infection. He was
> discharged from the hospital on the

nineteenth day and healed without scar

tissue formation on the leg. (Erwin 274)

Hypnosis, then, is no trick. It is an undeniable reality, not yet fully understood by science, which can be used by trained professionals to alleviate pain and promote healing. Like open heart surgery or radiation therapy, it is better left to those trained to use it. Hypnosis should not be regarded as a spectator sport. It has no more business in a theater or night club floor show than brain surgery has on a carnival midway--and for the same reason: such a casual use can be dangerous to the subject.

This danger is only increased by the ignorance of the general public on the subject of hypnosis. Unaware of the scientific research, they understandably doubt the reality of hypnotism and either take it too lightly or, half believing that it might be real, fear it for the wrong reasons. In fact, the more a typical layman has heard about hypnotism, the more likely he is to be seriously misinformed and thus--if the occasion arises--to willingly take part in "entertainment" that is truly dangerous.

It is perfectly understandable that an intelligent layperson would doubt the reality of hypnotism as it is popularly portrayed. The very notion that someone he knows well could, in just a few minutes, be plunged into such a strange state of consciousness naturally seems as unreal to him as the witch doctors and voodoo spells he has seen in grade B movies.

Knight 5

Nor does the widespread circulation of
sensational books on hypnotism give him any reason to
be open-minded. Their claims are often so outlandish
and their evidence so meagre that only a child could
take them seriously. Indeed, the cover of one
otherwise responsible book promises that with self-
hypnosis you can "stop smoking . . . lose weight . . .
shed your inhibitions--through the power of your inner
mind" (LeCron). More sensational books, available in
novelty shops or through mail-order houses
specializing in occult items, explain how hypnotism
can be used to bring out latent telepathic powers,
promote clairvoyance, and launch subjects on spiritual
journeys through time (Edmunds).

Such extravagant claims are easily laughed off by
those who have been cajoled, at one time or another,
into helping a stage hypnotist "put one over" on the
audience and have gone along with his fake
demonstrations for the amusement of the crowd. Neither
they nor the friends to whom they have later revealed
the deception have any way of knowing that what they
took part in is not what researchers, physicians, and
even other entertainers mean by "hypnotism."

Understandable as it is, such skepticism itself
introduces an element of danger when hypnotism is used
for casual entertainment. One major problem stems from
the fact that a subject hypnotized before a group,
unlike a patient in the clinic, is not alone with the
person who hypnotized him. At a party, for instance,
there are often one or two outspoken skeptics who will

Knight 6

try to "expose" the fakery, often by inflicting pain on the hypnotized person. Such "tests" amount to little more than torture. In one case the hypnotist was moved to demonstrate that his volunteer was actually in a trance by suspending her "with her head on one chair and her feet on another. He then stood on her abdomen" (Harding 163). The volunteer was in so much pain after the performance that she went to a hospital emergency room. She was subsequently admitted to the hospital for seven days, underwent extensive testing, was released and continued to suffer from headaches, backaches, and nerve conduction disturbances for at least six months (Harding 164).

In his book Hypnotism: Its Power and Practice, Peter Blythe records another such incident. The hypnotist placed a subject in a trance and instructed him that henceforth he was deaf, he could hear nothing. The hypnotist then fired a gun to demonstrate how effective his suggestion had been. The subject did not even flinch. However, when the hypnotist told the subject to awake, the subject failed to respond. He remained hypnotized because the hypnotist had told him he was deaf. As a result he could not "hear" the hypnotist's instructions to awake (Blythe 123).

Real harm can also occur accidentally when the process is not taken seriously by the subject's family and friends. Let's say for example that three or four people are hypnotized at a party and told that they are covered with itching powder. The hypnotist is aware of the dangers that audience interference poses,

so he has warned them to be absolutely silent while
the demonstration is taking place. The audience is
quiet and all goes well. But at the end of the
demonstration, the hypnotist either fails to wake one
of the people (possibly not realizing that she was
really hypnotized) or he wakes her incorrectly by not
emphasizing the suggestions necessary to remove
suggestions given during hypnosis. As the party goes
on the subject who was incorrectly wakened from her
trance continues to scratch because the itching powder
is still real to her. Her family and friends do not
take this scratching seriously because they think she
is simply carrying on the performance to get
attention. Finally the person scratches so much that
she develops skin lesions which subsequently become
infected. At this point, hopefully, her family finally
takes her problem seriously and seeks professional
help.

Hypnotism is not a parlor trick: It is not for an
amateur with a how-to-do-it book on hypnosis and no
training in psychology. Only a competent professional
should be allowed to practice hypnosis, and then only
when it is beneficial to and in the best interests of
the patient.

While hypnotism may look simple, it actually
involves much more than the repetition of a few words.
The hypnotist must safely, efficiently and accurately
determine who should and should not be hypnotized. He
is trained therefore to be aware of the two factors
that affect hypnotizability: the confidence of the

hypnotizer in the procedure and the resistance of the
subject (Blythe 25-27). A subject's resistance to
hypnotism can be the result of a variety of factors
including unconscious resistance, fear of losing
control, individual personality, bad past experience
with hypnosis, and lack of motivation (Cheek and
LeCron 21-22). The trained hypnotist knows how to
locate such resistance and to judge whether it is
resolvable or whether it eliminates a person as a
candidate for hypnotism.

Hypnotism is not a cure-all. The professional
understands its benefits, dangers, and limitations. He
understands what to watch and how to make allowances
for individual differences between patients. Not every
patient who can be hypnotized should be hypnotized.
Experts generally agree, for example, that it is
extremely dangerous to hypnotize someone who has
psychotic tendencies.

The responsible hypnotist can deal with
unexpected problems, such as the patient who has
difficulty in coming out of the trance state, or the
patient who acquires an unexpected behavior as the
result of hypnosis. One patient who was hypnotized and
"returned to his childhood" during a session reported
that in the week which followed, he found himself
reacting, and even sometimes thinking like a child.
Because the psychiatrist who hypnotized the patient
understood hypnotism, he was able to immediately
identify the problem. During the previous session he
had omitted to tell the patient, before bringing him

out of the trance, "and now you are no longer five years old, you are with me now, the date is . . . and you are . . . years old" (Blythe 124).

A responsible hypnotist is also careful to act within his own area of expertise. The dentist who uses hypnotism to relax or even anesthetize his patients before surgery knows he could be asking for trouble if he practices hypnotism at cocktail parties. One dental hypnotist who failed to recognize this fact was responsible for causing his patient to have a nervous breakdown. The dentist was at a cocktail party one evening and, as a source of amusement, he rehypnotized a male patient of his who also happened to be attending the party. While the patient was hypnotized, the dentist instructed him to act like a woman. This suggestion seems harmless enough, but it resulted in an acute psychiatric reaction because the patient had latent homosexual tendencies (Gerschman, Reade, and Burrows 474).

In the final analysis, hypnotism is a tool. It is not, in and of itself, any more dangerous than the use of general anesthesia, if it is used by a competent professional. Like anesthesia, hypnosis should not be used for general amusement or simply to satisfy casual curiosity. And in both cases you wouldn't allow a professional to treat you who didn't consider the treatment as something to be used carefully, in a controlled environment, under competent supervision. After all, hypnotism is not a parlor trick: It shouldn't be treated as one.

Knight 10

Works Cited

Blythe, Peter. Hypnotism: Its Power and Practice. New
    York: Taplinger Publishing Company, 1971.

Burrows, Graham D., and Lorraine Dennerstein. Handbook
    of Hypnosis and Psychosomatic Medicine. New York:
    Elsevier/North-Holland Biomedical Press, 1980.

Cheek, David B., and Leslie M. LeCron. Clinical
    Hypnotherapy. New York: Grune and Stratton, 1968.

Edmunds, Simeon. Hypnosis: Key to Psychic Powers.
    N.p.: n.d. N. pag.

Erwin, Dabney M. "Hypnosis in Burn Therapy." Hypnosis
    1979: Proceedings of the 8th International
    Congress of Hypnosis and Psychosomatic Medicine,
    Melbourne. Ed. Graham D. Burrows, David R.
    Collison, and Lorraine Dennerstein. New York:
    Elsevier/North-Holland Biomedical Press, 1979.
    269-276.

Gerschman, Jack A., Peter C. Reade, and Graham D.
    Burrows. "Hypnosis and Dentistry." Burrows and
    Dennerstein 443-475.

Gorskey, Benjamin H., and Susan R. Gorskey.
    Introduction to Medical Hypnosis. Garden City,
    NY: Medical Examination Publishing Co., 1981.

Harding, H. Clagett. "Complications Arising from
    Hypnosis for Entertainment." Hypnosis at its
    Bicentennial. Ed. Fred H. Frankel, and Harold S.
    Zamanski. New York: Plenum Press, 1976. 163-168.

Hilgard, Ernest R. "Hypnosis in the Treatment of
    Pain." Burrows and Dennerstein 233-267.

LeCron, Leslie M. Self Hypnotism: The Technique and

Knight 11

its Use in Daily Living. 1964. New York: Signet,
    1970.

McGill, Ormond. The Encyclopedia of Stage Hypnotism.
    N.p.: Abbott, n.d.

Miller, Michael M. Therapeutic Hypnosis. New York:
    Human Sciences Press, 1979.

Nelson, Alan R. Pseudo-hypnotism and Hypnotism by
    Radio. Unpublished manuscript, n.d.

Orne, Martin T., and A. Gordon Hammer. "Hypnosis."
    Encyclopaedia Britannica: Macropaedia. 1974.

Sample Research Paper in APA Format

Dangers of Public Skepticism

Toward Hypnosis

James Knight

Oldham University

Running head: DANGERS OF SKEPTICISM TOWARD HYPNOSIS

Hypnosis

2

Abstract

Scientific history shows the reality of hypnosis to
be established beyond doubt by its successful use
in medicine, dentistry and psychiatry. Yet the
public, being ignorant of this, fails to recognize
dangers in today's widespread abuse of hypnotism.
Evidence is presented to demonstrate that this is a
serious problem, and the conclusion is reached that
hypnosis can properly be used only by a qualified
professional working within his area of expertise
to perform services for the benefit of the
hypnotized subject.

Dangers of Public Skepticism

Toward Hypnosis

Since early childhood all of us have been
exposed to the popular views of hypnosis. We have
seen it practiced by cartoon characters like Tom
and Jerry. We have heard that The Shadow of comic
book and pulp fiction fame attributed his
invisibility to a "special form of hypnotic
suggestion." Many of us even sent in boxtops or
bubble gum wrappers for books claiming to give us
the secrets of hypnotism, much as we ordered
similar books on fortune telling, ventriloquism,
and magic.

As adults, we may see hypnotism on the stage,
in night clubs, and on TV. So it is not surprising
that most of us tend, unconsciously, to think of
hypnotism in much the same way that we regard the
simple magic tricks we used to order from the backs
of comic books when we were children--as a hoax
that can be perpetrated by anyone who owns the
right gimmicks and can repeat the right patter.

But hypnotizing a human being is quite
different from picking coins out of the air or
restoring cut ropes. Hypnosis is no parlor trick.
In fact, almost two centuries of scientific
evidence attests to the fact that hypnosis is a
very real phenomenon. Though it is not yet fully
understood, doctors, dentists, and psychologists
have long used hypnotism as both a treatment in

itself and an adjunct to other treatments.

In 1843, before chemical anesthesia was widely available, one English surgeon reported that he had performed many surgical operations using hypnosis as the sole pain-killer (Hilgard, 1980). In India, at about the same time, a young Scotch surgeon named James Esdaile used hypnotism to control pain and surgical trauma in over three hundred major operations and thousands of minor ones (Miller, 1978, p. 19). Only the development of ether, which was quicker, surer, and less dependent on the psychological makeup of individual patients, prevented hypnosis from becoming the nineteenth century surgeon's anesthetic of choice (Gorsky & Gorsky, 1981, p. 25).

Psychiatrists from the days of Freud to the present have used hypnosis as a method of unlocking patients' subconscious minds to help them identify and resolve hidden conflicts. In fact, it was Freud's opinion that, in order for psychotherapy to become widespread, it would be necessary to use hypnotism as a short cut (Miller, 1979). And because the hypnotic state is so puzzling psychologists continue to study it (Orne & Hammer, 1974).

As a result, an increasingly wide range of uses have been discovered for hypnosis within the past thirty years. Doctors are once again finding uses for hypnotism, especially in pain control and

in the reduction of pre- and post-surgical trauma.
Faced with evidence that patients who fear surgery
have a much higher death rate than those who are
calm, doctors are increasingly turning to hypnosis
as a means of ridding patients of debilitating
fears and unconscious conflicts (Cheek & LeCron,
1968). In fact, for some minor surgical procedures,
hypnosis is once again the only anesthesia used
(Cheek & LeCron, 1968; Miller, 1979).

An especially fruitful application of hypnosis
has been in teaching patients to cope with chronic
or long-term pain. With guidance, patients with
cancer and similar illnesses can be taught to use
self-hypnosis in the management of their pain. This
significantly reduces the amount of medication they
need and thus increases their clarity of mind,
their sense of control, and their ability to
maintain the integrity of personality and the
dignity which contribute to making life desirable.

Hypnosis is also being used to treat burn
victims. One surgeon reports that, if it is used
soon after the burn occurs, hypnotism can actually
limit the severity of the injury, decrease healing
time, and increase resistance to infection. As
evidence, he cites the case of a 28-year-old man

> whose leg was immersed in molten aluminum at
> 950 degrees Centigrade; he was hypnotized
> within 30 minutes, developed only a second
> degree burn, and although antibiotics were not

used, had no infection. He was discharged from
the hospital on the nineteenth day and healed
without scar tissue formation on the leg.
(Erwin, 1979, p. 274)

Hypnosis, then, is no trick. It is an
undeniable reality, not yet fully understood by
science, which can be used by trained professionals
to alleviate pain and promote healing. Like open
heart surgery or radiation therapy, it is better
left to those trained to use it. Hypnosis should
not be regarded as a spectator sport. It has no
more business in a theater or night club floor show
than brain surgery has on a carnival midway--and
for the same reason: such a casual use can be
dangerous to the subject.

This danger is only increased by the ignorance
of the general public on the subject of hypnosis.
Unaware of the scientific research, they
understandably doubt the reality of hypnotism and
either take it too lightly or, half believing that
it might be real, fear it for the wrong reasons. In
fact, the more a typical layman has heard about
hypnotism, the more likely he is to be seriously
misinformed and thus--if the occasion arises--to
willingly take part in "entertainment" that is
truly dangerous.

It is perfectly understandable that an
intelligent layman would doubt the reality of
hypnotism as it is popularly portrayed. The very

notion that someone he knows well could, in just a few minutes, be plunged into such a strange state of consciousness naturally seems as unreal to him as the witch doctors and voodoo spells he has seen in grade B movies.

Nor does the widespread circulation of sensational books on hypnotism give him any reason to be open-minded. Their claims are often so outlandish and their evidence so meagre that only a child could take them seriously. The cover of one such book, for instance, promises that with self-hypnosis you can "stop smoking . . . lose weight . . . shed your inhibitions—through the power of your inner mind" (LeCron, 1964/1971). Similar books, available in novelty shops or through mail-order houses specializing in occult items, explain how hypnotism can be used to bring out latent telepathic powers, promote clairvoyance, and launch subjects on spiritual journeys through time (Edmunds, n.d.).

Such extravagant claims are easily laughed at by those who have been cajoled, at one time or another, into helping a stage hypnotist "put one over" on the audience and have gone along with his fake demonstrations for the amusement of the crowd. Neither they nor the friends to whom they have later revealed the deception have any way of knowing that what they took part in is not what researchers, physicians, and even other entertainers mean by "hypnotism."

Understandable as it is, such skepticism
itself introduces an element of danger when
hypnotism is used for casual entertainment. One
major problem stems from the fact that a subject
hypnotized before a group, unlike a patient in the
clinic, is not alone with the person who hypnotized
him. At a party, for instance, there are often one
or two outspoken skeptics who will try to "expose"
the fakery, often by inflicting pain on the
hypnotized person. Such "tests" amount to little
more than torture. In one case the hypnotist was
moved to demonstrate that his volunteer was
actually in a trance by suspending her "with her
head on one chair and her feet on another. He then
stood on her abdomen" (Harding, 1978, p. 163). The
volunteer was in so much pain after the performance
that she went to a hospital emergency room. She was
subsequently admitted to the hospital for seven
days, underwent extensive testing, was released and
continued to suffer from headaches, backaches, and
nerve conduction disturbances for at least six
months (p. 164).

In his book Hypnotism: Its Power and Practice,
Peter Blythe records another such incident. The
hypnotist placed a subject in a trance and
instructed him that henceforth he was deaf, he
could hear nothing. The hypnotist then fired a gun
to demonstrate how effective his suggestion had

been. The subject did not even flinch. However, when the hypnotist told the subject to awake, the subject failed to respond. He remained hypnotized because the hypnotist had told him he was deaf. As a result he could not "hear" the hypnotist's instructions to awake (1971, p. 123).

Real harm can also occur accidentally when the process is not taken seriously by the subject's family and friends. Let's say for example that three or four people are hypnotized at a party and told that they are covered with itching powder. The hypnotist is aware of the dangers that audience interference poses, so he has warned them to be absolutely silent while the demonstration is taking place. The audience is quiet and all goes well. But at the end of the demonstration, the hypnotist either fails to wake one of the people (possibly not realizing that she was really hypnotized) or he wakes her incorrectly by not emphasizing the suggestions necessary to remove suggestions given during hypnosis. As the party goes on the subject who was incorrectly wakened from her trance continues to scratch because itching powder is still real to her. Her family and friends do not take this scratching seriously because they think she is simply carrying on the performance to get attention. Finally the person scratches so much that she develops skin lesions which subsequently become infected. At this point, hopefully, her

family finally takes her problem seriously and
seeks professional help.

Hypnotism is not a parlor trick: it is no
place for an amateur with a how-to-do-it book on
hypnosis and no training in psychology. Only a
competent professional should be allowed to
practice hypnosis, and then only when it is
beneficial to and in the best interests of the
patient.

While hypnotism may look simple, it actually
involves much more than the repetition of a few
words. The hypnotist must safely, efficiently and
accurately determine who should and should not be
hypnotized. He is trained therefore to be aware of
the two factors that effect hypnotizability: the
confidence of the hypnotizer in the procedure and
the resistance of the subject (Blythe, 1971, chap.
1). A subject's resistance to hypnotism can be the
result of a variety of factors including
unconscious resistance, fear of losing control,
individual personality, bad past experience with
hypnosis, and lack of motivation (Cheek & LeCron,
1968, chap. 1). The trained hypnotist knows how to
locate such resistance, and to judge whether it is
resolvable, or it whether eliminates a person as a
candidate for hypnotism.

Hypnotism is not a cure-all. The professional
understands its benefits, dangers, and limitations.
He understands what to watch and how to make

allowances for individual differences between patients. Not every patient who can be hypnotized should be hypnotized. Experts generally agree, for example, that it is extremely dangerous to hypnotize someone who has psychotic tendencies.

The responsible hypnotist can deal with unexpected problems, such as the patient who has difficulty in coming out of the trance state, or the patient who aquires an unexpected behavior as the result of hypnosis. One patient who was hypnotized and "returned to his childhood" during a session, reported that in the week which followed, he found himself reacting, and even sometimes thinking like a child. Because the psychiatrist who hypnotized the patient understood hypnotism, he was able to immediately identify the problem. During the previous session he had omitted to tell the patient, before bringing him out of the trance, "and now you are no longer five years old, you are with me now, the date is . . . and you are . . . years old" (Blythe, 1971, p. 124).

A responsible hypnotist is also careful to act within his own area of expertise. The dentist who uses hypnotism to relax or even anesthetize his patients before surgery knows he could be asking for trouble if he practices hypnotism at cocktail parties. One dental hypnotist who failed to recognize this fact was responsible for causing his patient to have a nervous breakdown. The dentist

was at a cocktail party one evening and, as a
source of amusement, he rehypnotized a male patient
of his who also happened to be attending the party.
While the patient was hypnotized, the dentist
instructed him to act like a woman. This suggestion
seems harmless enough, but it resulted in an acute
psychiatric reaction because the patient had latent
homosexual tendencies (Gerschman, Reade & Burrows,
1980, p. 474).

In the final analysis, hypnotism is a tool. It
is not, in and of itself, any more dangerous than
the use of general anesthesia, if it is used by a
competent professional. Like anesthesia, hypnosis
should not be used for general amusement or simply
to satisfy casual curiosity. And in both cases you
wouldn't allow a professional to treat you who
didn't consider the treatment as something to be
used carefully, in a controlled environment, under
competent supervision. After all, hypnotism is not
a parlor trick: it shouldn't be treated as one.

Hypnosis

13

References

Blythe, P. (1971). Hypnotism: Its power and
    practice. New York: Taplinger Publishing
    Company.

Burrows, G. D., & Dennerstein, L. (1980). Handbook
    of hypnosis and psychosomatic medicine. New
    York: Elsevier/North-Holland Biomedical Press.

Cheek, D. B., LeCron, L. M. (1968). Clinical
    hypnotherapy. New York: Grune and Stratton.

Edmunds, S. (n.d.). Hypnosis: Key to psychic
    powers. N.p.: n.p.

Erwin, D. M. (1979). Hypnosis in burn therapy. In
    G. D. Burrows, D. R. Collison, & L. Dennerstein
    (Eds.), Hypnosis 1979: Proceedings of the 8th
    International Congress of Hypnosis and
    Psychosomatic Medicine, Melbourne (pp. 269-276).
    New York: Elsevier/North-Holland Biomedical
    Press.

Gerschman, J. A., Reade, P. C., & Burrows, G. D.
    (1980). Hypnosis and dentistry. In G. D. Burrows
    & L. Dennerstein (Eds.), Handbook of hypnosis
    and psychosomatic medicine (pp. 443-475). New
    York: Elsevier/North-Holland Biomedical Press.

Gorsky, B. H., & Gorsky, S. R. (1981). Introduction
    to medical hypnosis. Garden City: Medical
    Examination Publishing Co., Inc.

Harding, H. C. (1976). Complications arising from
    hypnosis for entertainment. In F. H. Frankel &

Hypnosis

14

H. Zamanski (Eds.), <u>Hypnosis at its bicentennial</u>
(pp. 163–168). New York: Plenum Press.

Hilgard, E. R. (1980). Hypnosis in the treatment of
pain. In G. D. Burrows & L. Dennerstein (Eds.),
<u>Handbook of hypnosis and psychosomatic medicine</u>
(pp. 233–267). New York: Elsevier/North–Holland
Biomedical Press.

LeCron, L. M. (1971). <u>Self hypnotism: The technique</u>
<u>and its use in daily living</u>. New York: Signet.
(Original work published in 1964.)

McGill, O. (n.d.). <u>The encyclopedia of stage</u>
<u>hypnotism</u>. N.p.: Abbott.

Miller, M. M. (1979). <u>Therapeutic hypnosis</u>. New
York: Human Sciences Press.

Nelson, A. R. (n.d.). <u>Pseudo–hypnotism and</u>
<u>hypnotism by radio</u>. Unpublished manuscript.

Orne, M. T. & Hammer, A. G. (1974). Hypnosis. In
<u>Encyclopaedia Britannica: Macropaedia</u> (pp. 133–
140). Chicago: Helen Hemingway Benton.

10

Doing Some
Primary Research
of Your Own

For the most part, the library research explained in this book deals with what are called *secondary sources*. It puts you in touch with accounts of events that you did not witness and reports of research that you yourself did not conduct. This kind of secondary research is always important; it gives you the background and perspective you must have in order to conduct your own firsthand research.

When a researcher gathers her own data, conducts her own analysis, and reaches her own conclusions, she is engaged in *primary* research. You may remember the quick overview of research at the beginning of this book. Most of the kinds of research described in chapter 1 were examples of primary research. To give you a detailed mastery of all those methods of conducting primary research is beyond the scope of this book. Indeed, few scholars ever become at home with all of them, for each demands its own kind of precise thinking and is suited only to a certain range of questions addressed only to certain kinds of data.

Your future college work is sure to contain parts of courses, if not whole courses, that will show you how the principles of analysis and investigation described there apply to research in your field. Whether your future responsibilities require you to conduct research yourself or merely to read reports of it and evaluate its relevance for your work, you will need some specialized instruction in research methodology to equip you fully for what lies ahead.

Meanwhile, the purpose of your work in this course will be more apparent if you have a reasonably good idea of the kind of research methods you may find yourself concentrating on when the opportunity arises to use what you have learned here. For that reason, we explain below a

249

few informal methods for developing new knowledge and suggest that you try your hand at using one or two of them, just to get a feel for the thinking that goes into this kind of work.

In many everyday situations, where the cost of a mistake is not great or where a limited amount of primary research is needed to confirm judgments arrived at by other means, the informal methods described here may be sufficient. Journalists, for instance, depend heavily on interviews in their day-to-day work. Politicians and administrators often use informal surveys without going to the trouble and expense required to ensure fully the dependability of their findings. And direct observation has long been used to develop information needed by clinicians and field workers in a wide range of professions. When used with integrity and discretion, therefore, even these informal methods of investigation, "quick and dirty" though they are, can make important contributions to knowledge.

THE INTERVIEW AS A RESEARCH METHOD

It often happens that the information needed by the researcher is already known to someone else. Depending on the circumstances, the person with that information may realize its importance but be uncertain just who could make proper use of it. Or he may do research in a related field, where experts take for granted facts that would be of crucial importance to researchers in another. He may even be an ordinary person—a private soldier, a consumer, a teenager—whose location or experiences put him in possession of information of great interest to the researcher.

The obvious procedure for the researcher in such cases is to locate the person with the information needed and ask him to share it. The interview is therefore a simple and effective research tool, though not always an easy one to use. Its proper use requires that the researcher (1) identify the person with the information she needs; (2) enlist the cooperation of that person; (3) conduct the interview in a manner that develops the necessary information without distortion or bias; and (4) if possible, develop a record for later reference.

Many times, the first of these requirements, finding a person with the information needed, is difficult if not impossible. For instance, it has been estimated that the federal government employs about 710,000 experts representing almost every conceivable area of human knowledge. Many of these experts are eager to share their knowledge with people who can make use of it. They owe their jobs to their ability and willingness to serve the public in this way.

But consider a commodity investor who suddenly learns that his vast holdings in potatoes have mysteriously doubled in value and who must decide within twenty-four hours whether or not to sell. How can he locate in that vast bureaucracy the *right* expert to tell him what is causing the sudden rise in potato prices and whether it is likely to continue?

This very problem was solved quickly and profitably in 1975 by Matthew Lasko, a Washington-based researcher who was hired by the broker. With a few phone calls, he identified the proper agricultural economist to talk to and arranged an interview, which turned out to take 2½ hours because, as he later wrote, the expert "had spent his lifetime studying the supply and demand for the potato and *finally* someone with a genuine need sought his expertise." That researcher's success, incidentally, was so phenomenal that in four years he had expanded his one-man operation to a million-dollar business with thirty-five employees—all specializing in locating information from governmental sources that is needed by clients willing to pay well for it.

The point to note, however, is that his success is not due to elaborate equipment or unusual modes of thought. In addition to skills in library research of the kind you learn in this book, his most important research tool is the personal interview.

The same observation could be made about the marketing coordinator of a chain of midwestern farm stores charged with the responsibility of suggesting operational changes that would improve sales. In such a situation, it might be almost as risky to rely on the advice of a distant expert as it would be to make changes at random and hope for the best. Instead of using Lasko's strategy of going to an expert, therefore, Mary Bouchard put the interview to work in a different way.

She arranged interviews with her customers—over ten thousand of them, during peak hours at forty stores—for she realized that, expert or not, customers know what they like in a store. If she could ask them in the right way, listen with understanding, and turn their collective answers into sound business recommendations, they would tell her exactly what she should do to win more of their business. These two examples, being so different, suggest correctly that interviews are useful in a wide range of research activities.

To make interviews work best, though, you should usually follow certain specific procedures before, during, and after each interview.

Before the Interview

Much of your most important work takes place before the interview. First, you must decide as specifically as possible just what it is that you wish to find out. Then you must choose one or more informants who have the information you need, contact them and persuade them to help you, and schedule interviews at agreeable times and places. Most important of

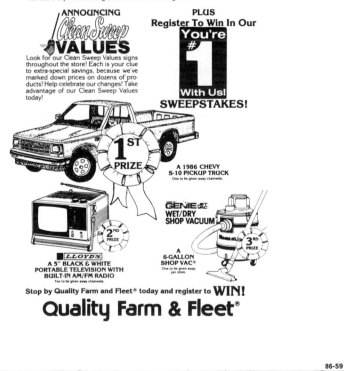

all, you must plan each interview, so that you will make the most of the time with your informant.

Defining Your Purpose. It is not essential that these preliminary trials be as strictly centered on one carefully phrased research question as is the case in the more formal investigations discussed in chapter 6. Still, you should give all research projects—these included—as much focus as possible.

This means that you should have a specific, limited goal in mind even before you contact your informant. You do not want to ask a World War II veteran to tell you "about" his war experiences. Such a vague undertaking gives no guidance to you or your informant. Plan to concentrate instead on something specific and attainable. How many of the innumerable foul-ups at Omaha Beach was he aware of during the invasion of Normandy, and how did he react to them at the time? Or perhaps, how were American soldiers received by French civilians from D-Day to the end of the war?

An ROTC student who knows from his study of military history about the incredibly bad luck of the American forces during the amphibious landing at Omaha Beach might well be interested in the first question, while a sociology or psychology major might be more interested in the second. In either case, however, the proper infomation is not likely to be developed unless the interviewer begins with a reasonably concrete goal in mind.

Finding an Informant. Genuine research almost always requires that you define your goal before deciding whom to interview; obviously, you must know what you wish to find out before you can judge who might be able to help you. With that understood, however, no great harm is done if—for the purpose of this introductory exercise—you simplify things by choosing a topic that capitalizes on the availability of a particularly valuable informant. So if you happen to know a professional wrestler, or a former associate of Martin Luther King's, or a person who has triumphed over great adversity, there is no reason that you should not shape your inquiry to draw on the human resource at hand. Indeed, the odds are overwhelming that you know a number of people whose memories and observations can help you to a fuller understanding of questions of interest to you. If you show interest in people's backgrounds, hobbies, and unusual jobs, you are sure to find some whose unusual accomplishments make them promising subjects to interview.

Regardless of the order in which you perform them, though, your first two steps should be to define the topic of your inquiry and locate an appropriate informant.

Winning the Cooperation of Your Informant. Unless you have some special reason to believe your informant will welcome an opportunity to be interviewed, you should be mindful that you are requesting a favor of him or her. This does not mean that you should be intimidated. (Most people enjoy being interviewed; wouldn't you?) However, it does mean that you should plan your approach so as to make it easy for him to say yes. Phone in advance and tell what you are studying and why you think his help would be particularly valuable to you. Explain that you would like to schedule a time when he has a few minutes to chat with you in some depth about your topic.

In this conversation, as in all subsequent contacts with your informant, you should be cheerful, open, optimistic, and—above all—courteous. You should also plan your call so that you can touch all the bases quickly and concisely. This suggests indirectly that the interview will not waste time with needless floundering. Whether or not the interview is granted, be modest on your own behalf and complimentary to him throughout. Often a source who is unable or unwilling to be interviewed himself will help you in other ways or refer you to another qualified informant, if you simply accentuate the positive.

When the informant agrees to be interviewed, be ready then and there to suggest several possible times. Know your own commitments so that you can concentrate on choosing a time and place that is convenient for your informant and favorable for the business of the interview.

Planning the Interview. The job of an interviewer is to make the informant comfortable in talking freely, to listen attentively, and to use questions where necessary to develop the information needed. It usually helps to write out twelve to twenty questions in advance, leaving space on your pad for notes on the answers given. Take care to sequence these questions so that you start with the easiest and least threatening and save until last any that your informant may be unable or unwilling to answer.

Take care also that you word your questions in such a way that the informant is encouraged to volunteer information that you might not think to ask about. Save questions about details and questions designed merely to confirm what you already know until late in the interview. Your first job is to listen to your respondent. So normally you should begin with your most general, most open-ended questions.

You should plan something like this for an opener: "I am trying to get an idea of what a typical work day would be like for a policeman in Old Hickory. What can you tell me that might give me a sense of what your job is and how you go about doing it?" Notice that such a question gives the informant a good deal of control over what he tells you; for that reason most subjects are likely to talk more freely.

Surprisingly enough, though, when an informant seems particularly reticent or suddenly clams up in mid-interview, it sometimes helps to reverse the procedure and go with short-answer questions directed to specific facts that are well known to him. These are usually less threatening, so some sources warm to the interview better while dealing with them.

Plan follow-up questions to ensure that you cover your subject thoroughly, and be sure that all those questions lead the conversation towards rather than away from your topic of investigation. But word them so that they too invite the informant to give full, expansive answers rather than crisp perfunctory ones. Ask, "What are some of the things you like most and some of the things you hate most about your job?" rather than, "Do you feel that policemen in a small town get the respect they deserve?"

During the Interview

Make sure that you arrive on time, fully equipped, and prepared to begin on a friendly but businesslike basis. Bring with you the stenographic pad with your list of questions, an ample supply of sharpened pencils, and, if you have one, a small, battery-powered tape recorder in good working order. It is better, though, if none of these things are obvious when you introduce yourself. Keep them in a briefcase or large purse until they are needed.

When you have thanked the informant for his time, and exchanged pleasantries, remind him of the purpose of your study, and ask the first question. Do this without bringing out your note pad; some people become uneasy when they realize that you will take down what they say. Let your infomant warm to the topic a little first. When your informant is talking comfortably, casually explain that his information is important to your study and you do not want to rely totally on your memory of it. Ask for permission to record your conversation or, if you have no recorder, to take a few notes. Even after permission is given, it is better to set the recorder where you can see it but where it will be out of sight of the informant.

With those essentials out of the way, concentrate on getting your informant to tell you what you need to know. Listen carefully, take appropriate notes, and test your understanding when you are in doubt by repeating what you understand him to be saying. Avoid asking leading questions or expressing your own judgments about what you are told, particularly if they might be taken as disapproval of your informant.

As he talks, follow your list of prepared questions, noting when each has been answered sufficiently. Make notes of follow-up questions you need to ask to clarify obscure points or to complete partial answers. As the interview draws to a close, ask any questions from your prepared list that have not been touched on. Then ask the follow-up questions listed in your notes, and conclude by giving the informant a chance to add any further thoughts that he thinks might be helpful. Thank him, and as you take your leave, ask if he would mind your phoning if you find, in writing up your report, that you are uncertain exactly what he said or what he meant on some important point.

After the Interview

As soon as possible, find a private place and go over your notes, writing out the thoughts behind any abbreviations or personal symbols you used. If you taped the interview, listen to it with your notes at hand while you focus on the purpose of your interview. Decide how all your information bears on your purpose, and begin while your memory is still fresh to plan your report. Memory fades fast once you turn to other activities. If you find that a follow-up call is necessary, wait until you have identified all the outstanding questions so that you will not have to call your informant more than once. Be sure to send him a note of thanks.

EXERCISE 10.1:   Doing Some Interview Research of Your Own

Find one or more persons whose backgrounds enable them to shed additional light on some event, period, or person that you have read about or studied in school. Conduct the necessary interview(s), and write a four–five page summary of your findings. Be sure to restrict your inquiry to one predetermined aspect of your chosen topic. Use the following examples to start you thinking about the interview possibilities available to you.

1. Find out from your grandmother or some other appropriate person what life was like for housewives during World War II. How were they affected, for instance, by rationing, scrap iron collections, the campaign to save bacon grease, and the absence of men who had been drafted?

2. Find out from someone who joined and later dropped out of an extremist political group or religious cult how he now views his own motivations at the time of those decisions. Are his perceptions consistent with what you learn about such groups in your sociology or psychology courses?

3. Find the oldest person you can locate, and ask him or her to tell you how limitations on transportation or communication made his or her childhood different from yours. What was life like when cars were still a novelty, gravel roads were called highways, and talking movies, radio, and TV were all beyond imagination?

4. Talk with one veteran who served willingly in Vietnam and one man who intentionally avoided the draft. Compare their perceptions of the war and its effects on the country.

5. Interview someone who has succeeded quite well in some line of endeavor. Find out what advice they would give a young person starting out in the same field today, what it takes to win promotion in that field, and what college courses they wish they had taken to prepare better for it. (If you do

not know a person established in your field of interest, perhaps your college placement service can put you in touch with someone; many placement of-fices keep files on alumni who are willing to talk with students.)

THE SURVEY AS A RESEARCH PROCEDURE

It often happens that the information needed by the researcher is not in the possession of any one person. A great many people may each have a fragment of the truth she is trying to get at. Was your high school English teacher a good one? Do the college librarians give courteous service? Interviewing is, at best, a hit-or-miss way of going about answering questions like these. The answers you get will obviously depend on whom you happen to ask. But what you want to know is how *most* students react to the teacher and how the conduct of the librarians is *generally* perceived. To trace such general patterns, you must bring together information about the reactions of a great many people—more than you could possibly interview in depth with the time and money that is likely to be available.

One common solution is to construct a questionnaire that can be quickly answered and that will tell you just what you want to know about one person's knowledge or opinion of the subject under investigation. Getting a large number of the right people to answer the questions on such a questionnaire is called a "survey." The people whose answers are tabulated in a survey are called "respondents."

Because the questionnaire puts identical questions to every respondent and gets answers that are easily combined, the tabulated results can give a good picture of how many people hold which views. To be positive that this picture is accurate, the researcher has to take special steps in writing the questions, in order to ensure the statistical integrity of the answers given. She must also use special techniques to make sure that the people who complete the questionnaire are genuinely representative of the group she wants to study and to analyze accurately and perceptively the tabulated answers.

Even without such sophisticated checks, however, surveys can develop suggestive evidence that is useful in making many everyday decisions. A teacher interested in improving his own classroom performance can ask his students to complete questionnaires giving their anonymous ratings of various aspects of his teaching. A college student who wonders whether others are upset as she is about the substandard food served in her dorm could survey fellow students to see whether she would have support for an official complaint.

Using survey research productively requires that the following steps be taken, more or less in the order shown: (1) defining the goal of the study; (2) writing appropriate questions; (3) formatting the questionnaire;

(4) testing and revising the questionnaire; (5) administering the questionnaire; and (6) tabulating and reporting the results.

Defining Your Goal

Because you must target the questions on your questionnaire to get the infomation you need, it is very important that you begin your survey with a well-defined purpose in mind. Often you can only define your purpose after a certain amount of background reading. Often, too, it helps to interview people with special knowledge of or interest in your topic, while you are clarifying the goal of your study.

Suppose, for instance, you belong to a small community improvement organization that has been barely holding together during its five years of existence. Your ten or twelve regular members have not gotten results from the city government when they have petitioned for corrective action, because the officials doubt that such a small group speaks for anybody other than its own members. Given the attitude of the city officials, it seems, the group cannot succeed at its efforts unless it has more members, and it cannot attract more members until it has chalked up some successes. At the last meeting, the question was asked, "What goals could we adopt immediately that the people in this community *would* support wholeheartedly?"

After a good bit of rambling discussion that got nowhere, you realized that the organization will surely fall apart unless it quickly adopts new projects popular enough to attract new members. So you volunteered to survey the adults who use the local community center, to see what concerns are uppermost in their minds. How should you proceed?

Your goal is to determine what projects stand the best chance of winning widespread support. So you would be wise to talk with a number of people while you are deciding which possibilities will be named in your questionnaire. Finally, though, you come up with a list of nine worthwhile projects that were mentioned at the meeting or by the people you interviewed.

Writing Appropriate Questions

Multiple choice and true/false questions of the kind you have seen on objective tests are examples of "forced-choice" questions. They are called that because respondents must choose one of the answers provided; they are not free to compose their own. Though harder to write, forced-choice questions produce survey data that are easier to process and interpret than those produced by the open-ended questions you were encouraged to use in the interview.

We recommend that for your first effort you use forced-choice questions for all except the last item on your questionnaire. The last question might then be something like this: "Please use this space to tell us anything else you know of that might help us find ways that the Neighborhood Improvement Coalition could better serve this community." Such an open-ended question makes it possible for interested respondents to clarify earlier answers or contribute good ideas that you might have overlooked when you wrote your forced-choice questions.

Much of the skill of the survey researcher consists in shaping forced-choice questions that will develop precisely the data needed. The following samples illustrate the forms most frequently used in survey research.

Two-Choice Questions

Please tell us a little about yourself and your past experience with the Neighborhood Improvement Coalition (NIC). [Place check marks in the appropriate blanks.]

__ man	__ married	__ have children at home
__ woman	__ single	__ no children at home

__ I have never been a member of the NIC

__ I am now or have been a member of NIC

Checklists

Please check each item that names an important reason you have never attended a NIC meeting.

__ I have never heard of NIC.

__ I do not know enough about NIC to know whether I would be interested.

__ The projects that NIC has undertaken are of little or no importance to me.

__ I disagree with some of NIC's goals.

__ It is a waste of time; NIC never accomplishes anything.

__ I do not think NIC goes about things in the right way.

__ All my time is already committed.

Multiple-Choice Questions

About how many times in the past two years have you or some members of your immediate family had property vandalized? (Check one.)

__ never

__ once or twice

__ three or four times

__ five times or more

What is your estimate of the total dollar value of your family's losses from vandalism during the past two years?

___ zero

___ $1–150

___ $151–300

___ $301–450

___ more than $450

Agree/Disagree Scales

Place the appropriate number in the blank before each statement to show how strongly you agree or disagree with it.

Number	*Meaning*
1	strongly agree
2	agree
3	agree with reservations
4	no opinion
5	disagree with reservations
6	disagree
7	strongly disagree

___ Police protection in this neighborhood is not as good as that in most other neighborhoods that I know about.

___ I would be willing to attend a meeting to help the police organize a crime watch in my neighborhood.

___ The most important need in this neighborhood is for better child care facilities for working mothers.

Ranking Questions

Several suggested community needs are listed below. Put the number 1 in the blank before the need you consider most important, a 2 beside the second most important need, and continue until you have ranked all the needs listed.

___ day care facilities for children of working mothers

___ recreational facilities for teenagers

___ security lights in alleys, parks, and isolated areas

___ control of vandalism

___ health care for the needy

___ home visitation for the disabled

___ recreation for senior citizens

Formatting the Questionnaire

If possible, have a couple of friends read through the questions you have written and point out where they find the wording awkward or the meaning unclear. Then revise, not only at those locations but everywhere else you find an opportunity to shorten, simplify, or clarify a question. Unless you plan to mail your questionnaire along with a cover letter as explained below, your next step should be to draft a short introduction for the questionnaire. Begin with a statement of the purpose of the survey and the use to which the results will be put. Estimate how long it will take to complete the questionnaire, and mention some good reasons that the respondent might want to devote that much time to such a worthwhile project. (Remember, the value of all survey research depends on the willingness of the right people to provide information; a high percentage of returns, therefore, is important to the validity of your survey.)

Eliminate all questions about nonessentials and all that duplicate information requested by other questions. Then arrange the remaining questions in the most logical order. Usually it is better to keep questions on the same topic together because that makes them easier to understand. When possible, keep questions in the same format together, for if all the checklists, all the multiple-choice questions, etc., are grouped together, the completion instructions can be simpler and less repetitious.

Read through the questionnaire from the beginning, imagining that you are a respondent seeing it for the first time. Be sure that all the necessary instructions are included, located properly, and worded for easy comprehension. Experiment with various formats until you're sure you have found the most inviting one.

Testing and Revising the Questionnaire

No matter how confident you are at this point, find a group similar to the one you plan to survey and get them to complete the questionnaire. At the very least, have several people complete it, and interview them to see whether they have comments or suggestions about how it could be improved. Then study their answers carefully, looking for answers that appear to be irrelevant or to contradict each other. These usually indicate that either the questions or the completion instructions confused the respondent. Make the necessary revisions, and arrange for the questionnaire to be reproduced in sufficient quantity.

Administering the Questionnaire

Most survey research is conducted through the mail. Questionnaires are mailed to a randomly chosen sample of respondents from the group to be studied, accompanied by a cover letter and a preaddressed, stamped return envelope. The cover letter is carefully worded to persuade the respondent to participate in the study. It usually underscores the importance of the survey, the tangible benefits or improvements that may be made on the basis of its findings, and the importance of having each respondent's views so that the researcher's information will be accurate and complete.

We suggest that, for this first effort, you try to deliver your questionnaires in person. Depending on the nature of your project, it may be possible for you to distribute them to certain classes or to position yourself where logical respondents are passing by so that you can hand them out as people come and go. Personal delivery allows you to explain orally the points normally explained in a cover letter and usually increases the response rate.

At the time the questionnaires are delivered, be sure that each respondent knows exactly how and when to return them. If possible, get an address or phone number so that if the questionnaire is not returned on time, you can phone or send reminder cards to the laggards. This usually makes quite an improvement in the return rate. Returns are often higher, also, if respondents are assured of anonymity. So if it is not important that you know which information comes from which people, do not have respondents identify themselves. Emphasize this anonymity on the questionnaire and in the cover letter. When you do that, of course, you make it impossible to contact those who have not responded. So you should decide in advance whether it is procrastination or reluctance to be identified that is likely to have the most dampening effect on your response rate.

Tabulating and Reporting the Results

Take a blank questionnaire and go through the questionnaires one at a time, tallying their answers in the appropriate spaces on your blank. For instance, if thirty-two respondents completed a questionnaire containing this item, the results might look like this:

What is your estimate of the total dollar value of your family's losses from vandalism during the past two years?

___ zero   //   (6%)

___ $1–150   ﷼ ﷼ ﷼ //   (53%)

___ $151–300   ﷼ ///   (25%)

___ $301–450   ////   (13%)

___ more than $450   /   (3%)

After all tallies are completed, they should be totalled and turned into percentages, as shown in the circled figures above.

Then you should read through the answers to that final open-ended question, to see what you can learn from them. Pay particular attention to suggestions or observations that are made more than once; in fact, you should make a note of each of them and put a tally beside the appropriate notation every time you encounter a repetition. Underline any particularly interesting comments so that you can find them quickly if you want to mention or quote them while drafting your report.

By reviewing your tally sheet and glancing over the underlined passages, you should now have a pretty good idea of the answer to the research question or questions you set out to investigate. It is time to summarize those findings in a report.

Here is one good way to organize your paper:

Background. Begin by explaining what problems, needs, or questions made your survey necessary or desirable. Why would anyone need or want to know what you set out to learn?

Statement of the Problem. Explain exactly what you set out to learn. Make clear what is and is not included in that goal.

Explain Your Research Procedure. How did you go about designing the questionnaire? With whom did you talk? From whom did you accept suggestions for topics to explore in it? Whose answers did you hope to record with your survey? How did you deliver your questionnaire? What percentage of the group you hoped to study actually received questionnaires? What percentage of those who got questionnaires returned them? Insofar as their answers to your questions are concerned, what reason do you have for believing that your respondents are or are not representative of the total group you hoped to study?

Present Your Findings. The tabulated answers constitute the raw data for your findings, which will be presented in your report in one of two ways, either by verbal summary or visually, in charts and graphs. Unless you have a computer that will prepare visuals, rely on verbal summary for this informal survey. So as not to bore your readers with excessive detail, select for inclusion only the figures that seem to shed light on the questions under investigation. However, you should always include any data that seem puzzling. Academic honesty requires that these be included, especially if they run counter to your final conclusions. A summary of the tabulation shown above might read, "Although most of the losses due to vandalism were small (53% were less than $150), almost everyone (94%) had experienced some loss, and 13% reported losses in the $301–450 range. One respondent's losses were greater than $450. Vandalism is clearly a significant problem to these respondents."

Draw Conclusions and Make Recommendations. Use the data just summarized to give pointed answers to the question or questions you set out to investigate. Account for answers that do not seem consistent with your expectations or conclusions, if you can. If not, acknowledge the difficulty, and give your reason for drawing the conclusions you do in spite of it. If it is appropriate for you to make recommendations and if your findings warrant doing so, conclude by stating what those recommendations are and showing how they follow from the evidence you have presented.

EXERCISE 10.2:   Conducting Your Own Survey

Identify a problem that could be clarified by getting members of some group to pool their knowledge and perceptions. Construct a questionnaire that will develop the necessary information, and administer it to as many respondents as you can get. (We suggest that you choose a study which will produce 25–50 questionnaires.) Tabulate the results and report your findings in a 7–10 page report. Use the following examples to help get you started.

1. Survey a group of students in your dorm to find out how many of them have and how many have not participated in student government in any way. What are the reasons for their participation or lack of it?
2. Survey a group of college freshmen to learn how well their high school English classes prepared them for the work now required of them in freshman English.
3. Survey a group of high school students to find out what academic subjects (or musical groups, or styles, or fads) are most popular with them and why.
4. Look up Wentworth and Flexner's *Thesaurus of Slang* in your college library, and compile a list of twenty-five slang words from some earlier period. Then survey a cross-section of today's college students to see how many have heard them and know their meanings.

FIELD OBSERVATION AS A RESEARCH METHOD

In the 1920s the great Swiss psychologist Jean Piaget began a long series of intensive observations of young children at the Rousseau Institute in Geneva. At different times, he watched for different behaviors. For a long while, he watched preschoolers at play, observing who talked to whom about what, noticing particularly the differences in conversational skills between younger and older children. At another time, he singled out individual youngsters, and concentrated on the questions they asked. During one period, for instance, he listed every "why" question asked by one youngster so that he could later classify those questions according to the kind of information that the child seemed to be trying to obtain.

In this famous example of scientific field observation, Piaget filled his notebooks with details of child behavior that must have puzzled, vexed, and frustrated countless mothers and nannies through the centuries. But Piaget did not ask, as most parents do when faced with what seems to be willful childishness, "When will they learn to play without fighting?" or "Will they *ever* grow up?"

He asked a more objective, more tolerant kind of question when he reviewed his data. "What clues do we have here to the way the child's mind works at this age?" "How does he see the world and his place in it?" "What is he trying to accomplish in his own world as he perceives it at this point in his development?" By contemplating questions like these, by working with the data from those early observations, and by supplementing them with a wide variety of other research procedures over a lifetime of investigation, Piaget produced a theory of child development that has guided research in this area for over half a century.

Piaget's early work is such a classical case of how field observation can uncover new knowledge with far-reaching implications that we will often mention it as an example during this discussion. First, though, let us consider a couple of other examples, so that we can begin to appreciate the flexibility, the power—and the difficulty—of field observation as a research technique. One example deals with something that you have probably looked at but never seen, the other with something that you have almost certainly never had an opportunity to see.

What you have no doubt glanced at, if you have spent any time in an American city, are the small groups of men who congregate in informal groups on certain street corners in working-class neighborhoods. This informal "hanging out" is so common that most urban dwellers take it for granted. We look at it occasionally, but we do not see it. At the very most, we may notice that the same faces seem to appear on the same corner day after day. But of the people behind those faces, of the human needs they satisfy in their street-corner congregations, and of the implications of such groups for us as taxpayers, business people, educators, and government administrators we know nothing. How could we?

About the only way to gain that kind of understanding would be to adopt the method used by the urban anthropologist Elliot Liebow. He moved into one of those neighborhoods, won admittance to such a street-corner society, and spent several months observing it from the inside. He tried to ensure that the only difference between him and the other members was that, after hanging out with them, he would always go directly to his room and write a detailed log of what had just happened. Many of his most important observations, along with his professional evaluation and interpretation of what that group meant to the human experience of its members, are summarized in the book *Tally's Corners*, which is required reading in many sociology and anthropology courses. If yours happens to be one of them, then you have before you an excellent example of how field observation can extend a researcher's understanding into previously uncharted territory.

Perhaps an even better example is that of Jane Goodall, whose interests in chimpanzees went far beyond anything she could find out in even the most realistic laboratory setting or zoo. She wanted to know how they organized themselves, found food, fled from or fought enemies, and raised their young in their *natural* habitat. So this extraordinary woman moved to the African jungle, lived where the chimpanzees lived, stayed until she became a natural feature of the location, and watched, made notes, and studied aspects of chimpanzee behavior that no qualified observer had ever seen before. Such are the advantages of observation in the field, where whatever is being investigated can be studied in its natural surroundings, with a minimum of interference or distortion from the researcher's procedures.

Basic Principles of Field Observation

Each of the examples cited, particularly that of Piaget, illustrates several principles of personal observation as a research method. It is these principles that distinguish scientific observation from casual watching. For that reason, we state them here as guidelines to be followed, or at least approximated, when you try your hand at field observation.

1. *Decide in advance exactly what you will observe.* Remember, Piaget did not study "children"; at any given moment he was studying the "why" questions of a particular child, or the conversations of small groups of children at play, or something else equally specific. Similarly, an education major should not set out to observe "disruptive behavior" in a classroom until she has defined exactly what does and does not qualify as "disruptive." Throwing a book would obviously be disruptive, but what of negativism expressed through nonverbal body language? What of off-the-wall answers to questions, and irrelevant comments? And if it is decided to count the latter as disruptive, on what basis will the investigator distinguish deliberate instances of verbal disruption from innocent stupidity or harmless pleasantry?

2. *Decide on the objectives of your study as early as possible.* Piaget, for instance, decided early that he wanted his observations to help him understand the characteristic thinking processes of young children. To pursue this goal, he adopted many specific objectives at different points in his work. Some play conversations he watched specifically to see how much attention children of different ages paid to each other while they talked. At other times, he made quite different observations for quite different purposes. The point is that until you have a clear objective in mind, you cannot be sure that any observations you make are going to help in accomplishing it.

3. *Develop and master a consistent method of recording your observations.* Be sure to record all and only information that bears on the goal of your study. While Piaget was studying that boy's "why" questions, he had an associate list them and confined his attention to that one aspect of the child's speech. It met his purposes to categorize those questions according to the kind of information the boy seemed to be seeking. Similarly, you should set up a system for categorizing your data that matches the goals of your study. Then practice using that system in several dry runs before you begin making actual observations in the field. Once your study begins, you should be free to concentrate on making observations; recording them should be automatic and effortless, never distracting.

4. *Distinguish observations from interpretations.* One advantage of rigorously defining what you plan to observe is that having those definitions in mind helps keep you aware of the numerous judgments and interpretations that an observer necessarily adds to the raw data he or she is there to record. Those interpretations are not bad in themselves; it is from them that all scientific understanding ultimately springs. But they must not be confused with observation. An educational psychologist does not *see* Jimmy "disrupt the class" at 2:05 P.M. She only sees him make a face at the teacher when her back is turned. If that is one of the disruptive behaviors she is there to observe, of course, she should record it. If not, and if it seems to her that Jimmy's clowning has a disruptive effect, then she should note that too, as a personal judgement, separately from the notes on her systematic observation. Even that side note, however, should be in behavioral terms, recording what Jimmy did, what the other students did, and what the teacher did. Viewed objectively, Jimmy did not "disrupt" the class; he made a face. In a different class, with an extremely popular teacher, the other students might have behaved differently. They might even have shunned Jimmy for "thinking he's smart" and "showing off"; so his disruption would have been minimal if not nonexistent. Field observation depends crucially on the investigator's success in distinguishing observations from evaluations and interpretations.

Forms of Note Taking for Field Observation

There is only one absolute, when deciding how to record your observations: The note-taking format you use should match the purpose of your investigation. That is, it should be capable of capturing efficiently all the information you need to record in a form that, when examined later, will make it possible for you to answer the research question or questions you set out to answer. For that reason, observers use a variety of note-taking strategies.

Anecdotal Records or Diaries. Researchers studying aspects of social adjustment often keep diaries describing instances of behavior that seem either very characteristic or highly exceptional for the individuals or situations under study. This, for instance, was the method of the anthropologist who recorded his observations on Tally's corners.

Periodic Summaries. When it is impossible to record data during or immediately after each observation, practitioners and researchers sometimes write periodic summaries. That is, they make their observations as opportunity presents itself. Then at regular intervals they sit down and record those that seem significant for the purpose at hand. This has the advantage of enabling the investigator to concentrate on larger patterns, likely to be more important than some of the trivia that usually encumber more systematic recording procedures.

Frequency Counts. Often some simple count of the number of times a given type of event takes place within a given time or given number of opportunities provides data of great significance to the researcher. Some experts believe, for instance, that the proportion of student-initiated comments in a classroom is a fairly good index to the effectiveness of instruction. By student-initited comments, they mean comments made by a student in response to something that has just been said by another student, without any intervention from the teacher. To test this claim, a researcher would probably find it necessary to use frequency counts of student-initiated comments.

Checklists and Rating Scales. Where the subject under investigation is complex enough to require numerous observations, it is usually better for the researcher to prepare checklists to guide his observations so that he does not fail to note one or more of the features he needs to record. It is also fairly common for the field observer to work with concepts that vary quantitatively rather than qualitatively. That is, the differences he is interested in are not differences in kind but differences in amount. This is especially true of certain concepts of great practical importance in everyday life which—though unmistakable in practice—defy definition in terms of the explicit information presently available.

For instance, long before psychologists and anthropologists perfected systems for the scientific description and interpretation of body language, psychiatrists, school counsellors and other professionals worked daily with individuals whose body language had to be taken into account. For that reason, researchers could not afford to ignore this important aspect of the practitioner's work. In cases of this sort, where it is necessary in effect to measure the indefinable, rating scales are sometimes useful. Thus instead of spinning their wheels trying to define conventionally recognized signals of the common emotions, researchers could devise scales of this general type:

How anxious did this patient seem today? (Circle the appropriate number.)

1	2	3	4	5	6	7	8	9	10
Extremely anxious				Somewhat anxious					Not at all anxious

If it is known that qualified judges are generally in agreement in their ratings and that those ratings have significance for the research at hand, then rating scales may give the field observer a convenient and efficient way of recording data.

EXERCISE 10.3: Conducting Your Own Observation

Choose one of the following projects, or think of a similar one of your own. Make the necessary observations, record your data in an appropriate form, and write a seven–ten page report explaining the purpose of your observation(s), reporting your findings, and stating your conclusions. Do not forget to get permission from the appropriate person in advance if your observation will require a visit to a place where your presence could conceivably upset or inconvenience anyone.

1. It is generally accepted that children need a generous amount of praise if they are to develop healthy personalities. Observe a day care center or classroom to see how much of what children are told is praise, how much is scolding or casting blame, and how much is neutral, task-oriented communication to inform.

2. One index to the quality of care in a nursing home, day care center, classroom, or other helping facility might be the amount of interaction between the clients and the professionals who are presumably there to help them, i.e., the amount of individual attention paid to each patient, student, etc. Develop a recording procedure that will enable you to observe how staff members in such a facility spend their time and estimate how much time each client spends in getting individual assistance from one or more staff members. Then visit such a facility, conduct your observation, and report your findings.

3. Find an employee whose job requires a variety of tasks and whom you can observe at work. Note how much time he spends at each. Pretend you are an efficiency expert charged with finding ways that his employer can make more productive use of his time. Report your findings and include the recommendations you would make to the employer.

4. Go to the library and look up a book or two on verbal interaction analysis. This is an observational system used often to evaluate classroom instruction. Learn one system for classifying the verbal interaction that takes place in a

classroom setting. Then use it to observe a class you are taking which you consider either particularly interesting or particularly boring. Indicate in your report whether or not the systematic evaluation corroborated your own impression.

THE EXPERIMENT AS A RESEARCH METHOD

Essentially, an experiment is just a systematic way of arranging observations that will determine whether or not one thing causes another. The researcher deliberately introduces a suspected cause into a situation and watches carefully for the expected effect. Because both the supposed cause and its effect can be present in varying numbers or amounts, they are called *variables*. The suspected cause that is manipulated by the experimenter is called the *independent variable*. The possible effect is the *dependent variable;* if a causal connection exists, the effect on the dependent variable hinges on the presence of the independent variable.

The underlying logic of experimentation, like most important intellectual accomplishments, is elegant in its simplicity. However, it is also demanding and unforgiving. Experiments requiring great investments of time and money can be rendered worthless by momentary oversights or unexamined assumptions. Furthermore, experimental research has a specialized vocabulary, designed to help researchers put the mathematics of probability to work to ensure the soundness of their conclusions. For the most part, the concepts behind that vocabulary are not difficult, but they do require careful explanation and clear understanding if the concepts are to become tools for convenient use.

Study of the basic forms of thought that go into experimental design is usually easier and more interesting to students when they can try them out on subjects that they are informed about and at home with. The usual practice in college, therefore, is to give students some guided practice in running simple experiments in basic science courses, but to delay serious study of experimental design until the last two years when they have already chosen their majors. By then, most students will be working to their own strengths while they are mastering the tricky points of experimental design.

For these reasons, we will not discuss the theory of experimental research in any detail. But in order to give you some practice in the general principles of thinking and writing about this kind of research, we will have you do informal approximations of experiments. These approximations fall far short of the scientific rigor required for valid experimentation. But we think that you will find some of them interesting in themselves. At any rate, they will give you an idea of how the experimenter organizes and reports his or her work.

Organizing a Report on Experimental Research

The conventions for reporting on experimental research vary somewhat from one branch of study to another, but the form described here is in fairly common use. Moreover, it emphasizes the pattern of thought that characterizes most experimental research. Even if you find yourself using a different format in the specialized work you do later, the chances are that you will see the logic of that format more easily after practicing with this one.

Most experimental research can be summarized clearly and effectively by answering the following questions in order as shown:

1. *What is the problem under investigation?* Why is there a need for the information that will be gained from the experiment? Good experimental research grows out of uncertainty about something of importance; so explain at the outset where that uncertainty comes from and why it is important. Assume, for instance, that previous research has consistently shown that appropriate physical contact, touching, is a highly-valued experience in interpersonal relations. Put beside that fact the well-known taboos about, for example, touching strangers and touching members of the opposite sex. Doesn't the juxtaposition make you wonder where the dividing line is? Doesn't it raise questions about whether and how casual, innocent touching might color interpersonal contacts in routine business transactions? To point out in this way the possibility that previous research findings may not hold true in the case under consideration is to identify a research problem. Begin your report with a statement of that problem.

2. *State the exact hypothesis to be tested or the precise question to be answered.* Hypotheses are usually phrased as statements so that, ideally, they can be either accepted as true or rejected as false on the basis of findings from the forthcoming experiment. For the purposes of this chapter, however, you should be able to succeed just as well if you formulate a carefully defined research question, as you were instructed to do on pages 140–143 in chapter 6. Notice, though, the questions that are used to guide thinking about experimental research should almost always be the kind of questions that can be answered by a yes or a no.

In this part of the report, then, we can offer a hypothesis. "Hypothesis: Library patrons who are touched casually by the librarians who help them will evaluate the library more favorably than those who are not touched." Or we can put the same proposition in the form of a yes/no question: "*Will* library patrons who are touched casually . . ." We cannot, however, ask an open-ended question, such as, "What effect will it have on patrons' evaluation of the library if the librarians who assist them touch them casually?" At best, our experiment will only tell us about the connection between the independent and dependent variables. It cannot possibly enlighten us about the multitude of other effects that might be covered by such an open-ended question.

3. *Describe the independent variable.* The possible cause to be tested in the experiment should be described in detail. If a drug is being administered to an experimental animal, the exact dosage and manner of dispensing should be explained. If the hypothesis requires casual touching of library patrons, it should be made clear that in the experiment the casual touching always took the form of a light contact on the back of the hand. A point to keep in mind is that the report should be detailed enough that the readers could replicate the experiment themselves.

4. *Describe the dependent variable.* What, exactly, is the researcher going to observe? How will those evaluations of the library be collected and recorded? What method of measurement will be used? This is the point in the paper to explain that questionnaires will be administered after the patrons have left the library and that those questionnaires will include rating scales designed to learn respondents' evaluations of various aspects of the library's operation. One or two sample rating scales might well be included to complete the description of the dependent variable.

5. *Explain the procedure followed.* How many subjects were used? Who were they, and how were they selected? Describe any apparatus used and exactly how it operated during the experiment. If assistants were used to administer the questionnaire to patrons leaving the library, who were they and what training were they given? What steps were taken to ensure that their personalities or their manner of approach did not affect respondents' evaluations?

6. *Summarize the results.* Present the results of your tabulations or observations, just as they came out, omitting any unnecessary commentary.

7. *Analyze the results.* Examine your data carefully to see precisely where your findings do and do not seem to support the hypothesis you set out to test. Are there reasons to believe that some of the results were influenced by unintended factors that were overlooked in the design of the experiment or that could not be controlled when they appeared? If so, suggest what those factors might be, explain what features in your data may be taken as evidence of their existence, and show how their presence affects the relevance of your experiment to the hypothesis under investigation.

8. *State your conclusions.* Write a very brief summary of your experiment which brings you to a final set of explicit statements designed to give your readers a clear answer to the question or questions you set out to investigate.

For easy comprehension, reports of experiments usually include major subheads to identify most of the sections called for in the above list.

We suggest the following subheads: Statement of Problem (1), Design of Experiment (2, 3, and 4), Procedure (5), Findings (6 and 7), and Conclusion(s) (8).

EXERCISE 10.4: Doing Your Own Informal Approximation of an Experiment

Select one of the following designs for arranging planned observations. Follow the directions given, and write up your findings in the format given for a report on an experiment.

1. *Observe the effect of dress on social status.* Decide on a short trip that you can take repeatedly by train or bus. An ideal choice would be a train trip of about an hour. However, any trip that will bring you into contact with a large number of people representing a cross-section of the adult population and last long enough to enable you to observe a good many individuals will serve the purpose. Try also to choose a trip that is unlikely to produce a chance meeting with any of your acquaintances.

   First make a field observation by taking the trip while dressed nicely but conservatively. Stay where the people are, and interact with as many of them as you can without behaving unnaturally or inappropriately. Observe people's reactions to you closely. As soon as possible after the trip, record your observations as fully and as accurately as you can recall them. Arrange to repeat the trip as soon as you can, only this time wear work clothes that are clean but well-worn. Try to dress as you imagine a "poor but honest" person might dress. Again, interact with as many people as possible and observe their reactions to you. Again, write down your recollections as soon after the trip as you can. Then compare your two sets of data to see whether you find any pattern of differences in the way strangers reacted to you on the two trips. What reasons do you have for believing these differences are or are not the result of the difference in your dress?

2. *Study the effect of reinforcement on verbal behavior.* Get a friend to engage someone in conversation while you observe, unobtrusively. Use a tally/time system to indicate who is talking. Simply write their names and adopt a rhythm so that, at regular intervals, every second or so, you place a tally beside the name of the person talking. Observe the conversation for ten minutes, building a record of the subject's natural conversational behavior.

   Then give your friend a signal, and have him start "reinforcing" every utterance by the other person. (Reinforcement, in this case, means simply appropriate verbal and nonverbal encouragement. "Really?" "Amazing!" "Wow!" "Oh." "Yeah." "Uh huh." Such expressions as these, accompanied by appropriate gestures and facial expressions, normally function as positive reinforcers.) Allow exactly the same amount of time to build your time/tally record of the conversation during reinforcement. Compare the two records to see whether you can draw any conclusions about the effect of reinforcement on talkativeness.

3. *Double check the law of large numbers.* Conventional wisdom has it that the greater the number of observations of a chance event, the closer it will come to the mathematical probabilities. Test this out by flipping a penny ten times and recording how many times it comes up heads. Turn your total into a percentage, and record it in a column headed "Percentage this series." Make

another column headed "Cumulative percentage," and copy the figure into it from the first line of the "Percentage this series" column. Then flip the penny ten more times and enter the percentages from this second set in the appropriate column. Combine the figures for all twenty tosses, and calculate the cumulative percentage. Enter this in the column prepared for that statistic.

Continue doing this until you hve recorded 200 tosses. Then examine your data and write a report explaining what you have done and stating whether your findings are consistent with what the statisticians would expect. Does the cumultive percentage come closer and closer to 50 percent as the total number of tosses rises?

11

Practical Applications and Future Possibilities

In the best of all possible worlds, what you have already learned about research reports would be enough. In the real world, however, important problems arise which are not mentioned in the idealized scheme presented so far. The rest of this book is devoted to alerting you to the existence of these problems and equipping you to deal with them.

SPECIAL FORMAT PROBLEMS

A rather frequent complication arises when the client or agency that sponsors a research project also prescribes the format of the report. When this happens, you may find it necessary to adapt the format described in this book slightly, in order to meet those special requirements. Governmental funding agencies, for instance, almost always prescribe their own format for the cover sheet. It is common practice also for clients, funding agencies, and college instructors to specify the major topics they want to see covered in a report. If the report you prepare for such readers is also to be submitted to others, with different expectations, it may even be necessary to prepare two or more versions.

In general, such special requirements are only minor inconveniences, requiring mechanical adjustments of no real importance to the content of the report. A more serious problem is encountered when, as often happens, a publication, sponsoring agency, or instructor imposes strict space limitations. Special measures are required when writers are forced to balance the scholarly requirements of accuracy and complete-ness against an arbitrary limit on the number of words or pages they may submit.

These steps can only take two directions: (1) reducing the number of words and (2) reformatting the report.

Cutting Excess Words

Until you see that the space limitation will be a problem, your work properly focuses on presenting the necessary information in an under-standable form. The excellence attained in this way, however, will be wasted unless your report is, finally, acceptable to the instructor, em-ployer, or publication for whom you prepared it.

So if your final draft runs over the allotted space, you have no choice but to shorten it. Obviously, your first step is to reassess the value of every bit of information in the paper. If you have used special opening and clos-ing strategies, check to see whether it is possible to shorten the introduc-tion and conclusion. Often you can cut half-a-dozen sentences with no loss of effectiveness.

If this is not enough and if your special opening and closing both contribute significantly to your report, try the other strategies listed below to cut out words. But be aware that, as a last resort, you may have to cut one or both of these nonessential passages or strike the best tradeoff you can among some other passages that you would like to keep.

Letting Out the Air. Before making drastic cuts, however, go through the document, line by line, ruthlessly cutting out every unneces-sary word. The following list suggests the innumerable opportunities that will present themselves to a sharp eye.

1. *Redundant Expressions.* Phrases that express the same meaning more than once waste words. Cut the redundant words.

> EXAMPLES:
>
> "full and complete"   [*Since both items in each pair mean exactly*
> "hope and trust"   *the same thing, just choose one.*]
> "and so on and so forth"
>
> "sudden crisis"   [*In each case the modifier is redundant; the*
> "future plans"   *noun says it all.*]
> "free gift"

2. *Huwhiches.* Often the words *who, which,* and *that* force writers to use whole clauses where short phrases would serve just as well.

EXAMPLE:

Change this	to this
"Freud was fascinated by mistakes which are so common in everyday life."	"Freud was fascinated by mistakes in everyday life."
	OR
	"Freud was fascinated by everyday mistakes."

3. *Stock Phrases.* Substitute single words for standard phrases that fail to earn their space.

EXAMPLES:

Change this	to this
"Make the acquaintance of"	"meet"
"In the event that"	"if"
"Despite the fact that"	"even though"

4. *Useless Passives.* A sentence is in the *active voice* if its verb expresses action performed *by* the subject. This is normally the simplest and clearest way of expressing an idea.

ACTIVE: "Gregor Mendel demonstrated the basic principles of heredity in 1865."

SIMPLER AND USUALLY BETTER THAN

PASSIVE: "The basic principles of heredity *were demonstrated* in 1865 *by* Gregor Mendel."

Notice that the main verb in both versions is *demonstrated*. But the active sentence names Gregor Mendel, the person who did the demonstrating, first, as the *subject* of that verb. In the passive version, the true performer of the action is mentioned at the end in what appears to be an unimportant prepositional phrase, "by Gregor Mendel." The *by* in that phrase and the *were* before the main verb are there merely to signal that the verb is passive. Neither is necessary when the same meaning is expressed in the active voice.

EXAMPLES:

Change this	to this
"Hypnosis was discovered by James Braid."	"James Braid discovered hypnosis."

| "Fear is struck into the hearts of millions by the name Svengali." | "The name Svengali strikes fear into the hearts of millions." |

The Power of Footnotes and Endnotes. When space is a problem, study carefully the description of the format prescribed in the directions you were given. Often these directions do not require that you follow either the MLA or the APA style exactly. Sometimes they name other style manuals that you can follow or permit modifications. If possible, consult copies of reports that have been found acceptable by your readers. Check to see whether endnotes or footnotes are used and whether they are single or double spaced. You can save a few lines by using endnotes if you have a choice. If notes can be single spaced, you can save still more space by shifting peripheral material from your double-spaced text into notes.

Tables and Figures. Researchers often find it necessary to interpret complex data or summarize findings that are hard to put into words and too involved for readers to hold in memory. In such cases, summarizing the evidence in tables (i.e., in brief entries arranged clearly in columns and rows) makes much of the information self-explanatory. The writer can simply refer to the proper lines and columns in the table. In other situations, the use of graphs, line drawings, or other figures offers many of the same advantages.

Advantages of Appendices. Sometimes the page limitation applies only to the main portion of your report. Business and technical reports addressed to decision-making officials, for instance, are often required to follow an "administrative format." This means that the body of the report contains only the findings and recommendations along with a very brief summary of the research methodology.

The detailed evidence and the full explanation of how that evidence led to the findings reported are placed in one or more annexes or appendices. The body of the report may be arbitrarily limited to two to four pages. But an appendix can be of any length, and there is usually no limit to the number that can be attached.

Whenever you have difficulty fitting your report into an arbitrary space limitation, find out whether the limitation applies to appendices as well as to the report proper. If not, consider moving the following kinds of material into appendices.

1. *Any long list or body of data under discussion.* A sociolinguist's report on the jargon, the special language, of oil field workers, for instance, would focus on trying to find some pattern, some significance, in the way the workers used their slang. Having collected eighty or ninety such expressions, the investigator should not try to include them all in the body of his report. At best he should mention *representative* phrases and generalize from them. The complete list should go into an appendix. This would enable readers to concentrate on the discussion in the report without being distracted by unnecessary information. But the evidence would still be available to interested readers who wanted to consult it, possibly to test the validity of the researcher's generalizations.

2. *Sample forms or documents, for instance questionnaires, interview checksheets, or historical documents with evidential value.*

3. *Side arguments and supplementary evidence concerning crucial presumptions too important to leave unmentioned.*

SOME OBSTACLES TO REAL-LIFE RESEARCH

Beginners are often frustrated by a number of obstacles that, sooner or later, every researcher encounters. Most of these obstacles have causes which—though not identical—are closely related.

The Explosion of Knowledge. Viewed in perspective, even a major research accomplishment is only a tiny stick of driftwood in a huge logjam of information. With human knowledge doubling every fifteen years and with over 60 million pages of scientific and technical literature being created every year, no single research project weighs heavily when balanced against the whole.

That is why the ideal picture given in chapter 1 of research as a cooperative search for truth, in which all parties share information freely and give recognition generously—though essentially true—is incomplete. It takes no notice of the high-stakes competition that is sure to be generated when such huge sums are spent for such important human undertakings. This competition is one impediment to free exchange of scientific information.

Publication Costs. A related impediment is the fact that the careers of individual researchers hinge on which reports are circulated, published, and accepted by their peers. Resources are always too limited to make use of all the worthwhile research. That is why publications and sponsoring agencies insist on keeping their reports short. This allows more studies to be evaluated and published. Wider representation keeps the total research enterprise in better balance and makes it fairer for individual researchers, to whom success means publishing more and publishing first.

Professional Caution. Occasionally, the inordinate pressure to "produce," coupled with the intense competition among colleagues, leads to an honest confusion over who was first or—worse—to an unfortunate lapse in professional integrity. When many people are investigating the same topic, the odds increase that two or more will be pursuing the same clue at the same time. It is not unheard of, either, for a competing researcher to rush into print with a report taking credit for a discovery by a colleague. In some fields, the rights to patents, worth possibly millions of dollars, tempt susceptible researchers to lay claim to the fruits of work done by others. Though rare, such episodes have a dampening influence on the free exchange of information.

Confidentiality. These realities force researchers to choose with care the colleagues to whom they speak freely about their work in progress. At times, sponsors and employers may impose further restrictions as a precaution against international espionage or industrial spying. More typically, however, researchers are deterred from sharing everything they know because they feel obligated to keep confidences with friends and colleagues whose work is vulnerable to piracy.

Despite these realities, however, investigators need to share the details of their work in progress, in order to help each other think through problems of research design and data interpretation. Such exchanges normally take place between colleagues whose work is related but not in direct competition. The success and continuation of these contacts depends on confidentiality. For this reason, the beginning researcher may not be given access to all information by every colleague.

FINDING "EVERYTHING" ON YOUR TOPIC

The obstacles just described, though real, are hardly typical. Few professions, considered as a whole, offer more mutual generosity, assistance, and support among individual practitioners than does research. Beginners usually find senior colleagues eager to help them get started.

As soon as your specialized training is complete enough to enable you to profit from them, therefore, do not hesitate to try some of the time-saving techniques explained in the following paragraphs. But be aware, as you do so, that on any given project some of the impediments to free discussion may limit their value to you. This is especially true at first. When you become known as a researcher with competence and integrity, the shortcuts described below will be even more valuable to you.

More Advanced Bibliographical Sources

To a great extent, the technical or professional competence of a modern worker is equivalent to familiarity with the standard references in his or her field. Being a real estate appraiser *means*, for example, knowing how to use the *Residential Cost Handbook* published by Marshall and Swift of Los Angeles and being familiar with the various references published in Chicago by the American Institute of Real Estate Appraisers. To be a public accountant one must know how to use the *Federal Tax Coordinator*, published by the Research Institute of America, and the various references it cites in explaining how the tax laws apply to specific cases. Similarly, an essential part of an attorney's training is learning to find relevant passages in legal codes, periodicals, and publications by commercial services that specialize in preparing summaries for legal specialists.

It is obviously impossible for an introductory text to do more than suggest the nature of the advanced references that you will probably work with in the normal progress of your career. However, Appendix D lists a selection of recent references which will guide you to sources close to your interests while you are working to perfect your research skills.

There are, however, two advanced bibliographical sources of sufficient general interest to deserve special mention here. Though not quite as useful as the *Guide to Reference Works*, which you learned about in chapter 4, they do prove helpful in a wide range of situations.

Bibliographic Index. Published twice yearly, the *Bibliographic Index* lists sources in which you will find bibliographies of fifty or more entries written in Germanic and Romance languages. Because it brings together information about all bibliographies, regardless of whether they first appeared in books, periodicals, or pamphlets, the *Index* can be a great time-saver. Being a bibliography of bibliographies, it can guide you quickly to a large number of works on almost any topic.

PAIS Bulletin. If your research deals with contemporary public issues, then you should certainly consult the *PAIS Bulletin*, published by the Public Affairs Information Service, Inc. This semimonthly bulletin lists sources of information on such diverse topics as alcohol abuse, national security, public morality, and the space race. Its primary purpose is to identify sources of information useful to legislators, policy makers, and researchers concerned with public policy.

The *PAIS Bulletin* itself only indexes publications in English; however, a companion publication, the *PAIS Foreign Language Index*, covers materials written in French, German, Italian, Portuguese, and Spanish. Both cover infomation published in books, periodicals, pamphlets, government documents, and even unpublished reports by private organizations. Their emphasis is on factual and statistical information.

So when your topic is an aspect of law, sociology, administration, political science or any similar subject with public policy implications, be sure to check the *PAIS Bulletin*.

HOW EXPERTS CUT CORNERS

Precisely because they are experts, established researchers seldom start as close to the beginning as you did in your project this semester. Because they have a general familiarity with work in their specialty, they seldom need to spend as much time on background reading as you did. To a large extent, their technical training is their background reading. That training, along with suggestions sparked by their previous research, usually makes it easier for them to begin formulating each new research question.

However, it is after the topic has been identified that the competent researcher will make use of her most valuable shorcuts. Not all of these time-savers are equally appropriate in every situation, but all are worth considering when the occasion arises. They may save you the time, trouble, and embarrassment of duplicating research already begun by others.

Conferences. Perhaps the first way in which you can appropriately cut some corners is by discussing your project with trusted colleagues who are familiar enough with research in the field to help you put things in perspective. Such people can often point you quickly to two or three sources which, taken together, list and interpret most of the studies of relevance to your project. In minutes they can give you information that will save you hours of bibliographical searching.

More importantly, well-informed researchers will know of a good deal of important research that has not yet been written up in print. Their range of professional contacts gives them a pretty good sense of who is working on what. In some fields, cooperative research goes forward at such a rapid rate that creative scholars cannot afford to await the formal publication of important research reports. Linguists, for instance, have a well developed "underground" network through which the best scholars circulate reports to each other informally, while they are awaiting formal publication. It is not uncommon for one of these papers to have sparked still further advances which are already written up by other linguists before the first report appears in print.

Even in areas where informal networks among researchers are less well organized, most established professionals have an orientation to their field which beginners have yet to develop. This orientation gives them a general sense of which questions are ready to be addressed, given the current state of knowledge, of what techniques could be used to answer those questions, and of who among the established researchers would be most likely to be working on each question.

So in addition to referring you to current published material, the senior colleagues with whom you confer can often name other researchers who are likely to be working on questions related to yours. They may even be able to introduce you, either in person or by telephone.

Networking. When colleagues begin to refer you to key people in your area of research, you soon learn that human resources, like bibliographical sources, can quickly pyramid. Thus as each person refers you to two or three others and to two or three (possibly unpublished) papers, you are quickly led to possession of a great deal of organized information. At the same time, the people with whom you discuss your project may raise questions that help you see ambiguities in your terminology or problems in methodology that you have not yet identified.

This technique of organizing a succession of professional conferences with knowledgeable researchers is called *networking*. Most networking depends heavily on the telephone, for it seldom happens that the best experts on a problem are located nearby. While you are getting started, and even later, when you are approaching a stranger without benefit of an introduction, it is wise to write in advance, explaining what you are working on, where you learned of the colleague's expertise, and what kind of assistance you hope to get. Then suggest a time when you will call, to see whether the colleague is free for a professional chat and—if not— to schedule a second call at a more convenient time.

The important thing to remember, in all such transactions, is that it is you who are asking favors of the people you call. So common courtesy requires that you arrange your schedule to accommodate theirs.

Letters of Inquiry. Different research disciplines have quite different customs concerning the propriety of asking advance clearance for a research project not yet undertaken. Even within the same field, different professional journals take opposite views of the so-called query letters that writers sometimes use to determine in advance whether a report might be viewed with favor. Usually, the most prestigious journals do not wish to answer such questions from researchers whose work is unknown to them. However, most funding agencies send out special publications indicating the kind of research they prefer to sponsor, and many have special staff personnel to respond to inquiries. Obviously, they cannot judge a proposal before it is submitted, but they *can* warn you away from an ill-suited project before you invest a lot of effort, and often they can suggest modifications that would bring your project into the scope of their interests.

PUTTING IT ALL INTO PERSPECTIVE

Throughout this book, and especially in this chapter, you have been encouraged to see the research report not as a mere school exercise but as a professional tool that you can and probably will use to advantage throughout your life. For this reason, the points covered in the preceding pages were necessary to make the discussion consistent and complete.

These facts, possibilities, and procedures are seldom mentioned to students during their first experience with the research paper. They are usually learned informally in the course of research by more advanced students and on the job by beginning researchers. We chose to include them here precisely to encourage you to begin now to think of yourself as a beginning researcher.

College students vary greatly in their access to the shortcuts and problem-solving strategies explained in this chapter. Even those who know experts willing to grant them time for interviews, for instance, may find that some instructors prefer them to carry out assignments without benefit of such assistance. In school, as elsewhere, all such instructions should be followed to the letter. However, it is equally true that neither in school nor on the job are researchers obliged to hem themselves in more than is necessary. Being aware of the possibilities mentioned in this chapter should help to raise questions that clarify just what is and is not permissible in any given assignment and to take advantage of opportunities that might otherwise go unnoticed.

One risk of mentioning these shortcuts and exceptions to beginning students, however, seems important enough to demand special attention. It would be a serious mistake for any student to read this chapter as a retraction of anything said earlier in the text about the requirements of sound research work or adequate research reports. Conferencing, networking, and writing query letters are merely faster and more efficient ways of formulating and carrying out your research. They are *not* substitutes for basic library work of the kind you were asked to do in developing your report. No matter how much current material you glean from such shortcuts, *your research is not complete until you have considered everything available that bears on your question.*

Remember, research is the development of *new* knowledge. To know what is new and to understand how it fits into the emerging pattern, a researcher *must* know what has already been said on his topic. For beginners and titans alike, there is no substitute for doing one's homework.

A similar caution applies to the pointers for shortening your report to fit arbitrary space limitations. None of that advice was meant ever to encourage students to ignore the designated style manuals or other instructions given to guide them in choosing their report format. Always find out exactly what is expected of reports like yours before using any of the space savers mentioned. Use them only when you can do so without violating direct instructions. Some of them are usually permitted, others only rarely. But remembering the right one at the right time can save you hours of fruitless drudgery. Those are hours that you can spend more profitably on a new and different research project.

LOOKING AHEAD

If you have applied yourself diligently to your study of the research report, you have now gained a great deal. Not only are you equipped to do the numerous term papers and short reports assigned in college courses; you have also acquired an intellectual tool that will help you in a variety of ways.

If you are alert to the possibilities, your research skills can help you exploit many personal and career opportunities that would otherwise go unnoticed. No matter what your vocation, the possibility exists that your ability to carry out library research and write effective reports can make advancement swifter and easier for you. To define precisely the question at issue, to assemble all available information bearing on the question, to organize and interpret that information and thus to produce the best possible answer to your question—these are abilities that figure in almost any kind of professional or personal success.

You have a good start on developing this competence. Why not resolve now to make the most of this beginning? Here are some specific suggestions to get you started.

1. *Keep in practice.* The natural temptation, after finishing such a demanding task as a research paper, is to congratulate yourself, celebrate a little, and put the whole thing behind you. Resist that temptation. Studies show that writing skills learned in course work deteriorate rapidly unless special steps are taken to maintain them. Plan now to take those steps. Look for opportunities in future college courses to put your report-writing skills to work. When given a choice, elect to submit written reports instead of other forms of class projects. Then guide yourself through as much of the report-writing process as seems appropriate to the assignment.

Above all, *never permit yourself to turn in carelessly written papers.* Do not allow sloppy work to erode the good writing habits you have developed in this course. Every time you write, you are practicing *some* kind of habit; it is up to you to see that the habits you practice are the ones you want.

2. *Take charge of your own learning.* As soon as you have settled on a major and chosen a career field, you will be in a better position than anyone to guide your further learning about report writing. Find out what style manual is used by researchers in your field and get a copy of it. Learn it thoroughly, and follow it in all college assignments unless you are instructed otherwise. It will soon become second nature to you; and from that point on, documentation will almost take care of itself. You will be free to concentrate on putting your information to use.

Talk to successful people in your chosen field and do some purposeful reading to find out what kinds of research are commonly done and how written reports figure into the total effort. In almost every case, there will be standard reference works and professional journals known to everyone in the field. Become familiar with them, and get to know the intellectual style and idiom of practitioners in your area. Your reports are sure to benefit when the nuances in your wording show that you are at home in the field.

3. *Recognize upcoming decisions ahead of time.* You learned early in this book that research is the development of *new* knowledge. If you read closely, however, you also noticed in later chapters that, practically speaking, not all new knowledge is equal. One good way to estimate which knowledge will be valuable in the immediate future is to look ahead to the decisions that will have to be made. Whether you are affiliated with a corporation, a governmental organization, or an academic discipline, you will find that decision makers always value information that bears on their immediate decisions.

The midwestern insurance man who surveyed agencies around the country to find out how they were using computers came to recognize the value of viewing his research in terms of the decisions being faced by others. His firm had bought one of the first personal computers, and Harold was developing his own programs to streamline office management at his agency. So it seemed natural for him to send out questionnaires to gather ideas from other agencies. As soon as those innovations were in place in his own office, he could easily have forgotten his survey.

Instead, he realized that the information which had been helpful to him would be equally useful to the hundreds of other agencies who were then deciding how to use their own newly purchased computers. So he published a report on his survey in a national trade magazine. His colleagues not only found the report as valuable as he had hoped; they also rewarded him in a variety of ways that he never anticipated: with a press release that brought him local publicity and new business, with the presidency of his state association of insurance agents, and with a prestigious lectureship at a nearby university.

Other qualifications obviously entered into Harold's success story. But he himself attributes all his later opportunities to the publication of that research report which first won him recognition and attention when he was just another small-town insurance agent. Because he gave some thought to the decisions his colleagues would be facing, he was able to publish the research they needed at just the time it was most helpful.

4. *Try to define everyday decisions as researchable questions.* Not every problem can be framed so neatly that the wording of the question suggests the evidence needed to answer it. But most decisions will be sounder after a careful assessment of the evidence. The employee or group member who assembles the evidence needed for rational choices performs an especially valuable service. By shifting the emphasis from who is right to what is right, and helping to ground judgments in solid evidence, he or she can contribute to the sense of order and purpose in almost any kind of cooperative effort.

Whether the decision has to do with locating a new business, reorganizing an old one, or opening a new line of research and development, it can be informed by library research and often can be dealt with more efficiently if the research is first developed in a well-written report.

5. *Use research reports to help with special problems.* Whenever your supervisor or employer faces a special problem in an area for which you have responsibility, you may have a unique opportunity to use your research skills. Such an opportunity came to Miriam who, though well trained, had been unsuccessful in finding a position as a college English teacher. Finally, about ten years ago Miriam got a meagre part-time job at a large university, tutoring students who were having unusual difficulty in freshman English.

Realizing that the English department was concerned about these students and finding that many more of them needed help than she could see in her allotted six hours a week, Miriam did three things. First, she kept careful records of the students she tutored. On her own time, she followed up on them and found that their grades in English had indeed improved after she had worked with them. As part of this follow-up, she sent questionnaires both to the students and to their instructors to find out how valuable they considered her tutoring to be.

The second thing Miriam did was to approach the administration and ask whether they would welcome a formal report on the effectiveness of her work, including recommendations based on the evidence developed in her study. Thirdly, once she had been assured that such a report would be welcomed, Miriam headed for the library to find out how other schools gave assistance to students with similar needs.

Then, combining data from her own survey research with the findings from her reading, she submitted a report to the English department demonstrating the effectiveness of the tutoring she had done and recommending establishment of a well-staffed "writing laboratory" to provide similar services to many more students. The next year her hours were increased and some additional part-time assistance was given to her.

Again she gathered her data and submitted a year-end report, showing evidence of her success and repeating the recommendation. By then, the administration was convinced. They allocated money and space to establish the writing lab and created a new faculty position so that they could hire her to run it. By using a research report to help them with their special problem, Miriam won her first chance at a career that has since gained her national recognition as a leading expert in this aspect of English education.

LAST WORD

Of course, no one can assure you that your efforts to capitalize on your research-writing skills will succeed as well as those of Harold or Miriam or any of the four other people we considered telling you about to emphasize the importance of what you have learned. These people obviously had other talents that also figured in their success.

So do you. So did the ex-GI who entered the University of Kentucky in 1955, to work towards his goal of becoming a high school teacher. But it was the term paper he wrote in an introductory literature course that caught the attention of the instructor. And it was that instructor who helped in numerous ways when financial pressures threatened to force the student out of school and who eventually procured a fellowship to help him cover expenses while he completed his Master's degree—something he had not dared hope to accomplish for several more years.

You can be sure that your other abilities, like those of the people mentioned above, will pay greater dividends both to you and to others if they are augmented by competence in research, in report writing, and in assembling and evaluating data.

That, we think, is reason enough to continue on your own to cultivate and perfect the skills that you have learned from this book.

EXERCISE 11.1:   Taking Stock and Planning Ahead

1. Review the five suggestions near the end of this chapter, considering them in the light of your present situation and your immediate plans. How many of them are you in a position to follow in the weeks ahead? Choose those that appeal to you and decide exactly what you can do now to make the most progress toward your own goals.

Appendix A
MLA DOCUMENTATION: SPECIAL CASES

This appendix shows you how to handle the most common complications you will encounter in your documentation. As you learned in chapter 5, it is always desirable to incorporate citations in the text when you can do so gracefully. Do not repeat the information thus incorporated in your parenthetical *citations*. Remember, though, that the information in the works cited list should *always* be complete.

If, for example, you write that "in Carl Sagan's book *Cosmos*, he talks about the library of Alexandria, noting that . . ." and go on to quote the book, you should include only the page number in the parentheses after the quote. If you found that you could appropriately include the page number in the text (as you occasionally can in relatively informal writing that cites only one or two sources), then no parenthetical citation would be necessary. In either case, the works cited list would contain all the usual data on Sagan's *Cosmos*.

Remember that the examples which follow assume that none of the parenthetical information has been mentioned in the text.

HANDLING CITATIONS IN SPECIAL CASES

Corporate Author

A publication by an organization such as the American Red Cross or General Motors is said to have a *corporate author*. In citing works by corporate authors, use that name, or a shortened version of it, as the author.

EXAMPLE:
(Chrysler 83)
[*Shortened reference to Chrysler Motors Corporation*]

Multivolume Reference

If you are citing from a work that has more than one volume, give the volume and page numbers.

> EXAMPLE:
> (Thorndike 2: 218)
> [*The reference is to volume 2, page 218.*]

To refer to an entire volume, you must use the abbreviation "vol."

> EXAMPLE:
> (Thorndike, vol. 2)

Literary Works

If you are referring to certain types of literary works, such as plays or long poems, it may be more appropriate to give other information in place of or in addition to the page number. Such information might include the chapter, the book, the act, scene, and line numbers.

> EXAMPLES:
> (Simpson; ch. 4)
>
> (Macbeth 4.1)
> [*The second reference is to Act 4, Scene 1, of the play entitled* The Tragedy of Macbeth *by William Shakespeare. Note that when classic literary works by well-known writers are cited, a shortened form of the title is cited rather than the author's name.*]

Short Works and Works Included in Alphabetized References

If you are citing a work which is only one page long, or is an article in a work that is arranged aphabetically, such as an encyclopedia, you may omit the page number in the parenthetical citation. The interested reader will find it when he or she checks the works cited list.

PREPARING THE WORKS CITED LIST

Follow the format shown in Figure 9–5 (page 211) and the instructions that accompany it. In general, all entries are arranged in alphabetical order, using the author's last name. If the author is unknown, alphabetize the entry, using the first important word in the title.

MLA REFERENCE LIST FORMAT FOR SPECIAL CASES

Solutions to most common problems are represented in the following examples. Just find the example that matches your case and follow it. If you have a reference that does not fit into these classifications, check the *MLA Handbook for Writers of Research Papers,* which is available in most college libraries. Or better yet, if yours is a major that will require you to follow MLA documentation, buy a copy for permanent reference. It is available at most college bookstores; or if you prefer, you can purchase it from The Modern Language Association of America, 62 Fifth Avenue, New York, New York 10011.

References to Books and Parts of Books

The general principle in ordering information within book references is that the information present should be listed in the following order. The *order* holds for all entries even though not all the information listed can appropriately be included in a particular entry. It is often convenient to refer to this list for guidance when you must decide on questions not directly answered in the *MLA Manual.*

1. Author's name
2. Title of the part of the book
3. Title of the book
4. Name of the editor, translator, or compiler
5. Edition used
6. Number of volumes
7. Name of the series
8. Place of publication, name of publisher, and date of publication
9. Page numbers

COLLECTIONS

Collection with One Editor or Compiler

> Wells, Carolyn, Comp. A Nonsense Anthology. New York: Dover,
>
> 1958.

Collection with an Editor/Translator

> Grimm, Horton, ed. and trans. Stories of Black Magic in the
>
> Middle Ages. New York: Bezzel Press, 1980.

Work with More Than One Author

> Gates, Edward Paul, and Thomas Billingsford. The International
>
> Guide to Political Cartoons. New York: Pnyn Press, 1978.

Two or More Books by the Same Author

> Tolkien, J. R. R. <u>Farmer Giles of Ham</u> and <u>The Adventures of Tom</u>
> <u>Bombadil</u>. London: Unwin Books, 1975.
>
> ———. <u>The Hobbit or There and Back Again</u>. Boston: Houghton,
> 1966.
>
> ———, trans. <u>Sir Gawain and the Green Knight, Pearl, and Sir</u>
> <u>Orfeo</u>. New York: Ballantine, 1975.

Book by Corporate Author

> American Red Cross. <u>Advanced First Aid and Emergency Care</u>. 2nd
> ed. Garden City, New York: Doubleday, 1979.
>
> Union Carbide Corporation. <u>Eveready Battery Engineering Data</u>.
> n.p.: Union Carbide Corporation, 1976.

Anonymous Book

> <u>Van Nostrand's Scientific Encyclopedia</u>. 2nd ed. New York: D. Van
> Nostrand Company, Inc., 1938.

Begin the entry with the title and alphabetize according to its first important word.

Work Included in a Collection

> Klaxton, Henry Q. "Socialization of Spider Monkeys."
> <u>Contemporary Studies in Animal Behavior</u>. Ed. Arthur E.
> Trent. New York: Sebastian Press, 1983. 572–96.

Introductions, Prefaces, Forewords, and Afterwords

> Sagan, Carl. Introduction. <u>Cosmos</u>. By Sagan. New York: Random
> House, 1980.

Multivolume Work

> Doyle, Arthur Conan. <u>The Annotated Sherlock Holmes: The Four</u>
> <u>Novels and the Fifty-six Short Stories Complete</u>. Ed.
> William S. Baring-Gould. 2 vols. New York: Clarkson N.
> Potter, Inc., 1967. vol. 1.

If only one volume is actually used, list the volume number directly after the date of publication, then simply give the appropriate page numbers within the text. If, however, you refer to more than one volume, then both volume and page numbers must be given at the point of each citation within the text.

Clemens, Samuel Langhorne. "Some Rambling Notes of an Idle

    Excursion." The American Tradition in Literature. Eds.

    Sculley Bradley, Richmond Croom Beatty, and E. Hudson Long.

    3rd ed. 2 vols. New York: Grosset and Dunlap, Inc., 1967.

    2: 223-26.

EDITIONS

The rule of thumb is that you begin the citation with the author's name rather than the editor's name if you refer primarily to the work itself. The editor's name is then listed after the title information is given. However, if most of your citations are to material added by the editor, e.g., notes, introduction or other commentary, then the entry should begin with the editor's name and should give the author's name after the title information.

An Edition in which You Refer Primarily to the Text Itself

    Melville, Herman. Moby Dick or, The Whale. Ed. Charles

        Feidelson, Jr. Indianapolis: Bobbs-Merrill, 1964.

An Edition in which You Refer Primarily to the Editor's Material

    Feidelson, Charles Jr., ed. Moby Dick or, The Whale. By Herman

        Melville. Indianapolis: Bobbs-Merrill, 1964.

TRANSLATIONS

A Translation in which Most of Your References Are to the Work Itself

    Chardin, Pierre Teilhard de. The Future of Man. Trans. Norman

        Denny. New York: Harper, 1964.

Republished Book

    Rhys, Jean. Wide Sargasso Sea. 1966. New York: W. W. Norton,

        1982.

Pamphlet

    McGuffy, Samuel. Flora and Fauna of the Wyoming Tide Water

        Regions. Cheyenne: Porites Press, 1983.

Government Publication, Other Than Congressional Document, Author Unknown

    Great Britain. Ministry of Defence. Military Readiness in the

        East Bloc Countries. 2 vols. London: HMSO, 1978.

    Arizona. Committee on Tourism. Investigation of State Park

        Facilities. Phoenix: Krugg Press, 1965.

United Nations. Center for National Resources. Grain Production
and Economic Aid in Developing Countries. Elmsford, NY:
Bezzel Press, 1983.

Government Publication: Congressional Document, Author Unknown

United States. Cong. Joint Committee on the Investigation of
Television Violence. Hearings on Television Violence. 91st
Cong., 2nd sess. 2 vols. Washington: GPO, 1970.

Congressional publications include the following:

bills (e.g.: S 23; H 77),
resolutions (e.g.: S. Res. 61; H. Res. 45),
documents (e.g.: S. Doc. 265; H. Doc. 325), and
reports (e.g.: S. Rept. 7; H. Rept. 62).

Government Publication, Author Known

Washburn, T. H. Chemical Contamination in Residential Areas.
U. S. 91st Cong. 2nd sess. H. Rept. 94, Washington: GPO,
1970.

United States. Cong. House. Chemical Contamination in
Residential Areas. By T. H. Washburn. 91st Cong. 2nd sess.
H. Rept. 94. Washington: GPO, 1970.

Multiple Publishers

Ketterman, Klaus. Science and Sacrifice in Aztec Society. Ed.
Geoffry Shaw. London: Poloneus; New York: Bezzel Press,
1976.

If the title page lists two or more publishers, list them in the usual
format, in the order given on the title page, separating them by a semicolon and a space.

Book with a Title within its Title

Short, William B. F. Seventeenth Century Interpretations of
"Samson Agonistes." New York: Shade Press, 1972.

Zembla, Ephram. Satire and the Sublime in Don Quixote. New York:
Bezzel Press, 1947.

If the enclosed title is normally indicated by quotation marks, retain the quotation marks and underline the entire title. (If the closing quotation mark is at the end, a period should precede it.) If it is normally underlined, as with a novel or play, the title within the work is neither underlined nor placed in quotation marks.

References to Articles in Periodicals

The following list shows the order in which information about periodical sources is normally arranged within entries. The *order* remains the same even though a particular entry does not require all kinds of information. Consult this list in making judgments about entries not clearly addressed in the *MLA Handbook*.

1. Author's name
2. Title of the article, in full
3. Name of the periodical
4. Series number or name
5. Volume number or name
6. Date of publication
7. Page numbers

Note how this information is arranged in the following examples.

Basic Periodical Reference

Ramsey, Herbert P. "Do You Hear What I Hear?" Language,

Linguistics, and Communication 56 (1982): 303–23.

Doyle, Kathy A. "Forensics of a Pottery Shard." Contemporary

Issues in Archeology 13.10 (1984): 50–68.

If the periodical numbers its pages continuously throughout the volume, follow the first example. Note that it gives no issue number. If each issue of the journal numbers its pages separately, follow the second example. This reference is to issue no. 10 in volume no. 13.

Article from a Weekly or Biweekly Periodical

Reed, William F. "The Prescription the Doctors Needed." Sports

Illustrated 12 Feb. 1979: 12–13.

Article from a Monthly or Bimonthly Periodical

Edson, Daniel. "Bin–Picking Robots Punch In." High Technology

June 1984: 57–60.

Article from a Daily Newspaper

> Fialka, John. "Simple Army Drone Grows Complicated, Expensive,
>   and Late." Wall Street Journal 23 Nov. 1984, midwest ed:
>   1+.

Signed Editorial

> Tate, Jane E. "Let's Stop Hiding Behind Semantics." Editorial.
>   Linguistic Forum Dec. 1972: 5

Unsigned Editorial

> "Challenging Students Through Puzzling Problems." Editorial.
>   Contemporary Issues in Modern Math 28 Mar. 1983: 18.

Anonymous Article

> "Rules of the Dig." Contemporary Issues in Archeology 12:10
>   (1983): 27–32.

Letter to the Editor

> Kingston, Geoffrey. Letter. Contemporary Issues in Archeology
>   12:10 (1983): 7–8.

Reply to a Letter to the Editor

> Kastel, William. Reply to the Letter of Geoffrey Kingston.
>   Contemporary Issues in Archeology 12:11 (1983): 5–6.

Review

> Brickley, Anne. "Zembla Misses the Joke." Review of Satire and
>   the Sublime in Don Quixote, by Ephram Zembla. Manchester
>   Literary Beacon 7 July 1947: 26.
> Glass, Kate. "Is Equality a Thing to Be Grasped?" Review of
>   Dolphins: Man's Intellectual Equal?, ed. Edward Porites.
>   Manchester Literary Beacon 19 Dec. 1978: 34–35.

Article whose Title Contains a Quotation or Title within Quotation Marks

> Langstrome, Julia. "Descriptions of a Battle in Wilfred Owen's
>   'Strange Meeting.'" Manchester Literary Beacon 6 Jan.
>   (1921): 21–22.

Replace the article's double quotation marks with single quotation marks and then list the information in the usual manner.

Article in a Series

> Tobias, Martha A. "Preserving Fragile Artifacts from a Delicate Dig." American Archeologist 52 (1982): 524–67; 53 (1983): 224–67, 332–68.
>
> Mann, David. "How Kids Disappear." Phoenix Guardian 9 Mar. 1984, late ed.: Al. Pt. 1 of a series.
>
> ———. "Missing Children." Phoenix Guardian 10 Mar. 1984, late ed.: Bl. Pt. 2 of a series begun on 9 Mar. 1984.

Computer Software

> Smith, Maryann. Third Dimension. Computer software. Bezzel Software, 1984. IBM PC, 264KB, disk.

Material from a Computer Service

> Green, Sandy E. "Magic, Mischief, and Mayhem in our Daily Society." Current Observations. May 1982: 114–32. SCANSEARCH file 341, item 11724 9889.

ACCEPTABLE ABBREVIATIONS FOR NAMES OF PUBLISHERS

Do not clutter up the reference list with the full names of publishers as they appear on the title page. Use the shortened forms on the list below. If you are using endnote citations, as described in Appendix C, use these forms in your notes as well.

Abrams	Harry N. Abrams, Inc.
Acad. for Educ. Dev.	Academy for Educational Development, Inc.
Allen	George Allen and Unwin Publishers, Inc.
Allyn	Allyn and Bacon, Inc.
Appleton	Appleton-Century-Crofts
Ballantine	Ballantine Books, Inc.
Bantam	Bantam Books, Inc.
Barnes	Barnes and Noble Books
Basic	Basic Books
Beacon	Beacon Press, Inc.
Benn	Ernest Benn, Ltd.
Bobbs	The Bobbs-Merrill Co., Inc.
Bowker	R. R. Bowker Co.

CAL	Center for Applied Linguistics
Clarendon	Clarendon Press
Columbia UP	Columbia University Press
Cornell UP	Cornell University Press
Dell	Dell Publishing Co., Inc.
Dodd	Dodd, Mead, and Co.
Doubleday	Doubleday and Co., Inc.
Dover	Dover Publications, Inc.
Dutton	E. P. Dutton, Inc.
Farrar	Farrar, Straus, and Giroux, Inc.
Feminist	The Feminist Press
Free	The Free Press
Funk	Funk and Wagnalls, Inc.
Gale	Gale Research Co.
GPO	Government Printing Office
Harcourt	Harcourt Brace Jovanovich, Inc.
Harper	Harper and Row Publishers, Inc.
Harvard Law Rev. Assn.	Harvard Law Review Association
Harvard UP	Harvard University Press
Heath	D. C. Heath and Co.
HMSO	Her (His) Majesty's Stationery Office
Holt	Holt, Rinehart, and Winston, Inc.
Houghton	Houghton Mifflin Co.
Humanities	Humanities Press, Inc.
Indiana UP	Indiana University Press
Johns Hopkins UP	The Johns Hopkins University Press
Knopf	Alfred A. Knopf, Inc.
Larousse	Librairie Larousse
Lippincott	J. B. Lippincott Co.
Little	Little, Brown, and Co.
Macmillan	Macmillan Publishing Co., Inc.
McGraw	McGraw-Hill, Inc.
MIT P	The MIT Press
MLA	The Modern Language Association of America
NAL	The New American Library, Inc.
NCTE	The National Council of Teachers of English
NEA	The National Education Association
New York Graphic Soc.	New York Graphic Society
Norton	W. W. Norton and Co., Inc.
Oxford UP	Oxford University Press, Inc.
Penguin	Penguin Books, Inc.
Pocket	Pocket Books
Popular	The Popular Press
Prentice	Prentice-Hall, Inc.
Princeton UP	Princeton University Press
Putnam's	G. P. Putnam's Sons
Rand	Rand McNally and Co.

Random	Random House, Inc.
Rizzoli	Rizzoli Editore
St. Martin's	St. Martin's Press, Inc.
Scott	Scott, Foresman, and Co.
Scribner's	Charles Scribner's Sons
Simon	Simon and Schuster, Inc.
State U of New York P	State University of New York Press
UMI	University Microfilms International
U of Chicago P	University of Chicago Press
U of Toronto P	University of Toronto Press
UP of Florida	The University Presses of Florida
Viking	The Viking Press, Inc.
Yale UP	Yale University Press

Appendix B

APA DOCUMENTATION: SPECIAL CASES*

The first part of this appendix deals with the most common complications you are likely to encounter when making citations in your text. The rest is devoted to exceptions in reference list entries. To resolve difficulties of either kind, simply find the example that matches your case and follow it.

If you happen to have a source that does not match any example, check the latest edition of the *Publication Manual of the American Psychological Association,* which is available in most college libraries. Or better yet, if yours is a major that will require you to use APA documentation for future college work, buy a copy for permanent reference. It is available at many college bookstores and can also be ordered from the American Psychological Association, 1200 Seventeenth Street, NW, Washington, D.C. 20036. You will refer to it many times in your college career.

HANDLING CITATIONS IN SPECIAL CASES

Remember to incorporate citation information into the text when you can do so conveniently and gracefully. However, do not repeat in parenthetical citations information so included. Reference list entries, on the other hand, should always be complete.

If, for example, you write that "Carl Sagan points out the impor-

*Based upon the *Publication Manual of the American Psychological Association* (3rd ed.), 1983, Washington, D.C.: American Psychological Association. Copyright 1983 by the American Psychological Association. Summarized in this form by permission of the publisher and fees paid to the publisher. Further reproduction or copying of this material or any material from the *Publication Manual* without written permission of the APA is strictly prohibited.

tance of stored knowledge when he says. . . ," you need only give the *date* of the source in your parenthetical citation.

Once you give the date in parentheses, there is no need to repeat the date *within the same paragraph* so long as the source cannot be confused with another one. In the example above, you would only need to mention the date again if you were quoting from two different works by Sagan.

Remember that the examples which follow assume that none of the parenthetical information has been mentioned in the text.

Work with No Named Author

If the title page identifies no author, corporate or otherwise, use the first two or three words of the reference list entry, followed by the date. In such a case, the title should be punctuated appropriately. Underline book titles and use quotation marks if the entry is the title of a chapter or article.

Authors with the Same Last Name

When citing authors who have the same last name, you should avoid confusion by listing their initials in all citations.

EXAMPLE:
B. F. Short (1984) and W. I. Short (1985) are in agreement on

this point.

Citing Two or More Works within the Same Parentheses

If you are citing two or more sources within the same parentheses, list them in the order in which they appear in the reference list. Works by the same author should be arranged in order of publication, from the oldest to the most recent.

EXAMPLE:
(Short, 1972, 1978, in press)

Notice that a work currently in the process of publication is considered the most recent.

Works by the same author(s) with the same publication date are arranged alphabetically by title in the reference list.

When citing two or more works by different authors in the same parentheses, arrange them alphabetically and separate the entries with a semicolon.

EXAMPLE:
(Short, 1982; Zimmermann, 1980)

References to Specific Parts of a Source

If you are referring to a specific part of a source, simply indicate the page or chapter number after the date.

EXAMPLE:

(Haney & Kimble, 1967, p. 16)

(Dawson & Drucker, 1967, chap. 4)

APA REFERENCE LIST FORMAT FOR SPECIAL CASES

Entries should be arranged in alphabetical order by the surname of the first author. If the author is unknown, alphabetize the entry using the first important word in the title.

References to Books and Parts of Books

Typically, the reference information should be listed in the following order. The *order* holds for all entries even though not all the information listed can appropriately be included in a particular entry. It is often convenient to refer to this list for guidance when you must decide on questions not directly answered in the *APA Publication Manual.*

1. Author or editor's name
2. Date
3. Title of the part of the book
4. Title of the book
5. Name of the editor, translator, or compiler
6. Edition used
7. Number of volumes
8. Place of publication, name of publisher
9. Page numbers

Two or More Books by the Same Author

> Tolkien, J. R. R. (1966). The hobbit or there and back again.
> Boston: Houghton Mifflin Company.
> Tolkien, J. R. R. (1975). Farmer Giles of Ham and The adventures
> of Tom Bombadil. London: Unwin Books.

Book by Corporate Author

> American Red Cross. (1979). Advanced first aid and emergency
> care. (2nd ed.). Garden City, New York: Doubleday.
> Union Carbide Corporation. (1976). Eveready battery engineering
> data. n.p. Author.

Anonymous Book

> Van Nostrand's scientific encyclopedia. (1938). (2nd ed.). New
>
> York: D. Van Nostrand Company, Inc.

Introductions, Prefaces, Forewords, and Afterwords

> Sagan, C. (1980). Introduction. In C. Sagan Cosmos (pp. i-xii).
>
> New York: Random House.

References to Articles in Periodicals

Normally, the information for periodicals is arranged in the order listed below. It often helps to consult this list when making judgments about questions not directly answered in the *APA Publication Manual.*

1. Author's name
2. Date, enclosed in parentheses
3. Title of article, in full, without underlining
4. Title of the periodical, underlined
5. Volume number
6. Issue number, in parentheses, if each issue begins with page 1
7. Inclusive page numbers of the article

In studying the following examples, note that the abbreviations *p.* (for "page") and *pp.* (for "pages") tend to be used in references to general interest magazines but not in references to specialized journals.

Basic Periodical Reference

> Ramsey, H. P. (1982). Do you hear what I hear? Language,
>
> Linguistics and Communication, 56, 303-323.
>
> Doyle, K. A. (1984). Forensics of a pottery shard. Contemporary
>
> Issues in Archeology, 12(10), 50-68.

If the periodical numbers its pages continuously throughout the volume, follow the first example. Note that it gives no issue number. If each issue of the journal numbers its pages separately, follow the second example. The reference is to issue no. 10 in volume no. 12. Note that the number of the volume is underlined. Note also that this form is used for journals, i.e., periodicals publishing mostly scientific studies, theoretical articles, and reviews. List references in general interest magazines as shown under the following headings.

Article from a Weekly or Biweekly Periodical

> Reed, W. F. (1979, February 12). The prescription the doctors
>
> needed. <u>Sports Illustrated</u>, pp. 12–13.

Article from a Monthly or Bimonthly Magazine

> Edson, D. (1984, June). Bin–picking robots punch in. <u>High</u>
>
> <u>Technology</u>, pp. 57–60.

Article from a Daily Newspaper

> Fialka, J. (1984, November 23). Simple army drone grows
>
> complicated, expensive, and late. <u>Wall Street Journal</u>, pp.
>
> 1, 22.

Note that when the pages are not continuous all pages are given,
separated by commas.

Appendix C
USING FOOTNOTES
OR ENDNOTES
IN THE MLA SYSTEM

As you learned in chapter 5, MLA still recognizes the system of using notes and a bibliography as a perfectly suitable method of documentation. Under this arrangement, the notes contain complete bibliographical information. It is traditional also to list all references alphabetically in a bibliography or works cited list for the reader's convenience. However, some instructors (and publishers) do not require this. Be sure you understand the instructions given you on this point.

CORRECT FORMAT AND HANDLING OF NOTES

Use endnotes instead of footnotes unless you are instructed otherwise. Notes are indicated by placing a raised arabic number at the appropriate location in the text. Write the actual note after a matching number, either at the end of the text (an endnote) or at the bottom of the page (a footnote). Notice in the examples which follow that the first line of the note is always indented five spaces.

Numbering Your Notes

Notes are numbered consecutively throughout the paper, starting with the number one. Place the note number at the end of the sentence unless clarity requires that it be located at the end of the clause or phrase in which the reference is made.

Format

Almost without exception, documentary notes and citations provide the same information as a list of works cited, only in a different form. Because those differences are important, it is instructive to compare the two.

Entries on the Works Cited List. The works cited form has three major divisions, each separated by a period: the author's name with last name first for alphabetizing, the title, and the publication information.

```
Sagan, Carl. Cosmos. New York: Random House, 1980.
```

Note form. A documentary note, on the other hand, has *four* major divisions: the author's name in *normal* order, the title, the publishing data in parentheses, and the page number(s) of the reference. Notice in the example below that the page number(s) appears one space after the publication information without any preceding punctuation or abbreviation. The author and title sections are separated by *commas;* the only period comes at the end of the note.

```
1 Carl Sagan, Cosmos (New York: Random House, 1980) 162.
```

All notes should be typed double spaced. If the note extends more than one line, the second line is begun at the left margin. This contrasts with the hanging indentation used for entries in the works cited list.

Placement of Endnotes and Footnotes

The placement of endnotes is explained in chapter 9, which deals in detail with preparing the final draft of your report. When footnotes are used, they should be located at the bottom of the page, four lines below the main text. Footnotes should be typed single space, with double spacing between footnotes.

Repeated References

Once a source has been fully documented in a note, repeated references to it can be made in shortened form. However, the information included must always be sufficient to identify the work.

```
1 Peter Blythe, Hypnotism: Its Power and Practice (New
York: Taplinger Publishing Company, 1971) 28.
2 Blythe 67-8.
```

Usually, the author's last name, followed by the relevant page numbers, is enough in a repeated reference. If, however, you have cited two or more works by the same author, or you have cited works by two or more authors with the same last name, more information, such as a short-ened form of the title, is needed. Suppose, for example, you have cited two books by Carl Sagan, *Cosmos,* and *The Dragons of Eden.* In this case, you would simply include a shortened form of the latter title in all subse-quent references. Second references to these works, therefore, would look like this:

> [6] Cosmos 47.
>
> [7] Sagan, Dragons 92.

The information given in a subsequent reference is repeated even if two references in sequence refer to the same work. The abbreviations "ibid." and "op. cit.," which you may have been taught in high school, are no longer used, according to the *MLA Handbook.*

Using Notes for Book Citations

The basic form for a first reference to a book was used above in the full citation of Peter Blythe's book on hypnotism. The examples below show how to deal with the most common problems that arise in footnote citations. Find the heading that identifies the source you are citing and follow the example that fits. If you happen to use a source unlike those listed, check the *MLA Handbook for Writers of Research Papers* for further guidance.

COLLECTIONS

Collection with One Editor, Compiler, or Translator

> [1] Carolyn Wells, Comp., A Nonsense Anthology (New York: Dover, 1958) 27.

Collection with One Editor/Translator

> [2] Horton Grimm, ed. and trans., Stories of Black Magic in the Middle Ages (New York: Bezzel Press, 1980) 34.

Book with Multiple Authors

> [3] Edward Paul Gates, and Thomas Billingsford, The International Guide to Political Cartoons (New York: Pnyn Press, 1978) 427.

Book by Corporate Authors

> [4] American Red Cross, Advanced First Aid and Emergency Care, 2nd ed. (Garden City, New York: Doubleday, 1979) 76.

Anonymous Book

[5] Van Nostrand's Scientific Encyclopedia, 2nd ed. (New York: D. Van Nostrand Company, Inc., 1938) 673.

Work Included in a Collection

[6] Henry Q. Klaxton, "Socialization of Spider Monkeys," Contemporary Studies in Animal Behavior, Ed. Arthur E. Trent (New York: Sebastian Press, 1983) 578.

Introductions, Prefaces, Forewords, and Afterwords

[7] Carl Sagan, introduction, Cosmos, by Sagan (New York: Random House, 1980) ii.

Multivolume Works

[8] Arthur Conan Doyle, The Annotated Sherlock Holmes: The Four Novels and the Fifty-six Short Stories Complete, Ed. William S. Baring-Gould, 2 vols. (New York: Clarkson N. Potter, Inc., 1967) 1: 296.

EDITIONS

Edition in which You Refer Primarily to the Text Itself

[9] Herman Melville, Moby Dick or, The Whale. Ed. Charles Feidelson, Jr. (Indianapolis: Bobbs-Merrill, 1964) 98.

Edition in which Most of Your Citations Are to the Editor's Notes, Introduction, or Other Support Material

[10] Charles Feidelson, Jr., ed., Moby Dick or, The Whale. By Herman Melville (Indianapolis: Bobbs-Merrill, 1964) 172.

TRANSLATIONS

Translation in which Most of the References in Your Paper Are to the Work Itself

[11] Pierre Teilhard de Chardin, The Future of Man, trans. Norman Denny (New York: Harper, 1964) 62.

Translation in which Most of the References in Your Paper Are to the Preface, Notes, and Other Material Written by the Translator

[12] Denny, Norman, trans., The Future of Man, By Pierre Teilhard de Chardin (New York: Harper, 1964) 97.

Republished Book

[13] Jean Rhys, Wide Sargasso Sea (1966; New York: W. W. Norton, 1982) 54.

Article in a Reference Work

[14] Arthur L. Schawlow, "Laser and Maser," Encyclopedia Britannica: Macropaedia, 1974 ed.

[15] "Atlantis," Encyclopaedia Britannica: Micropaedia, 1974 ed.

Pamphlet

[16] McGuffy, Samuel, Flora and Fauna of the Wyoming Tide Water Regions (Cheyenne: Porites Press, 1983) 51.

Government Publication

[17] Great Britain, Ministry of Defence, Military Readiness in the East Bloc Countries, 2 vols. (London: HMSO, 1978) 2:349.

Book that is Part of a Series

[18] Franz Ernst Gobel, German Romance Epics, trans. Sean Knight, Orlando Series 26 (New York: Bezzel Press, 1981) 127.

Book with Multiple Publishers

[19] Klause Ketterman, Science and Sacrifice in Aztec Society, Ed. Geoffry Shaw (London: Poloneus; New York: Bezzel Press, 1976)

Book with a Title within its Title

[20] William B. F. Short, Seventeenth Century Interpretations of "Samson Agonistes" (New York: Shade Press, 1972) 252.

[21] Ephram Zembla, Satire and the Sublime in Don Quixote (New York: Bezzel Press, 1947) 90.

Book without Stated Publication Information

[22] Henry P. Bosco, Legends of the Scottish Lochs. ([Bloomington]: [Indiana U Fac. of Humanities], n.d.) 204.

Use the following abbreviations for missing information:

n.p.   no place of publication given
n.p.   no publisher given
n.d.   no date of publication given
n.pag.   no page number given

Using Notes for Periodical Citations

Article in a Periodical with Continuous Page Numbering

[1] Herbert P. Ramsey, "Do You Hear What I Hear?" Language, Linguistics and Communication 56 (1982): 322–23.

Article in a Journal that Numbers Pages in Each Issue Separately

[2] Kathy A. Doyle, "Forensics of a Pottery Shard," Contemporary Issues in Archeology 13.10 (1984): 52.

Article in a Weekly or Biweekly Publication

[3] William F. Reed, "The Prescription the Doctors Needed," Sports Illustrated 12 Feb. 1979: 12.

Article in a Monthly or Bimonthly Publication

[4] Daniel Edson, "Bin-Picking Robots Punch In," High Technology June 1984: 58.

Article from a Daily Newspaper

[5] John Fialka, "Simple Army Drone Grows Complicated, Expensive, and Late," Wall Street Journal 23 Nov. 1984, midwest ed.: 1.

Editorial

[6] Jane E. Tate, "Let's Stop Hiding Behind Semantics," editorial, Linguistic Forum Dec. 1972: 5.

Anonymous Article

[7] "Rules of the Dig," Contemporary Issues in Archeology 12:10 (1983): 28.

Letter to the Editor

[8] Geoffrey Kingston, letter, Contemporary Issues in Archeology 12:10 (1983): 8.

Review

⁹ Brickley, Anne, "Zembla Misses the Joke," rev. of Satire
and the Sublime in Don Quixote, by Ephram Zembla, Manchester
Literary Beacon 7 July 1947: 26.

Articles whose Titles Contain Quotations or Titles within Quotation Marks

¹⁰ Julia Langstrome, "Descriptions of a Battle in Wilfred
Owen's 'Strange Meeting,' " Manchester Literary Research 6 Jan.
(1921): 21.

Using Notes to Cite Other Kinds of Sources

Computer Software

¹ Maryann Smith, Third Dimension, computer software, Bezzel
Software, 1984.

Material from a Computer Service

² Sandy E. Green, "Magic, Mischief, and Mayhem in our Daily
Society," Current Observations May 1982: 114 (SCANSEARCH file
341, item 11724 9889).

Appendix D

SELECTED MODERN REFERENCES IN SPECIALIZED FIELDS

AGRICULTURE

Agriculture Index. New York: Wilson, 1916 to 1963.
Biological and Agricultural Index. New York: Wilson, 1964–date.
CRC Handbook of Agricultural Productivity. 2 vols. Boca Raton: CRC, 1981.
United States Department of Agriculture. *Yearbook of Agriculture.* Washington: GPO, 1894–date.

ART AND ARCHITECTURE

American Art Directory. New York: Bowker, 1899–date.
Arntzen, Etta, and Robert Rainwater. *Guide to the Literature of Art History.* Chicago: American Library Assn., 1981.
The Art Index. New York: Wilson, 1929–date.
De la Croix, Horst, and Richard G. Tansey. *Art through the Ages.* 7th ed. New York: Harcourt, 1980.
Jacques Cattell Press, ed. *American Art Directory.* New York: Bowker, annual.
Jones, Lois S. *Art Research Methods & Resources: A Guide to Finding Art Information.* Dubuque, IA: Kendall, 1978.

ASTRONOMY

Milton, Simon. *The Cambridge Encyclopaedia of Astronomy.* Cambridge, Eng.: Institute of Astronomy, 1977.

BIOLOGICAL SCIENCES

Biological Abstracts. Philadelphia: U Of Pennsylvania P, 1926–date.
Biological and Agricultural Index. New York: Wilson, 1947–date.
Smith, R. C., and W. Malcolm Reid. *Guide to the Literature of the Life Sciences.* 9th rev. ed. Minneapolis: Burgess, 1980.

BOTANY

Willis, J. C. *A Dictionary of the Flowering Plants and Ferns.* 8th ed. New York: Cambridge UP, 1973.

BUSINESS

Accountants' Index. New York: American Inst. of Certified Public Accountants, 1921–date.

Business Periodical Index. New York: Wilson, 1958–date.

Heyel, Carl, ed. *Encyclopedia of Management.* 2nd ed. New York: Reinhold, 1982.

Standard and Poor's Industry Surveys. New York: Standard and Poor's Corp., 1959–date.

Wanerman, Paul, ed. *Encyclopedia of Business Information Sources.* 4th rev. ed. Detroit: Gale, 1980.

CHEMICAL ENGINEERING

Peck, Theodore P., ed. *Chemical Industries Information Sources.* Detroit: Gale, 1978.

Weekman, Vern W., Jr., ed. *Annual Reviews of Industrial and Engineering Chemistry.* Washington: American Chemical Soc., 1972–date.

CHEMISTRY

Chemical Abstracts. Easton: American Chemical Soc., 1907–date.

The Condensed Chemical Dictionary. 10th ed. New York: Van Nostrand Reinhold, 1981.

COMMUNICATION (See also Sociology and Psychology)

Blum, Eleanor. *Basic Books in the Mass Media: An Annotated, Selected Booklist Covering General Communications, Book Publishing, Broadcasting, Editorial Journalism, Film, Magazines, and Advertising.* 2nd ed. Champaign: U of Illinois P, 1980.

Communications Abstracts. Beverly Hills: Sage, 1978–date.

ECOLOGY

Parker, Sybil R., ed. *McGraw-Hill Encyclopedia of Environmental Science.* 2nd ed. New York: McGraw, 1980.

Pronin, Monica, ed. *Environment Index.* New York: Environment Information, annual.

ECONOMICS

Greenwald, Douglas. *Encyclopedia of Economics.* New York: McGraw, 1981.

EDUCATION

Child Development Abstracts and Bibliography. Chicago: U of Chicago P, 1927–date.

Educational Resources Information Center. *Current Index to Journals in Education* New York: Macmillan, 1969–date. York: Macmillan, 1973.

———. *Educational Documents Abstracts.* New York: Macmillan 1966–date.

United Nations Educational, Scientific, and Cultural Organization, Educational Clearing House. *Education Abstracts.* Paris: UNESCO, 1949–date.

United States Office of Education. *Publications of the Office of Education.* Washington, GPO, 1959–date.

ELECTRONICS AND ELECTRICAL ENGINEERING

Buchsbaum, Walter H. *Buchsbaum's Complete Handbook of Practical Electronics Reference Data.* 2nd ed. Englewood Cliffs, NJ: Prentice, 1978.

Graf, Rudolf F. *Modern Dictionary of Electronics.* 5th ed. Indianapolis: Howard Sams, 1977.

ENGINEERING

The Engineering Index. New York: Engineering Index, Inc., 1884–date.

Industrial Arts Index. New York: Wilson, 1913–date.

McGraw Encyclopedia of Science and Technology. 5th ed. New York: McGraw, 1982.

ENGLISH LANGUAGE AND LITERATURE

General

Holman, C. Hugh. *Handbook to Literature.* 4th ed. Indianapolis: Odyssey, 1980.

The MLA International Bibliography of Books and Articles on the Modern Languages and Literatures. (Formerly *American Bibliography,* 1921–55, *Annual Bibliography,* 1956–62.) New York: Modern Language Association, 1963–date.

Year's Work in English Studies. New York: Humanities, annual.

American Literature

Gohdes, Clarence. *Bibliographical Guide to the Study of Literature of the U.S.A.* 4th ed. Durham, NC: Duke UP, 1976.

Leary, Lewis, and John Auchard. *Articles on American Literature, 1968–1975.* Durham, NC: Duke UP, 1979.

Black Literature

Lindfors, Bernth, ed. *Black African Literature in English: A Guide to Information Sources.* Detroit: Gale, 1979.

British Literature

Harvey, Paul, and Dorothy Eagle, eds. *The Oxford Companion to English Literature.* 4th ed. New York: Oxford UP, 1967.

Mellown, Elgin W. *A Descriptive Catalogue of the Bibliographies of Twentieth Century British Poets, Novelists and Dramatists.* 2nd rev. and enl. ed. Troy, NY: Whitston, 1978.

Watson, George, ed. *The New Cambridge Bibliography of English Literature.* 5 vols. Cambridge, Eng.: Cambridge UP, 1969–77.

Drama

Chicorel, Marietta, ed. *Chicorel Theater Index to Drama Books and Periodicals, Volume Twenty-One.* New York: Chicorel Library, 1975.

Palmer, Helen H., and Anne Jane Dyson. *American Drama Criticism.* Hamden, CT: Shoe String, 1970. Supplement 1976.

Fiction

Baker, Ernest A. *The History of the English Novel.* 11 vols. 1927–36. New York: Barnes, 1975.

Coan, Otis W., and Richard G. Lillard. *America in Fiction: An Annotated List of Novels that Interpret Aspects of Life in the United States, Canada and Mexico.* 6th ed. Palo Alto, CA: Pacific, 1980.

Language

A Dictionary of American English on Historical Principles. Ed. Sir William Craigie and J. R. Hulbert. 4 vols. Chicago: U of Chicago P, 1938–44.

Oxford English Dictionary. Ed. James A. H. Murray et al. 13 vols. New York: Oxford UP, 1933.

The American Heritage Dictionary of the English Language. New college ed. 2nd ed. Ed. William Morris. Boston: Houghton, 1982.

Funk and Wagnalls Standard College Dictionary. New updated edition. Ed. Sidney I. Landau. New York: Funk, 1977.

The Random House College Dictionary. Ed. Stuart B. Flexner. New York: Random, 1979.

Webster's Ninth New Collegiate Dictionary. Ed. Henry Bosley Woolf. Springfield, Ill.: Merriam, 1983.

Webster's New World Dictionary of the American Language. 2nd ed. Ed. David B. Guralnik. Cleveland: William Collins and World, 1982.

Poetry

Preminger, Alex, ed. *The Princeton Encyclopedia of Poetry and Poetics.* Rev. ed. Princeton: Princeton UP, 1975.

World Literature

Bede, Jean-Albert, and William Edgerton, eds. *Columbia Dictionary of Modern European Literature.* 2nd ed. New York: Columbia UP, 1980.

Buchanan-Brown, John, ed. *Cassell's Encyclopedia of World Literature.* New rev. ed. New York: Morrow, 1973.

Harvey, Paul, and J. E. Heseltine, eds. *The Oxford Companion to French Literature.* Oxford: Clarendon, 1959.

FILM

Halliwell, Leslie. *The Filmgoer's Companion.* 7th ed. New York: Hill, 1980.

International Index of Film Periodicals. New York: Bowker, 1975–date.

FOREIGN LANGUAGES

General

MLA International Bibliography. New York: MLA, 1921–date.
Year's Work in Modern Language Studies. New York: Intl. Pub. Service, annually.

French

Cassell's French Dictionary. Ed. Denis Girard, et al. New York: Macmillan, 1977.
Grand Larousse Encyclopedique. 22 vols. Elmsford, NY: Maxwell Science, 1973. Supplements.

German

Betteridge, Harold T., ed. Cassell's German Dictionary: German-English, English-German. Rev. ed. New York: Macmillan, 1978.
Jones, Trevor, ed. The Oxford Harrap Standard German-English Dictionary. 3 vols. Oxford: Oxford UP, 1978.

Latin

Glare, P. G. ed. Oxford Latin Dictionary. New York: Oxford UP, 1968–75.
Hammond, Mason. A Historical and Linguistic Handbook. Cambridge: Harvard UP, 1976.

Russian

Harkins, William E. Dictionary of Russian Literature. 1956; rpt. Westport, CT: Greenwood, 1971.
Line, Maurice B., et al. Bibliography of Russian Literature in English Translation to 1945. 1963. Totowa, NJ: Rowman, 1972.

Spanish

Medina, Jeremy T. Introduction to Spanish Literature: An Analytical Approach. New York: Harper, 1974.
Peers, Edgar A., ed. Cassell's Spanish Dictionary: Spanish-English, English-Spanish. New York: Macmillan, 1977.

GEOGRAPHY

Harris, Chauncy D., and Jerome D. Fellmann. International List of Geographical Serials. 3rd ed. Chicago: U of Chicago Dept. of Geography, 1980.
The Statesman's Yearbook. New York: St. Martin's, 1961–date.
United Nations Statistical Office. Demographic Yearbook. New York: Intl. Pub. Service, 1962–date.
United States Bureau of the Census. Current Population Reports. Washington: GPO, 1870–date.

GEOLOGY

Bates, Robert L., and Julia A. Jackson, eds. Glossary of Geology. Falls Church, VA: American Geological Inst., 1980.

Bibliography and Index of Geology. Falls Church, VA: American Geological Inst., annual.

United States Bureau of Mines. *Minerals Yearbook.* Washington: GPO, 1933–date.

HEALTH AND PHYSICAL EDUCATION

Arlott, John, ed. *The Oxford Companion to World Sports and Games.* New York: Oxford UP, 1975.

Baseball Encyclopedia. 4th ed. New York: Macmillan, 1979.

Belknap, Sara. *Guide to Dance Periodicals.* 7 vols. Gainesville, FL: UP of Fla., 1950–date.

Besford, Pat. *Encyclopedia of Swimming.* 2nd ed. New York: St. Martin's, 1977.

Hollander, Zander. *The Modern Encyclopedia of Basketball.* Garden City, NY: Doubleday, 1979.

Kersley, Leo, and Janet Sinclair. *Dictionary of Ballet Terms.* New York: Da Capo, 1979.

Lovell, Eleanor C., and Ruth M. Hall. *Index to Handicrafts, Modelmaking, and Workshop Projects.* Westwood: Faxon, 1936. Supplements 1943, 1950, 1965, 1969, 1975.

Menke, Frank G. *The Encyclopedia of Sports.* 6th ed. New York: Barnes, 1978.

Treat, Roger. *Encyclopedia of Football.* Ed. Pete Palmer, 14th ed. South Brunswick, NJ: A. S. Barnes, 1976.

HEALTH SCIENCE AND MEDICINE

Cumulative Index to Nursing and Allied Health Literature. Glendale, CA: Glendale Advertisement Medical Center, 1977–date. (Formerly *Cumulative Index to Nursing Literature,* 1956–1976.)

Index Medicus. Washington: National Library of Medicine, 1960–date, monthly.

Morton, Leslie T. *How to Use a Medical Library.* 6th rev. ed. Philadelphia: International, 1979.

HISTORY

America: History and Life. Santa Barbara, CA: Clio, 1964–date.

Dictionary of American History. Rev. ed. 8 vols. New York: Charles Scribner's Sons, 1976.

Gwatkin, H. M., et al. *The Cambridge Medieval History.* 8 vols. New York: Cambridge UP, 1966–date.

Historical Abstracts. Santa Barbara, CA: Clio, 1955–date.

International Bibliography of Historical Sciences. New York: Wilson, 1930–date.

Morris, Richard. *Encyclopedia of American History.* New York: Harper, 1976.

Notable Names in American History. 3rd ed. Detroit: Gale, 1979.

Sharp, Harold S. *Footnotes to World History: A Bibliographic Source Book.* Metuchen, NJ: Scarecrow, 1979.

HOME ECONOMICS

Simon, Andre, and Robin Howe. *Dictionary of Gastronomy.* 2nd ed. New York: McGraw, 1979.

United States Department of Agriculture. *Home Economics Research Report.* Washington, GPO, 1957–date.

MATHEMATICS

American Mathematical Society. *Mathematical Reviews Cumulative Indice.* Providence: American Mathematical Soc., 1966–date.

Gellert, W., et al., eds. *The VNR Concise Encyclopedia of Mathematics.* Florence, KY: Reinhold, 1977.

Index of Mathematical Papers, Vols. 9 & 10. Providence: American Mathematical Soc., 1979.

MUSIC

Barlow, Harold, and Sam Morgenstern, eds. *A Dictionary of Musical Themes.* Rev. ed. New York: Crown, 1976.

Mixter, K. E. *General Bibliography for Music Research.* 2nd ed. Detroit: Information Coordinators, 1975.

Music Index. Detroit: Information Coordinators, 1949–date.

Rosenthal, Harold, and John Warrack, eds. *The Concise Oxford Dictionary of Opera.* 2nd ed. New York: Oxford UP, 1979.

Sadie, Stanley, ed. *The New Grove Dictionary of Music and Musicians.* 20 vols. London: Macmillan, 1980.

Stambler, Irwin. *Encyclopedia of Pop, Rock, and Soul.* New York: St. Martin's, 1977.

Westrup, J. A., and F. L. Harrison, eds. *New College Encyclopedia of Music.* New York: Norton, 1976.

PHILOSOPHY

Baldwin, James M., et al. *Dictionary of Philosophy and Psychology.* New York: Gordon, 1977.

Copleston, Frederick. *A History of Philosophy.* 9 vols. Garden City, NY: Doubleday, 1977.

De George, Richard T., ed. *The Philosopher's Guide to Sources, Research Tools, Professional Life, and Related Fields.* Lawrence, KS: Regents Press of Kansas, 1980.

Flew, Anthony, ed. *Dictionary of Philosophy.* New York: St. Martins, 1979.

Guerry, Herbert, ed. *A Bibliography of Philosophical Bibliographies.* Westport, CT: Greenwood, 1977.

PHOTOGRAPHY

Abstracts of Photographic Science and Engineering Literature. New York: Columbia U Dept. of Graphics in cooperation with the Soc. of Photographic Scientists and Engineers, 1962–date.

Backhouse, D., et al. *Illustrated Dictionary of Photography.* New York: Intl. Pub. Service, 1974.

PHYSICS

Annual Review of Nuclear and Particle Science. Palo Alto, CA: Annual Reviews, 1952–date.

Lerner, Rita G., and George L. Trigg, eds. *The Encyclopedia of Physics.* Reading, MA: Addison, 1981.

Solid State Physics Literature Guides. New York: Plenum, 1972–date.

POLITICAL SCIENCE

Congressional Quarterly Almanac. Washington: Congressional Quarterly, 1945–date.

Congressional Quarterly Weekly Report. Washington: Congressional Quarterly, 1943–date.

Index to Legal Periodicals. New York: Wilson, 1952–date.

International Bibliography of Political Science. New York: Intl. Pub. Service, 1951–date.

Price, Miles O., et al. *Effective Legal Research.* 4th ed. Boston: Little, 1979.

Public Administration Organizations. Chicago: Public Administration Clearing House, 1932–date.

Staar, Richard F., ed. *Yearbook on International Communist Affairs.* Stanford, CT: Hoover Institution P, 1969–date.

The Statesman's Yearbook. New York: St. Martin's press, 1961–date.

The United States Government Manual. Washington: GPO, 1935–date, yearly.

The United States Organizational Manual. Washington: GPO, 1935–date.

Yearbook of the United Nations. Lake Success, NY: United Nations, 1947–date.

PSYCHOLOGY

Annual Review of Psychology. Palo Alto, CA: Annual Rev., 1950–date.

Child Development Abstracts and Bibliography. Chicago: U of Chicago P, 1927–date.

Eysenck, H. J. *Encyclopedia of Psychology.* 2nd ed. New York: Continuum, 1979.

Marken, Richard. *Introduction to Psychological Research.* Monterey, CA: Brooks, 1981.

Psychological Abstracts. Lancaster: American Psychological Assn., 1927–date.

RELIGION

American Theological Library Assn. *Index to Religious Periodical Literature.* Chicago: American Theological Library Assn., 1949–1980.

————. *Religion Index One: Periodicals.* Chicago: American Theological Library Assn., 1981–date.

————. *Religion Index Two: Multi-Author Works.* American Theological Library Assn., 1970–date.

Bach, Marcus. *Major Religions of the World: Their Origins, Basic Beliefs, and Development.* New York: Abingdon, 1977.

Broderick, Robert. *Catholic Encyclopedia.* Nashville, TN: Nelson, 1976.

Buttrick, George A., and Keith R. Crim. *The Interpreter's Dictionary of the Bible.* 5 vols. New York: Abingdon, 1976.

Jacquet, Constant H., Jr., ed. *Yearbook of American and Canadian Churches.* New York: Abingdon, 1980.

Kuenen, Abraham. *National Religions and Universal Religions.* New York: AMS, 1978.

Mead, Frank Spencer. *Handbook of Denominations in the United States.* 7th ed. New York: Abingdon, 1980.

Pilley, Catherine M., ed. *The Catholic Periodical and Literature Index.* New York: Catholic Library Assn., 1934–date.

Strong, James, ed. *Strong's Exhaustive Concordance of the Bible.* Rev. ed. Nashville: Abingdon, 1980.

Wigoder, Geoffrey, and Itzhak Karpman. *The New Standard Jewish Encyclopaedia.* New York: Doubleday, 1977.

SCIENCE AND TECHNOLOGY (GENERAL)

Applied Science and Technology Index. New York: Wilson, 1958–date. Before 1958 see *Industrial Arts Index.*

Dictionary of Scientific Biography. 16 vols. New York: Scribners, 1970–81 (supplement 1977, index 1981).

Garfield, Eugene, ed. *Science Citation Index.* Philadelphia: Institute for Scientific Information, 1982.

General Science Index. New York: Wilson, 1978–date.

Industrial Arts Index. New York: Wilson, 1913–57. Superseded by *Applied Science and Technology Index.*

McGraw-Hill Encyclopedia of Science and Technology. 5th ed. 15 vols. New York: McGraw, 1982.

McGraw-Hill Yearbook of Science and Technology. New York: McGraw, annually.

Science Abstracts. London: Institution of Electrical Engineers, 1898–date. Monthly.

Technical Book Review Index. New York: Special Libraries Assn., 1935–date.

SOCIAL SCIENCES (GENERAL)

Ferman, Gerald S., and Jack Levin. *Social Science Research: A Handbook.* Cambridge, MA: Schenkman, 1977.

Rzepecki, Arnold. *Book Review Index to Social Science Periodicals.* Ann Arbor, MI: Pierian, 1978–date.

United States Superintendent of Documents. *Monthly Catalog of United States Government Publications.* Washington, GPO, 1895–date.

SOCIOLOGY

American Indian Index. Chicago: J. A. Huebner, 1953–date.

Hallie Q. Brown Memorial Library Staff. *Index to Periodical Articles by and about Blacks.* Boston: Hall, 1950–date.

Henry, Jeannette, et al. *Index to Literature on the American Indian.* San Francisco: Indian Historian Press, 1970–date.

International Bibliography of Sociology. Chicago: Aldine, 1952–date.

London Bibliography of the Social Sciences. London: London School of Economics, 1931–date.

Sociological Abstracts. New York: Sociological Abstracts, 1952–date.

Thernstrom, Stephan, et al., ed. *Harvard Encyclopedia of American Ethnic Groups.* Cambridge, MA: Harvard UP, 1980.

Turner, John, ed. *Encyclopedia of Social Work.* New York: Nat. Assn. of Social Workers, 1965–date.

SPEECH AND DRAMA

American Educational Theater Association. *A Bibliography of Theatre Arts Publications in English.* Washington: American Educational Theatre Assn., 1963–date.

Auer, John J. *Introduction to Research in Speech.* 1959. Westport, CT: Greenwood, 1977.

Granville, Wilfred. *Theater Dictionary: British and American Terms in the Drama, Opera, and Ballet.* Westport, CT: Greenwood, 1974.

Herbert, Ian, ed. *Who's Who in the Theatre.* 17th ed. Detroit: Gale, 1980.

The New York Times Theatre Reviews, 1920–1974. 10 vols. New York: Arno, 1974.

Whalon, Marion K., ed. *Performing Arts Research: A Guide to Information Sources.* Detroit: Gale, 1976.

WOMEN'S STUDIES

Davis, Audrey B. *Bibliography on Women: With Special Emphasis on Their Roles in Science and Society.* New York: Science History, 1974.

Krichmar, Albert, et al. *The Women's Rights Movement in the Seventies: An International English-Language Bibliography.* Metuchen, NJ: Scarecrow, 1977.

———. *Women's Rights Movement in the U.S., 1948–1970: A Bibliography and Sourcebook.* Metuchen, NJ: Scarecrow, 1972.

Who's Who of American Women. Chicago: Marquis, 1958–date.

Index